Lecture Notes in Computer Science　　10158

Commenced Publication in 1973
Founding and Former Series Editors:
Gerhard Goos, Juris Hartmanis, and Jan van Leeuwen

More information about this series at http://www.springer.com/series/7409

Frédéric Cuppens · Nora Cuppens
Jean-Louis Lanet · Axel Legay (Eds.)

Risks and Security
of Internet and Systems

11th International Conference, CRiSIS 2016
Roscoff, France, September 5–7, 2016
Revised Selected Papers

 Springer

Editors

Frédéric Cuppens
Telecom Bretagne
Cesson Sevigne CX
France

Nora Cuppens
Telecom Bretagne
Brest Cedex 3
France

Jean-Louis Lanet
Inria
Rennes Cedex
France

Axel Legay
Inria
Rennes Cedex
France

ISSN 0302-9743   ISSN 1611-3349   (electronic)
Lecture Notes in Computer Science
ISBN 978-3-319-54875-3   ISBN 978-3-319-54876-0   (eBook)
DOI 10.1007/978-3-319-54876-0

Library of Congress Control Number: 2017933071

LNCS Sublibrary: SL3 – Information Systems and Applications, incl. Internet/Web, and HCI

Printed on acid-free paper

This Springer imprint is published by Springer Nature
The registered company is Springer International Publishing AG
The registered company address is: Gewerbestrasse 11, 6330 Cham, Switzerland

Preface

This volume contains the papers presented at the 11th International Conference on Risks and Security of Internet and Systems (CRISIS 2016), which was organized in Roscoff, Brittany France, during September 5–7, 2016. Each submission was reviewed by at least three committee members. The review process was followed by intensive discussions over a period of one week, after which the Program Committee selected 17 regular papers. The accepted papers cover diverse research themes, ranging from classic topics, such as intrusion detection, applied cryptography, formal methods and methodology for risk and security analysis, to emerging issues, such as ransomware and security of software-defined networking or virtualization techniques. The program was completed with two excellent invited talks given by Roberto di Pietro (Nokia) and Zonghua Zhang (Telecom Lille) and two thrilling tutorials by Ruan He (Orange Labs) and Sheikh M. Habib (Technische Universität Darmstadt).

Many people contributed to the success of CRISIS 2016. First, we would like to thank all the authors who submitted their research results. The selection was a challenging task and we sincerely thank all the Program Committee members, as well as the external reviewers, who volunteered to read and discuss the papers. We greatly thank the tutorial and publication chairs, Esma Aimeur (University of Montreal) and Fabrizio Biondi (Inria), and the publicity chairs, Hélène Le Bouder (Inria) and Said Oulmakhzoune (TELECOM Bretagne). We would like to thank most warmly the local organization chair, Ghislaine Le Gall (TELECOM Bretagne), for her great efforts to organize and perfectly manage the logistics during the conference. We also cannot forget our sponsors including the Brittany Region, the Pôle d'Excellence Cyber, and the Chair Cyber CNI on Cybersecurity of Critical Infrastructures for their support. Last but not least, thanks to all the attendees. As security becomes an essential property in the information and communication technologies, there is a growing need to develop efficient methods to analyze risks and design systems providing a high level of security and privacy. We hope the articles in this proceedings volume will be valuable for your professional activities in this area.

January 2017

Frédéric Cuppens
Nora Cuppens
Jean-Louis Lanet
Axel Legay

Organization

Program Committee

Esma Aimeur	University of Montreal, Canada
Luca Allodi	University of Trento, Italy
Jocelyn Aubert	Luxembourg Institute of Science and Technology, Luxembourg
Christophe Bidan	CentraleSupelec, France
Fabrizio Biondi	CentraleSupelec, France
Yu Chen	State University of New York, Binghamton, USA
Jorge Cuellar	Siemens AG, CT T
Frederic Cuppens	Telecom Bretagne, France
Nora Cuppens-Boulahia	Telecom Bretagne, France
José M. Fernandez	Ecole Polytechnique de Montreal, Canada
Simone Fischer-Hübner	Karlstad University, Sweden
Simon Foley	University College Cork, Ireland
Rose Gamble	Tandy School of Computer Science, USA
Joaquin Garcia-Alfaro	Telecom SudParis, France
Bogdan Groza	Politehnica University of Timisoara, Romania
Christos Kalloniatis	University of the Aegean, Greece
Barbara Kordy	IRISA, France
Igor Kotenko	St. Petersburg Institute for Informatics and Automation of the Russian Academy of Sciences (SPIIRAS), Russia
Jorge L. Hernandez-Ardieta	Indra, Spain
Jean-Louis Lanet	Inria Rennes Bretagne Atlantique, France
Axel Legay	Inria Rennes Bretagne Atlantique, France
Javier Lopez	University of Malaga, Spain
Benattou Mohammed	Tofail University, Moroco
Raja Natarajan	TIFR, India
Stephen Neville	University of Victoria
Claudio Pastrone	ISMB, Italy
Michael Rusinowitch	LORIA, Inria Nancy, France
Ketil Stoelen	SINTEF, Norway
Belhassen Zouari	University of Carthage, Tunisia

Additional Reviewer

Hélène Le Bouder	Inria Rennes Bretagne Atlantique, France

Contents

Protection of Personal Data

CLiKC: A Privacy-Mindful Approach When Sharing Data

Esma Aïmeur, Gilles Brassard$^{(\boxtimes)}$, and Jonathan Rioux

Département d'informatique et de recherche opérationnelle, Université de Montréal,
C.P. 6128, Succursale Centre-Ville, Montréal, Québec H3C 3J7, Canada
{aimeur,brassard,riouxjon}@iro.umontreal.ca

Abstract. We introduce *CLiKC*, a context-aware anonymization algorithm that takes advantage of external information available about the situation under consideration. This enables a more precise understanding of the resulting utility, thus reducing the risks of unfortunate disclosure. *CLiKC* was successfully applied to a Canadian life-insurance publicly available data set.

Keywords: *LKC*-privacy · Third-party data · Context-aware privacy

1 Introduction

Most people using the Internet are aware that their information and preferences are valuable to many online service providers. While this data-fuelled *gold rush* is now in the public eye, it is not something new. Credit scores, medical files and more traditional data sources now share the spotlight with search history and social media posts. Privacy has become a public concern and every data owner needs to have a tailored strategy to fit his or her needs.

This paper focuses on the point of view of the owner of some third-party data. To paraphrase Ref. [1], *when you're dealing with somebody else's information, the intrinsic value of privacy is quite different than when it's your own.* Accordingly, we do not have to search for a very long time to find some re-identifiable data [11]. While we are aware that perfect privacy is an impossible dream [4], we use the models and tools built over time to mitigate our risk. On the other hand, we have to acknowledge that most private data owners (social networks, financial and insurance companies, etc.) are *profit-driven.* While privacy should never be a mere afterthought, we have to provide a way to optimize for a specific context.

We improve on the canonical *LKC*-Privacy algorithm [10], reviewed in Sect. 2, by adding the concept of bonuses and maluses, allowing the user to tailor how the data will be refined. We then show an application example using insurance data. Our algorithm, which is one of the cornerstones of an end-to-end solution [12], has been successfully applied to a project led by a life-reinsurance company.

© Springer International Publishing AG 2017
F. Cuppens et al. (Eds.): CRiSIS 2016, LNCS 10158, pp. 3–10, 2017.
DOI: 10.1007/978-3-319-54876-0_1

2   Related Work

2.1   Syntactic Privacy Frameworks

Syntactic privacy methods depend on a hierarchy of the different attributes encountered in the data. They take advantage of the prevalent taxonomy to limit the information available while keeping its *truthfulness* [5]. Those methods are complementary to—notably—semantic privacy methods, including differential privacy [4]. The tools used to attain the syntactic privacy goals are:

- generalization of the piece of data: we are replacing the information by another one, still true but more general (e.g. Montreal → Province of Quebec);
- when generalization is not possible, we proceed with the suppression of the information (Montreal → *, where * means "Any").

The best-known framework for syntactic privacy is k-anonymity [13]. This method builds on the foundation of data depersonalization and provides a more robust basis to offer privacy guarantees. Briefly put, k-anonymity is obtained in a data set when, for every possible combination of quasi-identifiers[1], every possible row is present at least k times. By making sure that we have enough similar rows, we can avoid an individual being "singled out" and her information disclosed.

k-anonymity may be hard to apply in a real-world scenario, especially when we have a large number of attributes. Making sure that we have k rows for each combination of quasi-identifying attributes may force over-aggressive generalization and render our data virtually useless. This has been called the curse of high dimensionality [2], a concept unfortunately too often encountered. Numerous extensions have been proposed [6–8,18]. Several of those techniques have been grouped under the *LKC*-anonymity concept [10,14,16], which is highlighted in Table 1.

LKC-anonymity draws its k from k-anonymity and mitigates its shortcomings by putting boundaries on the opponent's knowledge. It draws its inspiration from the fact that, in real-life scenarios, an opponent will not have access to the full gamut of identifying attributes. Accordingly, we do not necessarily have to account for every possibility. Formally, we consider the opponent's *prior knowledge* to be the ensemble of all vectors of attributes known by her, from which she can launch an attack on our data set. *LKC*-anonymity is defined as follows:

Definition 1. *LKC-anonymity [10]: Let QID be the entire set of quasi-identifiers as defined by k-anonymity (i.e. without regard to length). Let L be the maximum number of attributes in the vectors forming the prior knowledge. Let Sens be the entire set of sensitive attributes from our data set and S be a (not necessarily proper) subset of those. A data table T satisfies LKC-anonymity if for any qid ∈ QID whose number of possible attributes, denoted #qid, is bounded by L,*

---

[1] A quasi-identifier is an attribute that does not lead to successful identification by itself, but may do so in combination with other attributes.

Table 1. k-anonymity and derivatives as a specific case of LKC-anonymity

Method	Parameters	LKC-anonymity equivalence
k-anonymity	k	$L = \#qid, K = k, C = 1$
Confidence bounding [17]	none	$L = \#qid, K = 1, C = 0$
(α, k)-anonymity [18]	α, k	$L = \#qid, K = k, C = \alpha$

1. $|T[qid]| \geq K$, *where $K > 0$ is an integer anonymity threshold[2], and*
2. $\mathsf{Prob}(s \mid qid) \leq C$ *for any $s \in S$, where $0 < C \leq 1$ is a real number confidence threshold, which may be written as a percentage.*

Here, L, K and C are determined by the data holder. We restrict the power of the opponent with the choice of parameter L: the range of her potential attacks is restricted by allowing only quasi-identifier vectors containing at most L attributes. The probability of successful identity linkage is bounded by $1/K$ and the probability of successful attribute linkage is bounded by C.

3   Utility Measures

Following an anonymization procedure, the next logical step is to assess the remaining utility of the data set. To this end, a few useful metrics are presented below. They not only provide a score that can be used to compare the end results, but they may also drive the whole process by giving a stepwise intermediate score.

The first choice is obvious: run the same algorithm on both the original data set and its anonymized version, and compare the end results. This is easily done and, when possible, gives a good overview of the information lost during the process.

Another measure is to compute the number of suppression/generalization steps during the anonymization procedure. The goal here would be to minimize this number, an NP-hard problem [9]. Unlike most other measures, this one is independent from the type of data encountered. While the top-down nature of the LKC-private algorithm presented in Ref. [10] makes this metric difficult to calculate, it may be a good fit for a bottom-up algorithm.

We can also borrow from the predictive modelling discipline [3] by splitting our data set in two parts, one for the training and one for the prediction. Provided we have enough data, this makes it possible to use rapid iterations with different parameters in order to find the best fit. Following the classification model, the difference between the Classification Error (CE) and the Baseline Error (BE, basically the classification error on the original data) is used as a benchmark.

When the post-anonymization analysis step is not known, the *discernibility score* is a popular proxy [15]. The idea is to give a penalty to a tuple when it

---

[2] Note the similarity with k-anonymity.

is identical to another. Using the quasi-identifiers, we collect the tuples into n groups G_1, G_2, ..., G_n having the same attributes. The discernibility score is defined as follows:

$$Score(t) = \sum_{i=1}^{n} |G_i|^2, \tag{1}$$

where $|G_i|$ is the number of tuples in G_i. The minimum score is obtained when every tuple is unique regarding their quasi-identifier vector.

Finally, for syntactic privacy frameworks, the *normalized average equivalence class size metric* [5] uses a parameter K and the number of groups to compute a score illustrating the loss of diversity from an anonymization procedure.

$$C_A = \frac{K \times \#\,\text{of tuples}}{\#\,\text{of groups}} \tag{2}$$

Unfortunately, there are no standard procedures that can guide us through the proper benchmarking of an anonymization procedure. Several tools are available, but they rely fundamentally on the "know-how" of the end-user.

4   Methodology

Our contribution is an extension of the main LKC-private algorithm PAIP, introduced in Ref. [10]. While we share a common goal, we add the concept of *helper information* to influence the choice of specialization during (at least) the few first top-down phases. Our method works by adding a bonus b highlighting how important a given specialization $v : A \rightarrow A_v$ is to our data sharing. While it is not an explicit goal, we can effectively short-circuit the whole scoring process by using carefully chosen bonuses, tailoring the final granularity of our data.

Applied to the discernibility score, we would then choose the specialization maximizing the following formula, called the *combined score*.

$$ScoreC(v) = e^{b_{A \rightarrow A_v}} \times \sum_{i=1}^{n} |G_i|^2 \tag{3}$$

The bonus b can take any numerical value: the greater b is, the higher the chance the algorithm will choose said specialization, provided it respects the privacy constraints. A negative b—which we call *malus*—will lower the odds. Finally, when $b = 0$, we are in the domain of regular LKC-privacy.

Putting this together, we get our algorithm, named *CLiKC* (for *Contextualized LKC-private algorithm*). In a way similar to PAIP, we use a top-down approach, where we initialize every tuple to the most general value. The set of distinct tuples available in the data set at this step is denoted A. We then scan all possible specializations $A \rightarrow A_v$ for which A could be transformed into an A_v, resulting in a potentially greater utility. The algorithm repeats this operation until no further specialization is possible.

Algorithm 1. Contextualized *LKC*-Private Algorithm (CLiKC)

1: Initialize all attributes for every tuple in T to their most general value
2: Initialize Cut_i to include the most general value
3: **while** some $x \in \cup Cut_i$ is valid **do**
4:     Find the specialization B in $\cup Cut_i$ having the highest combined score
5:     Apply B over T and update $\cup Cut_i$
6:     Update $ScoreC(x)$ for $x \in \cup Cut_i$
7: **end while**
8: Return T and $\cup Cut_i$

Our algorithm differs from PAIP by the introduction of the combined score, which provides a richer contextualization of the resulting data set. We obtain the generic PAIP algorithm by forcing all the bonuses to be equal to 0. The proof of *LKC*-privacy for our algorithm is given in Ref. [12].

5   Results

Fortunately for the customer but unfortunately for us, public insurance data is hard to come by, and sensitive data almost impossible by legal means. Therefore, we exploit a public data set published by the Canadian Institute of Actuaries[3] and used in their 2012–2013 mortality study. Furthermore, we draw on the study document included with this publication as a baseline for the minimal information we have to share. While the table has some sort of aggregation already done, it is nowhere near acceptable levels of *LKC*-privacy.

5.1   Contextual Attack on the Face Amount

Let us suppose that the *face amount*, *i.e.* the amount insured for a policyholder, is the sensitive information[4]. If we are using the available context to infer a hierarchy of classes for the insured amount, we obtain something similar to Table 2.

   If we take the fourth band ($100,000 to $249,999 inclusive), we have here more than enough insured individuals in that specialization to respect the K parameter of *LKC*-privacy. We can also make the reasonable assumption that the C parameter is satisfied as well, without loss of generality. Let us now suppose that we have 50 policies in band 4 and the total face amount for those individuals is $5,000,000, then we can successfully infer that every insured person has a face amount of $100,000. This is an example in which extensive knowledge of the data set at hand may reveal more than what catches the eye. A careful individual will not therefore give the rate band if the face amount is a sensitive attribute. Even the most stringent *LKC*-private data set falls short when we're not aware of the context surrounding our analysis.

---

[3] http://www.cia-ica.ca/fr/publications/détails-de-publication/215062.
[4] It usually isn't, but this illustrates our point quite well.

Table 2. Band as a function of the face amount

Band	Amount
1	< $10,000
2	$10,000 to $49,999
3	$50,000 to $99,999
4	$100,000 to $249,999
5	$250,000 to $499,999
6	$500,000 to $999,999
7	$1,000,000 and more

5.2 *LKC*-Privacy Applied to Our Data Set

While we shall not extensively show the chosen classification hierarchies (see Ref. [12] for details), we can highlight the most important facts. **Gender Information** and **Smoking statuses** are primordial to our analysis, and hence we effectively "short-circuited" our algorithm by putting a very high bonus ($b = 10,000$). Our goal was to reproduce all the tables in the study document available with the data set[5], with extra points if we were able to reproduce the ones in their Appendix, which are usually more granular. All the tables are akin to a `select ... from table group by ...` query in SQL, so testing was easily done. The results are illustrated in Table 3

Table 3. Result of the *CLiKC* algorithm on the IndLifeMDBtable

Field	Possible values
Gender	Male/Female
Smoker status	Smoker/Non-Smoker
Insurance product	PERM (Permanent)/TEMP (Temporary)
Age	0–34, 35–44, 45–54, 55+
Duration	Policy year 1 to 15 (select period), 16 and more (ultimate period[a])

[a]When one subscribes to a life insurance policy, the first few years are considered "select" since the person was recently underwritten. After that period, his or her experience is no longer considered better (or worse) than the average individual, and he or she joins the "ultimate" crowd.

CLiKC, as a syntactic privacy algorithms, does not provide a fine granularity when facing diversified fields such as Age or Duration. On the other hand, we were able to get most of the relevant information concerning the duration (*are we during the select or the ultimate period?*) and we can enjoy a modestly granular age gamut.

---

[5] Available at the aforementioned URL.

On the utility side, we had 32 different QID vectors after the anonymization procedure. On the original data set, keeping only the QID having an exposure over 0, we have 20,979 distinct QID vectors, giving us a discernibility ratio of 0.103. We can improve the relevance of this score by replacing the denominator by what we call an *ideal taxonomy*. This is computed by identifying the level of granularity required to compute all the tables in the study document. From the tables presented in the study document, we have 2 gender × 2 smoker status × 12 products × 9 age classes × 2 duration classes for a total of 864 QIDs, for an adjusted score of 0.74. This shows that, despite the dramatic loss of dimensionality regarding mostly the Age and Duration fields, we were able to reproduce the most important tables (Mortality score for Gender, Smoker Status, the type of product—Permanent vs. Temporary—and Select Period).

6 Conclusion

We presented the *CLiKC* algorithm, an *LKC*-private algorithm that provides a richer contextualization of the data at hand. Keeping the same guarantees as a well-known framework such as PAIP allows us to deliver strong privacy guarantees. We improve on the utility score using the extra information available from the given problem. *CLiKC* is also quite easy to implement and the intermediate results are shown visually in Ref. [12], making it easier to understand.

Our approach considers the privacy problem from a more goal-oriented fashion, starting with the question *what will this data be used for?* CLiKC acts as a stepping stone towards the recognition of privacy as a full-blown part of any data sharing. We cannot coerce a third-party into cumbersome privacy procedures and hope for the best: with an easy to understand, easy to implement solution, they have one excuse fewer.

References

1. Acquisti, A., John, L., Loewenstein, G.: What is privacy worth? J. Legal Stud. **42**(2) (2013). Article 1
2. Aggarwal, C.C.: On k-anonymity and the curse of dimensionality. In: Proceedings of the 31st International Conference on Very Large Data Bases, pp. 901–909. VLDB Endowment (2005)
3. Dagher, G.G., Iqbal, F., Arafati, M., Fung, B.C.M.: Fusion: privacy-preserving distributed protocol for high-dimensional data mashup. In: 21st International Conference on Parallel and Distributed Systems (ICPADS), pp. 760–769. IEEE (2015)
4. Dwork, C., McSherry, F., Nissim, K., Smith, A.: Calibrating noise to sensitivity in private data analysis. In: Halevi, S., Rabin, T. (eds.) TCC 2006. LNCS, vol. 3876, pp. 265–284. Springer, Heidelberg (2006). doi:10.1007/11681878_14
5. Fung, B.C.M., Wang, K., Chen, R., Yu, P.S.: Privacy-preserving data publishing: a survey of recent developments. ACM Comput. Surv. **42**(4), 1–53 (2010)
6. Li, N., Li, T., Venkatasubramanian, S.: t-closeness: privacy beyond k-anonymity and l-diversity. In: 23rd International Conference on Data Engineering (ICDE 2007), pp. 106–115. IEEE (2007)

7. Machanavajjhala, A., Kifer, D., Gehrke, J., Venkitasubramaniam, M.: *l*-diversity: privacy beyond *k*-anonymity. ACM Trans. Knowl. Discov. Data (TKDD) **1**(1), 3 (2007)
8. Martin, D.J., Kifer, D., Machanavajjhala, A., Gehrke, J., Halpern, J.Y.: Worst-case background knowledge for privacy-preserving data publishing. In: 23rd International Conference on Data Engineering (ICDE 2007), pp. 126–135. IEEE (2007)
9. Meyerson, A., Williams, R.: On the complexity of optimal *k*-anonymity. In: Proceedings of the 23rd ACM SIGMOD-SIGACT-SIGART Symposium on Principles of Database Systems (PODS 2004), pp. 223–228. ACM (2004)
10. Mohammed, N., Fung, B.C.M., Hung, P.C.K., Lee, C.-k.: Anonymizing health-care data: a case study on the blood transfusion service. In: Proceedings of the 15th ACM SIGKDD International Conference on Knowledge Discovery and Data Mining, pp. 1285–1294. ACM (2009)
11. Narayanan, A., Shmatikov, V.: Robust de-anonymization of large sparse datasets. In: Symposium on Security and Privacy (SP 2008), pp. 111–125. IEEE (2008)
12. Rioux, J.: PEPS : Un modèle rétroactif de réconciliation utilité-confidentialité sur les données d'assurance. Master's thesis, Université de Montréal repository (2016). https://papyrus.bib.umontreal.ca/xmlui/handle/1866/16180
13. Samarati, P., Sweeney, L.: Protecting privacy when disclosing information: *k*-anonymity and its enforcement through generalization and suppression (1998). http://epic.org/privacy/reidentification/Samarati_Sweeney_paper.pdf. Accessed 7 Feb 2016
14. Shmueli, E., Tassa, T., Wasserstein, R., Shapira, B., Rokach, L.: Limiting disclosure of sensitive data in sequential releases of databases. Inf. Sci. **191**, 98–127 (2012)
15. Skowron, A., Rauszer, C.: The discernibility matrices and functions in information systems. In: Słowiński, R. (ed.) Intelligent Decision Support: Handbook of Applications and Advances of the Rough Sets Theory, pp. 331–362. Springer, Heidelberg (1992)
16. Wang, K., Fung, B.C.M.: Anonymizing sequential releases. In: Proceedings of the 12th ACM SIGKDD International Conference on Knowledge Discovery and Data Mining, KDD 2006, pp. 414–423. ACM (2006)
17. Wang, K., Fung, B.C.M., Yu, P.S.: Handicapping attacker's confidence: an alternative to *k*-anonymization. Knowl. Inf. Syst. **11**(3), 345–368 (2006)
18. Wong, R.C.-W., Li, J., Fu, A.W.-C., Wang, K.: (α, *k*)-anonymity: an enhanced *k*-anonymity model for privacy preserving data publishing. In: Proceedings of the 12th ACM SIGKDD International Conference on Knowledge Discovery and Data Mining, pp. 754–759. ACM (2006)

Ransomware and the Legacy Crypto API

Aurélien Palisse[1]([✉]), Hélène Le Bouder[1], Jean-Louis Lanet[1],
Colas Le Guernic[1,2], and Axel Legay[1]

[1] High Security Laboratory - INRIA TAMIS, Rennes, France
aurelien.palisse@inria.fr
[2] DGA Maîtrise de l'Information, Bruz, France

Abstract. Ransomware are malicious software that encrypt their victim's data and only return the decryption key in exchange of a ransom. After presenting their characteristics and main representatives, we introduce two original countermeasures allowing victims to decrypt their files without paying. The first one takes advantage of the weak mode of operation used by some ransomware. The second one intercept calls made to Microsoft's Cryptographic API. Both methods must be active before the attack takes place, and none is general enough to handle all ransomware. Nevertheless our experimental results show that their combination can protect users from 50% of the active samples at our disposal.

Keywords: Malware · Ransomware · ECB mode · Replay attacks · Microsoft's Cryptographic API

1 Introduction

Motivation. Ransomware constitute a hot topic since they are rapidly spreading. The number of ransomware victims has increased significantly recently as shown in reports of various actors [1–3]. For example, Kaspersky [4] observes a 5-fold increase in the number of individuals infected between 2012 and 2015. Moreover victims are not limited to individuals, but important organizations are targeted too, such as hospitals [5,6].

Despite this, to the best of our knowledge there are only three scientific publications about ransomware. In our opinion, too few works have been done on this topic that is rapidly becoming one of the main security threat.

State of the Art. The first publication [7] demonstrates how to make an experimental ransomware with the Microsoft's Cryptographic API. At that time cryptographic libraries and capabilities were generally restricted by governments's legislation. The first solution against its malicious usage was zero-knowledge authentication. A second proposal was to allow public-key encryption only for trusted certificates verified by the kernel (and checked against revocation lists).

In fact the first ransomware could be bypassed by reverse-engineering [8]. At that time, the motto in ransomware development was: *"few investments, few*

© Springer International Publishing AG 2017
F. Cuppens et al. (Eds.): CRiSIS 2016, LNCS 10158, pp. 11–28, 2017.
DOI: 10.1007/978-3-319-54876-0_2

incomes, few risks". So only weak custom cryptography, RC4 encryption, or factorisable RSA key were used.

A more recent research [9], proposes an efficient and practical approach for ransomware detection. The authors perform an insight analysis on file system activities during infection. Distinguishable patterns have been found concerning Input/Output (I/O) operations on top of the Windows file system driver. Their solution is to place a filter driver between userland applications and the NTFS driver to intercept all I/O Request Packets (IRPs), to block ongoing attacks. Alternatively they suggest to monitor the Master File Table (MFT) with the advantage that files can be recovered. Unfortunately none of these protections have been implemented or experimentally evaluated.

Contribution. In this paper, new protections against ransomware are presented and we make a comparative study of the threat evolution dedicated to filecryptor. The first protection is based on the principle of a replay attack [10]. The main idea is to benefit from a weak chaining mode with cipher algorithm against the ransomware. The second protection uses the Microsoft's Cryptographic API to prevent malicious alteration of user files.

Organization. This paper is organized as follows. Section 2 introduces ransomware. A collection of ransomware and our classification are described in Sect. 3. Then our protections are detailed in Sects. 4 and 5. In Sect. 6, experimental results are presented. Finally the conclusion is drawn in Sect. 7.

2 Ransomware Overview

2.1 Definition

A malware is a software designed by an attacker to perform undesirable actions on the victim's computer, and usually without the knowledge of legitimate users. A ransomware is a form of malware that prevent legitimate users from accessing their device or data and asks for a payment in exchange for the stolen functionality. They have been used for mass extortion in various forms, but the most successful seem to be encrypting ransomware: most of the user data are encrypted and the key can be retrieved with a payment to the attacker.

To be widely successful a ransomware must fulfill three properties [8]:

Property P1: The hostile binary code must not contain any secret (*e.g.* deciphering keys). At least not in an easily retrievable form, indeed white box cryptography can be applied to ransomware[11].

Property P2: Only the author of the attack should be able to decrypt the infected device.

Property P3: Decrypting one device can not provide any useful information for other infected devices, in particular the key must not be shared among them.

2.2   Infection Distribution

The most common infection vectors to data have been through malicious email attachments, compromised software and drive-by downloads[1] exploit kits [12,13]. Other vectors include malvertisements[2], hacking or social engineering. It can also be downloaded as a payload by another malware.

2.3   Payment Method

The goal of a ransomware is to earn money. First ransomware used bank transfers and prepaid cards (MoneyPak, Amazon and Apple gift cards). In rare cases SMS or call to a overtaxed premium mobile number have been encountered. These methods are traceable by law enforcement agencies, thus large-scale campaigns were limited in order to not attract attention. That is why, new generation of ransomware relies on Bitcoin (BTC) almost exclusively. Bitcoin release has undeniably stimulated ransomware threats for massive attacks thanks to: confidentiality, rapidity of transfer, absence of central banking group. The Bitcoin protocol have been extended in 2014 and can be used to store 80 bytes not related to the transaction. The new variant of CTB-Locker uses this field as a side channel to send back the decryption keys once the ransom paid [14].

2.4   Command and Control

In order to fulfill property P2, the communication with the attacker is necessary. This is usually realize through a Command and Control (C&C) server. The minimal functionality is to provide the decryption key. In order to fulfill property P3, decryption key must be unique to each victim. Thus a unique identifier is computed. Different kinds of ransomware have been found, some of them require an initial connection to C&C in order to generate per-user key-pair or just to check its availability. A static central C&C can be easily disabled by law enforcement. Malware authors can circumvent this by Domain Generation Algorithm (DGA). Still it is not rare to analyze ransomware which tries to contact C&C without success, so their malicious payload stay inactive.

2.5   Obfuscation

Ransomware authors pack and obfuscate their payload to bypass anti-virus detection and evade analysis tools. Some modern ransomware are highly sophisticated pieces of code. Malware authors use Do-It-Yourself (DiY) malware kits and additional armoring techniques to generate new executable files based on the same code. An infinite number of variants based on an original sample can be generated. Automating the generation is named malware factory and can

---

[1] Drive-by download is a term used to describe how a piece of malware is installed on a user's computer without his knowledge when browsing a compromised website.

[2] Porte-manteau of malware and advertisement.

be compared to an assembly line. Some ransomware use malware factories techniques and morphing code to defeat hash based signature. New variants of Cerber are generated every 15 s thanks to on the fly server-side factories [15].

2.6   File Encryption

The seminal paper of Youg *et al.* [7] describes the use of both symmetric and asymmetric cryptography in conjunction with computer virus and trojan horse technology. They demonstrated with an experimental ransomware this concept on a Windows target using Triple DES [16] and RSA [17] implementation with a 1024-bits public-key. This proof of concept is based on public cryptographic services given to userland applications through the Microsoft's Cryptographic API (MS CAPI) framework. Distributed in 1996, MS CAPI provides a high degree of abstraction and significantly facilitates development of software with cryptographic primitives needs.

Implementation of standard algorithms (DES, Triple DES, RSA, PGP) in the 90s were not publicly available due to government legislation. At that time, cryptovirus required some crypto experts, and multiple precision library to manipulate large integer. The OpenSSL project only started two years later in 1998.

Nowadays plenty of free third-party cryptographic libraries can be used by criminals for malicious encryption purposes (OpenSSL, mbed TLS, libsodium). More recent cryptographic designs involve Elliptic Curve Cryptography (ECC) for shared secret and per-victim key-pair generation [18]. File encryption is performed almost exclusively by Advanced Encryption Standard (AES) with recent ransomware, difference can be pointed only on the chaining mode used. Ransomware authors might use the default setting of the system (MS CAPI) or library. In most situations files encryption is performed only superficially. The main objective is to make files unusable. In the remaining of the section, we present the two most used chaining mode.

Block Cipher Modes of Operation. A block cipher encrypts data of fixed-length n bytes. If the data are bigger than this fixed-length, data are split in different block of size n bytes each. If the size of data is not a multiple of n bytes, the last block is padded. The mode of operation describes how to repeatedly apply the encryption. The ransomware used two classic modes: Electronic Codebook (ECB) mode, Cipher Block Chaining (CBC) mode. In this paper, $\mathcal{F}$ denotes an encryption algorithm, T a plain-text, C a cipher-text and K a cipher-key. Plain-text is split in a set of blocks B_i of size n bytes.

Electronic Codebook Mode. The ECB mode encryption is a simple mode. The data are divided into blocks, and each block is encrypted separately (1).

$$C_i = \mathcal{F}(B_i, K_i). \tag{1}$$

Figure 1 illustrates this mode.

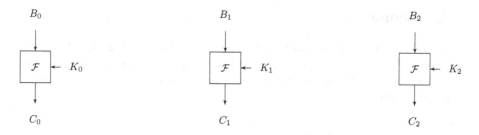

Fig. 1. Scheme of ECB mode encryption

Cipher Block Chaining Mode. In CBC mode, each block of plain-text is xored with the previous cipher-text block before being encrypted. An Initialization Vector (IV) is xored with the first block B_0. The relation is defined in (2).

$$\begin{cases} C_0 = & \mathcal{F}(B_0 \oplus IV, K_0) \\ C_{i+1} = & \mathcal{F}(B_{i+1} \oplus C_i, K_i). \end{cases} \tag{2}$$

Figure 2 illustrates this mode.

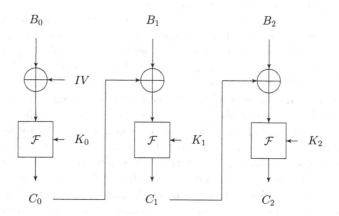

Fig. 2. Scheme of CBC mode encryption

Infection Mitigation. In order to mitigate the attacks, it is mandatory to realize backups daily to reduce the gap between the systems and the snapshots. The ransomware targets the network drives. Some attacks against Synology storage products have been done through a vulnerability exploited by the SynoLocker ransomware in 2014 [19]. To reduce the risks, off-site or cold backups need to be performed.

3 Taxonomy

With the advent of cryptographic libraries and APIs, the last decade saw a steady increase in the number of ransomware. We present a few of them in this section and try to address the most significant improvements from old to state of the art ransomware.

3.1 Ransomware Collection

One of the first studies about ransomware was published in December 2004 by Nazarov *et al.* [20]. This report make an insight analysis of **PGPCoder/GP-Code**. This ransomware was the first implementation of the model proposed by Young *et al.* encrypting over 80 different types of files on the disk.

CryptoLocker was first reported in September 2013 [21]. It is the first to implement all of the properties P1, P2 and P3. Files are encrypted using AES with a random key which is then encrypted thanks to a 2048-bits RSA public key. The corresponding private key, needed to decrypt the AES key, can be obtained by paying the ransom. Distribution was initially through spam messages containing malicious attachments. Then the main targets were the victims of the botnet Gameover ZeuS. It was disrupted by international law enforcement agencies during the authorities operation Tovar [22] in June 2014.

CryptoWall appeared in early 2014 [23]. It continues to gain notoriety and is still intensively developed [24]. It encrypts files using RSA and uses The Onion Router (Tor)[3] to obfuscate communications with the C&C. Each victim is registered and identified by a unique identifier and get from the C&C the corresponding RSA public-key. Infection vector was performed initially via exploit kits and then moved to more traditional spam email campaigns. File encryption does not occur if the RSA public-key is not received. It is one of the first requiring payment in Bitcoin only, and deleting the Shadow Copy. Moreover a list of all the encrypted files is stored in the registry to ease the decryption process.

Version 3.0 upgrades to AES symmetric encryption with Cipher Block Chaining (CBC) mode for files and communication with C&C was done over the Invisible Internet Project (I2P)[4] network. Due to the lack of reliability, they back up with a combination of compromised sites forwarding traffic to Tor server.

In version 4.0, an additional step in disruption is made by renaming files, including extension, with random characters. In order to avoid encrypting the same file again following superinfection, a hash corresponding to the RSA public-key given to the victim is prepended to the beginning of the file.

TorrentLocker ransomware was found in February 2014 [25] and shares many similarities with CryptoLocker. It adds captcha code and redirection to a spoofed site for infection. At the beginning, AES encryption was performed on all files with the same key and Initialization Vector (IV) using Counter (CTR) mode [26]. This can be exploited with one known plain-text and cipher-text in

---

[3] https://www.torproject.org/.

[4] https://geti2p.net/fr/.

order to extract the keystream and then apply it to a cipher-text to recover any original file (RannohDecryptor[5]). Recently, the authors have fixed this flaw with CBC mode. In certain network, Tor traffic can be forbidden or might trigger warnings, instead TorrentLocker uses HTTPS like any legitimate connections made by the browser. New features were added like: harvesting email contacts, free decryption service for a single file, and partial encryption in order to speed up the attack.

The **CTB-Locker** (Curve-Tor-Bitcoin) appeared in June 2014 [27], it is the first to use ECC to compute public keys and shared secrets based on secret keys generated at runtime [28]. An active Internet connection is no longer required to begin the encryption process, moreover a complex cryptographic design is used. It is the first one which preceded AES file encryption by a compression step using ZLib. Communication with C&C is established by proxy websites like the Tor2web service which acts as a relay to the back-end infrastructure build on Tor hidden service. Infection distribution is realized thanks to an affiliate program to a network of partners motivated by gain.

A new variant appeared in February 2016 that is designed specifically against websites [29]. Infection begins with the site hack and replaces the legitimate `index.html` with one that performs file encryption and displays a ransom note. To be successful the site needs to use a php module.

TeslaCrypt ransomware was uncovered in February 2015 [30], distributed through websites that redirect victims to an exploit kit (drive-by download). Angler is one of them which takes advantage of Adobe Flash (CVE-2015-0311[6]). Contrary to other ransomware, TeslaCrypt keep encryption keys on the disk during the attack. It is one of the first ransomware which specifically targets files used by video games. Similarly to CTB-Locker, encryption process occurs irrespectively of any communication with the C&C, but their cryptosystems design differ slightly. TeslaCrypt embeds an ECC public-key in its binary, shared across plenty of samples which is used to compute a shared secret involved in the generation of an AES session key. The system has an ECC master private key. It was surprisingly broadcast in May 2016 by the malware authors themselves during the ransomware shutdown process.

It can be noticed that **Crypvault** [31] ransomware uncovered in April 2015 uses a legitimate cryptographic tool GnuPG to process file encryption. Additionally, a password dump utility is used as well as a software provided by Sysinternals in order to definitively delete files on disk.

In February 2016 **Locky** ransomware [32] hit the Internet and spread to more than 100 countries worldwide. Attackers can get statistics on the encrypted files but also the corresponding list and their path. The United States and France are the most infected countries, authors concentrate the best of the previous ransomware to achieve a highly skilled threat.

---

[5] http://www.kaspersky.com/internet-security-center/threats/torrentlocker-malware.

[6] https://cve.mitre.org/cgi-bin/cvename.cgi?name=CVE-2015-0311.

The **Petya** ransomware discovered in May 2016 [33] infects the hard drive partition table and prevents the operating system to be launched. Victims are redirected to a special boot screen asking for a ransom with persuasive font. Besides partition table overwriting which is not a new feature for malware, a special structure managed by the file system driver called Master File Table (MFT) is also encrypted preventing file recovery from a live cd. To the best of our knowledge it is the first significant ransomware to possess an entire offline cryptosystem design and which is placed at low-level. The disk encryption is performed with the stream cipher *salsa20* [34]. First versions presented some cryptographic flaws [35] that were corrected later.

3.2 Classification

In this paper, these ransomware are classified according to the cipher algorithms and Command and Control (C&C) communication channel. Traditionally, encryption algorithms used by ransomware are the standards: RSA [17] for metadata encryption and AES [36] for file encryption. Communication with C&C is more heterogeneous, each group of authors can choose a different option in function of the degree of reliability and confidentiality. Moreover, offline cryptosystems begin to appear and are a way for criminals to reduce exposure.

4   Protection Against Ransomware Using Smart Encoding

In this part, we propose a protection against ransomware using block ciphers. The ECB chaining mode can be exploited. On the other hand CBC exploitation involves more processing and requires poor cryptographic usages.

4.1 Ransomware Using ECB Mode

In cryptography, the ECB mode has a big drawback. Identical plain-text blocks are encrypted into identical cipher-text blocks; thus, it does not correctly hide data patterns. Figure 3 illustrates this problem.

Fig. 3. ECB mode limitation (Tux pictures come from [37])

With such a mode, a replay attack [10] is possible. The main idea of our protection is to use the disadvantage of ECB mode to protect our data against ransomware. For this purpose, our protection consists in a smart data encoding.

The first step is to expend the data. Each byte of data is padded with 0 bytes to have block size n. In the case of the AES, $n = 16$. So a data file T of size m bytes, such as (3):

$$T = B_0, B_1, \cdots B_m;$$ (3)

is transformed in an expended data file such as (4):

$$\text{expended}T = B_0, \underbrace{0 \cdots 0}_{n-1}, B_1, \underbrace{0 \cdots 0}_{n-1}, \cdots, B_m, \underbrace{0 \cdots 0}_{n-1}.$$ (4)

Additionally a dictionary is created:

$$\text{dic} = \underbrace{0 \cdots 0}_{n}, 1, \underbrace{0 \cdots 0}_{n-1}, \cdots, 255, \underbrace{0 \cdots 0}_{n-1}.$$ (5)

If the ransomware uses the same key to encrypt all files, it also encrypts the dictionary file "dic". The user can retrieve all files thanks to it by matching the encrypted blocks of a file with the encrypted blocks of the dictionary for which the unencrypted values are known.

If the ransomware uses a different key for each files, the dictionary can be created at the beginning of each of them. So a file T as (3) is expended in "dic + expended$T$":

$$\text{dic} + \text{expended}T = \underbrace{0 \cdots 0}_{n}, 1, \cdots, 255, \underbrace{0 \cdots 0}_{n-1}, B_0, \underbrace{0 \cdots 0}_{n-1}, \cdots, B_m, \underbrace{0 \cdots 0}_{n-1}.$$ (6)

Another solution is to use the entropy of the original file. If T is a text, it can be supposed that the user knows the language used. In this case, no dictionary is necessary, text files are just expended (4) and the entropy is used to retrieve data with a classic basic cryptanalysis. Usually the file name is not encrypted, so the entropy could be stored in the file name to avoid the use of a dictionary.

4.2 Ransomware Using CBC Mode

If a ransomware uses a block cipher in CBC mode, the solution described in Sect. 4.1 fails, because of the xor at the start of block encryption. This paragraph presents a more complex protection for this mode working if the ransomware encrypts newly created file with the same key as the file you want to retrieve.

The data files are expended exactly as in (4). But the construction of the dictionary is different. The user does not create a dictionary file, but 256 files dic_b^0, one for each possible value of byte $b \in [0, 255]$ such as (7):

$$\text{dic}_b^0 = b, \underbrace{0 \cdots 0}_{n-1}.$$ (7)

The ransomware encrypts all data files and the 256 dictionaries dic_b^0. At this step, the user can retrieve the first and only the first byte B_0 of each encrypted files. Then she can create new dictionaries, one for each encrypted file and for each possible value of byte $b \in [\![0, 255]\!]$ such as (8):

$$\text{dic}_b^1 = (b, \underbrace{0 \cdots 0}_{n-1}) \oplus C_0. \tag{8}$$

Then the ransomware encrypts the new dictionaries. At this step the user can retrieve all second bytes B_1 of the files.

So the user can retrieve all bytes B_i by recurrence on the dictionaries byte (9).

$$\text{dic}_b^i = (b, \underbrace{0 \cdots 0}_{n-1}) \oplus C_i. \tag{9}$$

4.3 Limitation

The main problem to these countermeasures are the sizes of the files which significantly increase. The data size is multiplied by n. In our description, the size of dictionary elements is fixed to one byte. In practice, it can be any other size. The bigger the size element is, the bigger the dictionary and the file sizes. In future works, it would be interesting to optimize these sizes.

It is important to precise that the countermeasure against CBC mode is limited to a ransomware which:

– uses always the same key K and the same vector IV,
– encrypts all newly created files.

5 Monitoring Microsoft's Cryptographic API

Beginning with cryptoviral extorsion as presented by Young *et al.* in [7], ransomware may use Microsoft's Cryptographic API. This section presents a generic countermeasure against a malicious usage of this API.

5.1 Microsoft's Cryptographic API (MS CAPI)

Windows operating systems, starting with Windows 95, include an easy-to-use API that supply cryptographic services to userland applications through MS CAPI. Cryptographic primitives are embedded in dynamic link libraries and divided in Cryptographic Service Providers (CSPs) each one offering a set of primitives classified by their type (Hash, Signature, Encrypt). Its objective is to provide an abstraction layer for programming purpose by non cryptographic specialists. Moreover due to its extensible architecture design, it is possible to add cryptographic modules once Microsoft signs them. For example, Hardware Security Module (HSM) vendors can implement white-box or home-made cryptographic algorithms and comply to Federal Information Processing Standard (FIPS) approved algorithms standards. It can be noticed that no user authentication is performed in order to access the primitives, authentication relies exclusively on the operating system. The framework does not provide persistent storage of keys or archival directly, you should use separate API provided by Microsoft. Moreover each time a process instantiates a Dynamic Link Library (DLL), code is shared but data remains unique for each instance and thus no key is exposed at load time. Cryptomodule is dedicated to one process so compartmentalization is ensured. Extended details can be found in [7,38] which give a list of the exported functions and an in-depth documentation.

MS CAPI is old (appeared with Windows 95), but is still widely spread notably in banking infrastructure such as ATMs. For legacy or backward compatibility in newer Windows operating systems, MS CAPI is deprecated but still present; it is strongly recommended to use the Cryptography API Next Generation (CNG) beginning with Windows Vista. Despite this recommendation OpenSSL continues to initialize its Deterministic Random Bit Generator (DRBG) with some entropy coming from *CryptGenRandom* from MS CAPI.[7] No ECC is supported with default providers, National Institute of Standards and Technology (NIST) Suite B Cryptography is fully available in CNG as well as additional chaining modes (XTS, GCM, CCM) and DESX block cipher.

5.2   System Protection

Presentation. The main question is how to prevent malicious usages of MS CAPI without intrusive methods. We want to provide a fully transparent solution as simple as possible, ransomware must not be informed about any analysis.

Contrary to Bromium report [13] where an intrusive method based on the instrumentation library Detours [39] is chosen, we implemented a CSP and then plug it in the system. When incorporating a cryptographic module in the system, we are located in a legitimate position to observe malicious cryptographic behavior but also legitimate calls. We have to provide real services to user application and so we used the OpenSSL library for cryptographic primitives.

Implementation. The Software Development Kit (SDK) and the Cryptographic Service Provider Developer's Toolkit (CSPDK)[8] supplied by Microsoft are used. We integrated the OpenSSL primitives in collaboration with MS CAPI architecture sin order to get a functional provider. Version 1.0.2e dated from December 2015 has been used and the provider was statically linked with the resulting library. We provide the following services:

- AES with CBC and ECB chaining modes,
- RSA #PKCS1 v1.5 and v2.0,
- RSA textbook,
- MD5, SHA1 and SHA256,
- random source.

---

[7] see *RAND_poll* in crypto/rand/rand_win.c.
[8] http://www.microsoft.com/en-us/download/details.aspx?id=18512.

Table 1. Ransomware collection

Family	First seen	Most recent	Encryption algorithm	C& C
Gpcode	2004	2014	AES - ECB	∼ HTTP
CryptoLocker	2013	2014	AES	∼ HTTP
CryptoWall	2014	2016	AES - CBC	Tor
CTB-Locker	2014	2016	AES - ECB	Tor
TorrentLocker	2014	2016	AES - CTR|CBC *	Tor
TeslaCrypt	2015	2016	AES - ECB|CBC *	Tor
CrypVault	2015	2016	RSA - OAEP	
Locky	2016	-	AES - CTR|ECB *	∼ HTTP
Petya	2016	-	Salsa20	No

* Samples variation

The above algorithms represent a set of cryptographic primitives sufficiently exhaustive to fit the needs of ransomware based on observations and reports (Table 1).

Integration. Cryptographic providers on both 32 and 64-bit architectures are compiled as DLLs. Providers are then placed in the *System32* default path, and system integration is achieved through register entries[9]. Administrator rights are needed to plug a CSP in the system, registration is performed with *regsvr32.exe*. As explained in Sect. 5.1, system can not trust, and thus use, any provider until a valid signature from Microsoft is obtained. For our academic proof of concept, we patched the binary responsible for the authentication mechanism to successfully load our CSP. As described in Fig. 4, user applications start by calling MS CAPI exported functions *Crypt(*)* through *advapi32.dll*. In fact this is nothing more than an indirect jump to *cryptsp.dll* which contains the CSP authentication mechanism and most of the framework functionalities.

Still, a ransomeware may use another provider. Indeed, during the initialization phase, a call to *CryptAcquireContext* with the argument *pszProvider* lets the user choose between available providers.

```
BOOL WINAPI CryptAcquireContext(
   _Out_     HCRYPTPROV *phProv,
   _In_      LPCTSTR     pszContainer,
   _In_Opt   LPCTSTR     pszProvider,
   _In_      DWORD       dwProvType,
   _In_      DWORD       dwFlags
);
```

Listing 1.1. Provider selection

---

[9] HKEY_LOCAL_MACHINE\SOFTWARE\Microsoft\Cryptography\Defaults\ Provider.

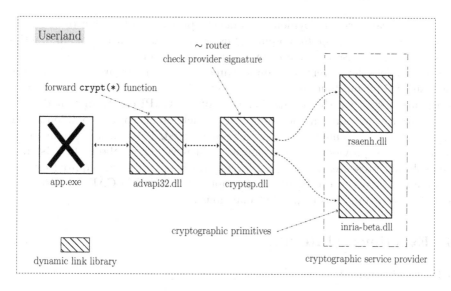

Fig. 4. Windows PE and Crypto API.

If the provider name is left *null*, a registry key indicates which is the default provider according to the requested type. So *cryptsp.dll* has been patched again to redirect all explicitly named provider to the default one. Final step is to set the name of the preferred cryptographic provider in registry as our own.

Detection. The malicious behavior must be stopped and the damage limited. In addition file recovery is needed to render ransomware harmless. We have the control on key generation, encryption, signature, randomness and integrity. At load time, no key exists within a CSP and usually deletion, exportation or public-key encryption is performed once operations are done. We can take advantage of this opportunity to monitor and store the secrets, if malicious activities are detected. Most interesting operations are logged in a special file prepended with a PE[10] header and extension to prevent ransomware encryption.

The difficulty is now to detect any abnormal behavior, no intelligence has been added to the module yet, but we investigate some possibilities. MS CAPI is marked as deprecated so very few applications on Windows down to Windows XP use its services. In any case, an intensive use is suspect, particularly encryption operations.

5.3   Limitation

As explained before, we had to place a patched *cryptsp.dll* in the ransomware directory. This is enough for our experimental purpose and characterization, but

---

[10] PE: Portable Executable, Windows executable file format.

not for any real world deployment. Signing our provider will allow it to be loaded by the legitimate *cryptsp.dll*. Forcing its use is still a theoretical issue, in practice most ransomware use the default one: our own provider.

To complete the current solution we can consider ransomware detection based on a supervised machine learning classifier. The provider can be deployed on legitimate hosts then the normal behavior of MS CAPI can train a model. We do not want to see machine learning as a miracle oracle so, user opinion has to be requested when a malicious behavior is suspected. This solution can be incorporated in the provider and ransomware will never know about its existence. The solution presented in Sect. 5.2 forces attackers to embed required cryptographic primitives in the binary. This approach avoids MS CAPI hijacking for manufacturers and aims to prevent malicious access.

6   Experimental Results

6.1   Environment

A bench of bare-metal hosts were used during the experiments. The Operating systems restoration is handled automatically in a few minutes. Moreover network traffic is captured through port mirroring and the hosts live in a completely open network. No malware analysis software were employed during ransomware execution, we aimed to be fully transparent regardless the threat complexity.

6.2   Results

The ransomware families considered are among the best known and the most diverse. Collection is composed of filecryptor (cf. Sect. 3). Unfortunately most of them do not trigger their malicious behavior. In most cases, C&C domains do not exist any more or are no more under attackers control. Due to this flaw, it seems important to note which one is active or inactive. CTB-Locker, TeslaCrypt and Petya do not require any C&C communication prior to begin encryption process. That is why good active rate is present with this families (Table 2).

Active samples have not yet been found for four families. CryptoWall, as noted by antivirus reports, uses MS CAPI to perform file encryption at least in these older versions [13]. Similarly Locky rely on MS CAPI [40].

Gpcode and CryptoLocker employ MS CAPI quite simply. First they acquire the context, the provider initializes some internal structures. Then they perform one or several AES key generations and quickly export them outside provider memory. Lastly prior to begin encryption, chaining mode is chosen. Encryption process is then performed through intensive calls to *CryptEncrypt()*.

6.3   Discussion

The main problem with ransomware is their high level of volatility. If C&C communication is required, reversing part of the network protocol is the only

Table 2. Results of our countermeasures on our ransomware collection. The first column gives the family. The second column indicates the number of ransomware collected. The third column indicates how many collected ransomware were actives, so tested in our experiments. The last two columns indicate if the ransomware families use ECB mode and/or the Crypto API, in positive cases ✓ is shown and the corresponding countermeasure is efficient. Unfortunately for families that do not have active ransomware, we are not able to know if the countermeasures work. Some families are divided in multiple rows, the separation represent significant variation between samples of the same family.

Family	# Samples	No. of Actives	Attack details	
			AES - ECB	Crypto API
Gpcode	4	4	✓	✓
	1	1	✓	×
CryptoLocker	7	0	-	-
	2	2	×	✓
CryptoWall	5	0	-	-
CTB-Locker	4	4	×	×
TorrentLocker	3	0	-	-
TeslaCrypt	2	2	×	×
	1	1	✓	×
	1	0	-	-
CrypVault	2	0	-	-
Locky	5	0	-	-
Petya	2	2	×	×
No. of Samples	39			
No. of Actives		16(41%)	6(37%) 6(37%)	
			8(50%)	

way to trigger the malicious behavior without intrusive methods. Ransomware samples have been found on different online repositories [41–43]. The samples quality is erratic especially for CryptoWall and Locky. Results are not relevant enough due to the small collection considered.

The low use of MS CAPI in the recent ransomware families could be partly explained with marketing purposes, no modern algorithms are available. It is more attractive to employ ECC cryptosystems with state of the art curve like *Curve25519* than the veteran RSA public key exchange algorithm. Petya uses Salsa20, in comparison MS CAPI contains the weak RC4 algorithm. A second explanation is that the generated keys are kept under the provider control through opaque structure. It can be one indication against a move to CNG.

In the future MS CAPI will be rare. The attackers have little control on MS CAPI and his successor CNG. Thus security checks may be embed as we presented. Strong cryptographic primitives are freely available contrary to the 90 s. One solution is to embed the cryptographic code in the binary. This approach is more stealthy and the attackers gain in control.

7 Conclusion

Few papers have studied ransomware threats and discussed about countermeasures. The taxonomy changes all days, protect files is complex within this context. Microsoft Windows is the principal target, on March 2016 the first significant ransomware on the OS X platform appeared. It would not be surprising that ransomware and worm capabilities will be mixed to enhance the incomes.

In this paper nevertheless, two new protections have been presented. One of them is based on the principle of a replay attack against a weak chaining mode in combination with a cipher algorithm. The second, more practical, exploit the Microsoft's Cryptographic API that many ransomware use. These two protections are placed at a different level and can be used complementary for best security, leading to a 50% success rate in our experiments. Unfortunately they are not efficient against all ransomware. Moreover these countermeasures are used after the attack, once the files have been encrypted. In our future works we would like to find an efficient protection that prevent files encryption by the ransomware.

Acknowledgments. The authors would like to thank Ronan Lashermes, Alexandre Gonzalvez and the anonymous reviewers for their valuable help and comments.

References

1. Trend Micro. By the numbers: Ransomware rising. http://www.trendmicro.com.ph/vinfo/ph/security/news/cybercrime-and-digital-threats/by-the-numbers-ransomware-rising
2. Paz, R.D.: Cryptowall, Teslacrypt and Locky: A Statistical Perspective. https://blog.fortinet.com/2016/03/08/cryptowall-teslacrypt-and-locky-a-statistical-perspective
3. Abrams, L.: The week in ransomware, 24 June 2016. http://www.bleepingcomputer.com/news/security/the-week-in-ransomware-june-24-2016-locky-returns-cryptxxx-apocalypse-and-more/
4. Kaspersky. Kaspersky Security Bulletin 2015. https://securelist.com/files/2015/12/Kaspersky-Security-Bulletin-2015_FINAL_EN.pdf
5. Lozhkin, S.: Hospitals are under attack in 2016, March 2016. https://securelist.com/blog/research/74249/hospitals-are-under-attack-in-2016
6. Lee, S.: Ransomware Wreaking Havoc in American and Canadian Hospitals, March 2016. http://europe.newsweek.com/ransomware-wreaking-havoc-american-and-canadian-hospitals-439714?rm=eu

7. Young, A.L., Yung, M.: Cryptovirology: Extortion-based security threats and countermeasures. In: IEEE Symposium on Security and Privacy, May 6–8, Oakland, CA, USA, pp. 129–140 (1996)

8. Gazet, A.: Comparative analysis of various ransomware virii. J. Comput. Virol. **6**(1), 77–90 (2010)

9. Kharraz, A., Robertson, W., Balzarotti, D., Bilge, L., Kirda, E.: Cutting the gordian knot: a look under the hood of ransomware attacks. In: Almgren, M., Gulisano, V., Maggi, F. (eds.) DIMVA 2015. LNCS, vol. 9148, pp. 3–24. Springer, Cham (2015). doi:10.1007/978-3-319-20550-2_1

10. Syverson, P.: A taxonomy of replay attacks [cryptographic protocols]. In: Proceedings of Computer Security Foundations Workshop VII, CSFW 7, pp. 187–191. IEEE (1994)

11. Josse, S.: White-box attack context cryptovirology. J. Comput. Virol. **5**(4), 321–334 (2009)

12. Wyke, J., Ajjan, A.: Sophos: the Current State of Ransomware, December 2015. https://www.sophos.com/en-us/medialibrary/PDFs/technical%20papers/sophos-current-state-of-ransomware.pdf?la=en

13. Kotov, V., Rajpal, M.S..: Bromium: Understanding Crypto-Ransomware (2014). https://www.bromium.com/sites/default/files/bromium-report-ransomware.pdf

14. Sinegubko, D.: How CTB-Locker Ransomware Uses Bitcoin and Blockchain. https://www.cryptocoinsnews.com/how-ctb-locker-ransomware-uses-bitcoin-and-blockchain/

15. Invincea endpoint security blog: Pat Belcher. Hash Factory: New Cerber Ransomware Morphs Every 15 Seconds. https://www.invincea.com/2016/06/hash-factory-new-cerber-ransomware-morphs-every-15-seconds/

16. National Institute of Standards and Technology. Data Encryption Standard (DES). http://csrc.nist.gov/publications/fips/fips46-3/fips46-3.pdf

17. Rivest, R.L., Shamir, A., Adleman, L.: A method for obtaining digital signatures and public-key cryptosystems. Commun. ACM **21**(2), 120–126 (1978)

18. Miller, Victor S.: Use of elliptic curves in cryptography. In: Williams, Hugh C. (ed.) CRYPTO 1985. LNCS, vol. 218, pp. 417–426. Springer, Heidelberg (1986). doi:10.1007/3-540-39799-X_31

19. Symantec. Trojan. Synolocker, 2014. https://www.symantec.com/security_response/writeup.jsp?docid=2014-080708-1950-99

20. Nazarov, D., Emelyanova, O.: Blackmailer: the story of Gpcode (2006). https://securelist.com/analysis/publications/36089/blackmailer-the-story-of-gpcode

21. Jarvis, K.: SecureWorks Counter Threat UnitTM Threat Intelligence. CryptoLocker Ransomware, December 2013. https://www.secureworks.com/research/cryptolocker-ransomware

22. Federal Bureau of Investigation (FBI). GameOver Zeus Botnet Disrupted. https://www.fbi.gov/news/stories/2014/june/gameover-zeus-botnet-disrupted

23. Allievi, A., Carter, E.: Ransomware on Steroids: Cryptowall 2.0. Cisco (2015). http://blogs.cisco.com/security/talos/cryptowall-2

24. Klijnsma, Y.: The history of Cryptowall: a large scale cryptographic ransomware threat. https://www.cryptowalltracker.org/

25. Léveillé, M.M.: TorrentLocker: Ransomware in a country near you (2014). http://www.welivesecurity.com/wp-content/uploads/2014/12/torrent_locker.pdf

26. Lipmaa, H., Rogaway, P., Wagner, D.: CTR-mode encryption. In: First NIST Workshop on Modes of Operation (2000)

27. Zairon.: CTB-Locker encryption/decryption scheme in details, February 2015. https://zairon.wordpress.com/2015/02/17/ctb-locker-encryptiondecryption-scheme-in-details

28. Bernstein, D.J.: A state-of-the-art Diffie-Hellman function. http://cr.yp.to/ecdh.html

29. Abrams, L.: CTB-Locker for Websites: Reinventing an old Ransomware. http://www.bleepingcomputer.com/news/security/ctb-locker-for-websites-reinventing-an-old-ransomware/

30. Talos Group. Threat Spotlight: TeslaCrypt Decrypt It Yourself, April 2015. http://blogs.cisco.com/security/talos/teslacrypt

31. Marcos, M.: CRYPVAULT: New Crypto-ransomware Encrypts and Quarantines Files. http://blog.trendmicro.com/trendlabs-security-intelligence/crypvault-new-crypto-ransomware-encrypts-and-quarantines-files/

32. Sinitsyn, F.: Locky: the encryptor taking the world by storm (2016). https://securelist.com/blog/research/74398/locky-the-encryptor-taking-the-world-by-storm

33. Sinitsyn, F.: Petya: the two-in-one trojan, May 2016. https://securelist.com/blog/research/74609/petya-the-two-in-one-trojan

34. Bernstein, D.J.: The Salsa20 family of stream ciphers. In: Robshaw, M., Billet, O. (eds.) New Stream Cipher Designs. LNCS, vol. 4986, pp. 84–97. Springer, Heidelberg (2008). doi:10.1007/978-3-540-68351-3_8

35. Leo-stone. Hack-petya mission accomplished. https://github.com/leo-stone/hack-petya

36. National Institute of Standards and Technology (NIST). Specification for the Advanced Encryption Standard, FIPS PUB 197, November 2001

37. Wikipedia. Block cipher mode of operation. https://en.wikipedia.org/wiki/Block_cipher_mode_of_operation

38. Microsoft. Microsoft Enhanced Cryptographic Provider, FIPS 140–1 Documentation: Security Policy (2005). http://csrc.nist.gov/groups/STM/cmvp/documents/140-1/140sp/140sp238.pdf

39. Hunt, G., Brubacher, D.: Detours: Binary interception of win 32 functions. In: 3rd USENIX Windows NT Symposium (1999)

40. Hasherezade. Look into locky ransomware. https://blog.malwarebytes.com/threat-analysis/2016/03/look-into-locky/

41. Malware online repository. https://malwr.com

42. Malware online repository. http://malwaredb.malekal.com

43. Malware online repository. https://virusshare.com

Risk and Security Analysis Methodology

A Formal Verification of Safe Update Point Detection in Dynamic Software Updating

Razika Lounas[1,3(✉)], Nisrine Jafri[2], Axel Legay[2], Mohamed Mezghiche[1], and Jean-Louis Lanet[2]

[1] LIMOSE Laboratory, Faculty of Sciences, University of Boumerdes, Independency Avenue, 35000 Boumerdès, Algeria
{razika.lounas,Mohamed.mezghiche}@univ-boumerdes.dz
[2] INRIA, LHS PEC, 263 Avenue Général Leclerc, 35042 Rennes, France
{nisrine.jafri,axel.legay,jean-louis.lanet}@inria.fr
[3] Xlim Laboratory, Limoges University, 123 Avenue Albert Thomas, 87060 Limoges, France
razika.lounas@xlim.fr

Abstract. Dynamic Software Updating (DSU) consists in updating running programs on the fly without any downtime. This feature is interesting in critical applications that must run continuously. Because updates may lead to safety errors and security breaches, the question of their correctness is raised. Formal methods are a rigorous means to ensure the high level of safety requested by such applications. The detection of points to perform safe updates is a critical issue in DSU. Indeed, an hazardous update point leads the updated system to erroneous and unexpected behavior. We present in this paper a mechanism to detect safe update points in DSU for Java Card applications. The mechanism is then formally verified using model checking against correctness properties: deadlock free, activeness safety and DSU-liveness.

Keywords: Dynamic Software Updating · Safe update point · Model checking · Update safety

1 Introduction

Context and Motivation. There are many classes of critical systems that must run continuously and that cannot be stopped. This is for example the case for operating systems [1,2], automation systems [3], embedded systems [4,5] and service oriented applications and real time systems [6]. One of the main challenge there is to be able to add new features and to eventually correct bugs without having to shutdown.

In order to guarantee this functionality, those systems implement a Dynamic Software Updating (DSU) procedure. The large interest of DSU and its use in many critical applications raise the question of its correctness. In fact, updates may introduce errors which may alter the application leading the system to an unexpected state and open security breaches. The study of DSU correctness

© Springer International Publishing AG 2017
F. Cuppens et al. (Eds.): CRiSIS 2016, LNCS 10158, pp. 31–45, 2017.
DOI: 10.1007/978-3-319-54876-0_3

relies on several criteria divided into two categories. The first category relies on common properties shared by all update mechanism such as type safety, consistency and no crash. The second category refers to specific behavioral properties related to the semantics of updated programs updates [7,8]. Over the past years, the use of formal methods to establish DSU correctness criteria has gained a wide interest. Indeed, techniques such as model checking [9] offer the right formalism to reason on system's behavior as well as to formally capture complex behavioral properties. Using formal methods will be the main objective of this paper.

It is worth mentioning that in critical applications where security issues are involved, applying updates must pass some certification procedure for example Common Criteria [10]. In this certification scheme, seven Evaluation Assurance Levels (EALs) are defined. These levels are a measure of assurance quality, where EAL 7 is the strongest. Assessment at the two highest levels, EAL 6 and 7, requires formal methods to give assurance that safety and security requirements are fulfilled by the system. Recently, the French ANSSI[1] has proposed a dedicated process [11] allowing to certify a product that can be dynamically changed, certifying only the update code and the loader. It defines the concepts and the methodology applicable to the evaluation of a product embedding a code loading mechanism and the usage of this loader as part of the assurance continuity process. It appears clearly that formal methods offer the high level of rigor required by critical applications in establishing DSU correctness.

Contribution. The main objective of this paper is to deploy formal methods to guarantee behavioral properties of DSU. We will mainly focus on Safe Update Points (SUP), one of the most critical part of the DSU. A SUP is a quiescent state where the system can be updated without introducing inconsistency or leading to application crash.

Here, we focus on the SUP of the DSU of Java Card applications. The considered system, called EmbedDSU [5,12] is based on two parts. The first one is the off-card part in which a module called DIFF generator computes the syntactic changes between the old and the new version of the application and generates a DIFF file (called also a patch). In a second step, this patch is then sent on the card to perform the on-card part: the update is interpreted by modules implemented by extending the Java Card virtual machine. A module of safe update detection allows to bring the system into a quiescent state to perform the update.

In this paper, we offer a model checking [9] approach to guarantee that the quiescent state satisfies a set of requirements. Model checking is a technique that consists that consists in a transition systems and a mathematical representation of all the executions of the system. This representation is suitable to verify complex temporal properties with powerful state-space exploration techniques [9] and automata-based representation. Most of existing model checkers rely on an unified intermediary representation language in order to be high-level language independent. One example of such language is the Promela representation [13] used by the SPIN (Simple Promela Interpreter) model checker [14,15]. The main

---

[1] Agence Nationale de la Sécurité des Systèmes d'Information.

drawback of those intermediary languages is that they often ignores complex features of high-level languages (arithmetic pointers, recursion, etc.). Fortunately, tools such as Modex [16,17] allows for a translation from the C language to Promela. Our objective is to satisfy the following three requirements:

1. *Deadlock free:* The studied module does not introduce deadlock into the system.
2. *Activeness safety:* The system does not introduce inconsistency by choosing to perform updates while no updated method is active (running).
3. *DSU-Liveness:* The mechanism of SUP detection leads to a quiescent state after every update request.

To achieve the objective, those requirements will be modeled via Linear Temporal Logic (LTL) [9], which is exactly the formalism accepted by the SPIN Model Checker. Starting from an initial C code implementation of the DSU, Modex produces a promela representation on which the LTL properties can be verified. In case the property is not satisfied, SPIN generates a counter example that allows us to refine the C code. The process is repeated until the requirements are all satisfied.

Organization. The rest of the paper is organized as follows: Sect. 2 describes the implementation of a DSU for java card applications. A mechanism for SUP detection is detailed in Sect. 3. Section 4 presents the properties that ensure the correctness of the mechanism and the methodology and tools to establish them. Finally, Related work and conclusion are given in Sects. 5 and 6, respectively.

2   A DSU System for Java Card

Smart Cards are small devices that embed high sensitive data and critical applications. These devices represent a target of attacks during their life time and must be upgraded to resist to threats. A good example is the electronic passport that must resist during 10 years to unknown attacks while delivered to the customer. So if a cryptographic algorithm used in a passport has been broken, the system needs to be updated to upload a new algorithm. The nature of the applications involved in smard cards require the use of DSU techniques.

EmbedDSU, introduced in [5,12], is a software-based DSU technique for Java-based smart cards which relies on the Java Card virtual machine. The Virtual Machine (VM) interprets Java Card programs once they are compiled to byte-code and loaded to the card. The system EmbedDSU is based on the modification of the VM and is divided in two parts as illustrated on Fig. 1

– In off-card, a module called *DIFF generator* determines the syntactic changes between versions of classes in order to apply the update only to the parts of the application that are really affected by the update. The changes are expressed using a Domain Specific Language (DSL). Then, the DIFF file result is transferred to the card and used to perform the update.

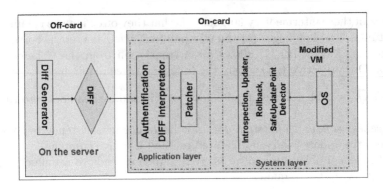

Fig. 1. Architecture of EmbedDSU

– The on-card part is divided into two layers: (1) Application Layer: The binary
DIFF file is uploaded into the card. After a signature check with the *wrapper*,
the binary DIFF is interpreted and the resulting instructions are transferred to
the *patcher* in order to perform the update. The *patcher* initialises data structures for update. These data structures are read by the *updater* module to
determine what to update and how to update, by the *safeUpdatePoint detector* module to determine when to apply the update and by the *rollbacker* to
determine how to return to the previous version in case of update failure. These
points require the introspection of the virtual machine. (2) System Layer: the
modified virtual machine supports the followings features: (1) *Introspection*
module which provides search functions to go through VM data structures
like the references tables, the threads table, the class table, the static object
table, the heap and stack frames for retrieving information necessary to other
modules; (2) *updater* module which modifies object instances, method bodies,
class metadata, references, affected registers in the stack thread and affected
VM data structures; (3) *SafeUpdatePoint detector* module permits to detect
SUP in which we can apply the update by preserving coherence of the system.

The system EmbedDSU is suitable for smart cards especially in term of resource
limitations. It was established that sending a DIFF file is less resource consuming
than sending the whole new version to the card and perform updates and that
the resources implied by the update modules are acceptable in term of memory
occupation [5]. The system EmbedDSU updates three principal parts:

– The bytecode: the process updates first the bytecode of the updated class
and the meta data associated with it *e.g.*, constant pool, fields table, methods
table...
– The heap: the process updates the instances of the updated class in the heap,
obtains new references for modified objects and updates instances using these
references.
– The frames: the process updates in each frame in the thread stack the references of updated objects to point to new instances.

To perform these updates, the mechanism uses the SUP detection module to bring the system to a quiescent state. This state is characterised by the absence of methods concerned by the update in the execution environment of the updated application. To obtain a safe point, the system uses introspection functions to go through the VM and block all calls to a class method to be modified in order not to have others frames related to a method to be modified in the stack thread. At starting point, all frames related to a modified method present in the stack thread are counted. If the value is not equals to zero, then the update is delayed, the virtual machine can continue to execute others applications. However, the value is decremented each time a method concerned by an update finishes its execution. When the value equals zero, then the safe update point is obtained and update is performed. The next section details the SUP mechanism by explaining the involved functions and concepts. This mechanism is verified using model checking with regard to three properties: deadlock free, activeness safety and DSU-liveness.

3   SUP Detection Mechanism

3.1   Methods and Language Description

In this work, we consider a target language containing five instructions. This language is used to study properties related to safe update point detection and thus the instructions are categorised in order to represent usual bytecode instructions, calling methods, locking and unlocking threads and returning:

- INST: This instruction is used to model the usual bytecode instructions. By usual, we mean all types of instructions except methods calls (arithmetics, stack operations and branching instructions...).
- INVOKE: This instruction is used to represent methods calls. An INVOKE instruction creates and initialises a new frame in the thread stack. This instruction is categorised to adapt the usual method invoke to make it suitable to SUP research functions.
- SETLOCK and UNLOCK instructions: The instruction SETLOCK is used to block the next thread in the threads table. The instruction UNLOCK is used by a thread to unlock a thread that it has already locked. These instructions are used to represent usual operations related to thread synchronisation in multi threaded languages.
- RETURN: this instruction is used to express the return from a method.

The detection of SUP is based on the notion of the quiescent state which is related to the absence of running updateable methods. the methods are so considered from activeness point of view. We notice four cases:

- **Active/Not active methods:** A method is active if it is running. This means that the method owns a frame in the execution stack because it has been invoked. Otherwise, a method is not active.

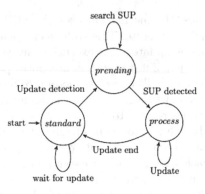

Fig. 2. Representation of VM modes

- **Restricted/Not restricted methods:** A method is restricted if it is active in the virtual machine (VM) and concerned by the update. A method is not restricted if it is not concerned by the update whatever it is active or not.

At a method invoke, the frame related to it is inserted in the thread stack. This frame initialisation contains with addition to standard information (such as its identifier and the identifier of the method) a data that indicates whether this frame is related or not to an updated method. This information is used by introspection and search SUP functions to lead the system to the quiescent state. These functions go through the VM structures and check for the existence of restricted method for each thread.

3.2 VM Modes and Threads Status

The research of the appropriate point to perform DSU is performed by a safe update detection algorithm. This algorithm ensures that no restricted method is executing during the update. The update process defines three modes for the virtual machine (Fig. 2):

- **The standard mode:** During this mode, the virtual machine works normally until detecting an update.
- **The pending mode:** At update detection, the virtual machine switches to seek a safe update point. A SUP is detected when the VM reaches a quiescent state.
- **The process mode:** After detecting a SUP, the update process is performed at the levels described in Sect. 2. The end of the update lead the VM to a standard mode.

A thread is mainly characterised by an identifier, a list of frames, its owner and its status. A thread passes trough different states. In standard mode, a thread is scheduled then executed (*Active* state). If it meets a sleep instruction, it goes to the sleeping state (*Locked* state). The thread gets blocked if it wants to acquire a lock but it cannot because another thread owns it, the active thread has to go to the blocked state and wait until another thread releases the lock (*Unlocked* state). A thread becomes inactive (*Idle* state) if its associated program terminates. In our mechanism, another state is necessary. The thread gets *DSU_locked* if the virtual machine enters the search SUP mode. This means that the thread is locked by the DSU mechanism if it has no frame related to restricted methods in its frame list, in order to force running restricted methods. The main idea is to force methods involved into an update to finish. This mechanism provides a highest priority to such methods that will be popped from the stack.

3.3   Search SUP Mode Functions

In order to detect a SUP, a function *searchSUP* introspects the frames for each thread of the running application. If the update is possible (no restricted method in the frames), then the VM is set to process mode. If restricted methods are present in the stack, we obtain the number of frames associated to restricted methods by VM introspection. It is stored in a variable nb_meth_stack. The search pending mode uses the following functions to lead the system to a quiescent state:

- *createFrame:* This function is used at every method invocation to create an associated frame. The frame is placed at the head of the frame list of the thread. This function is adapted to handle DSU mechanism at research SUP mode: at every created frame, a check is performed. If the thread has no frames related to a restricted methods in its execution stack then it is set to *DSU_locked* in order not to have others frames related to a method to be modified in the stack thread, otherwise it keeps executing. The goal is to let restricted methods finish their execution and lead them to inactive state. This accelerate the process of update.
- *releaseFrame:* This function is used at the end of the execution of a method to suppress its frame. In the search SUP mode, this function is adapted in order to check if restricted methods exist in the thread stack. If not, the thread is set to *DSU_locked*. The counter nb_meth_stack is decremented at every release of a frame associated to a restricted method. A safe update point is reached if this number reaches zero.
- *switchThread:* If the VM is in the normal mode, this function selects the next thread to be the active one. If the mode is pending and if all the remaining threads are blocked then it switches the process mode to update.

At the starting point, we count all frames related to a modified method present in the stack thread. If the value is not equals to zero, then the update is pending, the virtual machine can continue to execute other applications. However, the value is decremented each time these methods finished their execution. When the value equals zero, then the SUP is obtained and the virtual machine can switch to the update mode.

The algorithm *SUP_mechanism* shows the procedure of searching SUP mechanism. At the beginning, the normal execution of current methods is performed

```
     Data: UpdateSM, Instruction, nb_meth_stack;
 1   UpdateSM ← NoUpdate;
 2   repeat
 3   |   switch Instruction do
 4   |   |   case INVOKE
 5   |   |   |   CreateFrame();
 6   |   |   endsw
 7   |   |   case INSTR
 8   |   |   |   incr_pc();
 9   |   |   endsw
     |   |   /* Execution of a normal instruction, program counter
     |   |      incremented                                          */
10   |   |   case SETLOCK
11   |   |   |   lockThread();
12   |   |   endsw
     |   |   /* Locking the following thread in the threads table    */
13   |   |   case UNLOCK
14   |   |   |   unlockThread();
15   |   |   endsw
     |   |   /* Unlocking the previously locked thread, by the thread
     |   |      responsible of the lock                              */
16   |   |   case RETURN
17   |   |   |   ReleaseFrame();
18   |   |   endsw
     |   |   /* Deleting the frame associated to a terminating method,
     |   |      adapted to DSU                                       */
19   |   endsw
     |   /* Check for DSU request                                    */
20   |   if Notify_DSU() then
21   |   |   SearchSUP();
22   |   end
     |   /* Start searching SUP by counting restricted methods       */
23   |   if UpdateSM = Process then
24   |   |   Break;
25   |   end
     |   /* Exit if reaching SUP in SearchSup function               */
26   until ¬switchThread();
27   if UpdateSM = Pending ∧ nb_meth_stack = 0 then
28   |   UpdateSM ← Process; /* Set UpdateSM to process in the case of
     |      thread termination                                       */
29   end
```

Algorithm 1. SUP_mechanism

through the instructions defined by our language (lines 3 to 19). The systems checks the presence of update requests with the test *if Notify_DSU()* (line 20). If so, the function *SearchSUP* is called. This function checks the presence of restricted methods in the threads frames. The variable *UpdateSM*, initialised to *NoUpdate*, is set to *Process* if there is no restricted method, it is set to *Pending* otherwise. The *Pending* mode leads the functions *CreateFrames* and *ReleaseFrame* (lines 5 and 17) to execute in such way to get a quiescent state by especially setting threads to *DSU_locked*. This process is repeated until there is no more thread to schedule ($\neg switchThread()$). In this case, we have either reached *Process* or a check is performed after to set it to process in the case of a termination of threads without reaching *Process*.

4 Verification of Correctness Properties

In this section, we establish the correctness of the SUP detection mechanism with respect to three correctness criteria: *deadlock free*, *activeness safety* and *DSU_liveness*. We start with a brief presentation of the tools that will be used in the verification process. Then, we give a detailed description of the verification outcomes.

4.1 Methodology and Tools

As said in the introduction, our objective is to describe properties of systems with instances of the Linear Temporal Logic (LTL). This logic allows us to express 1. Boolean requirements on a specific state of the system (e.g., in current state, variable X is greater than 5), 2. hypothesis on the sequence of states that results from the execution of the system. For 1., the syntax relies on the classical Boolean first order logic. For 2., LTL offers various temporal operators. Given properties P, Q, and an execution $\pi = s_0, s_1...,$ ○ P (next P) expresses that in the next state s_1 P must be true. ◊ P (eventually P) express that there must exists a s_i where P is true. □ P (always P) requires that P is true in all the s_i.

SPIN Model Checker and Modex. There is a wide range of model checkers that can be used to verify LTL properties on a given system. In this work, we rely on the SPIN model checker that allows us to verify LTL properties on a system described in the Promela Language. This model-based language captures the features of several well-known high-level languages and allows us to use them in an independent manner (see [13] for more details).

To make the verification more efficient SPIN offers the implementation of several well-known optimization algorithms and heuristics. This includes Partial order reduction, State vector compression and Bitstate hashing [9]. One of the major advantages of Spin is its counter example generation process, that is when the properties is not satisfied, Spin will acts as a debugger for LTL and generate an execution of the system that does not satisfy the property.

Finally, in order to bridge the gap between our implementation and Promela, we propose to use Modex that automatically generates the Promela code corresponding to a C program. This translation exploits the embedding of C code into Promela and goes beyond the scope of this paper. A summary of our methodology is illustrated in Fig. 3

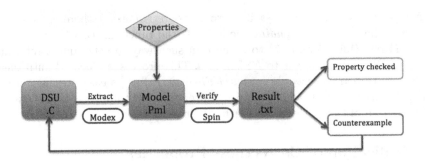

Fig. 3. Methodology of verification

4.2 Deadlock Free Property

We first use Spin to check for deadlocks. We describe a deadlock scenario and propose a solution to tackle it.

A Deadlock Scenario. Spin offers an automatic mechanism for deadlock detecting, that is at this stage we do not need to express the property with LTL. The application of the model checker on the implementation of the algorithm SUP_mechanism outlined the presence of a deadlock situation. This can be explained with a counter example involving two threads $T1$ and $T2$ with respectively frame lists $FT1$ and $FT2$. The elements of the frames lists are of the form (F_{ij}, R) if the frame F_{ij} correspond to a restricted method, and (F_{ij}, NR) if the frame F_{ij} correspond to a not restricted method. As illustrated on the Fig. 4, threads starts executing with the status *Active* corresponding to a normal execution. The virtual machine starts with the status *NoUpdate* corresponding to a standard execution. The vertical lines on the illustration represent events. The first event $e1$ corresponds to the execution of a *lock* instruction by $T1$. This leads the thread $T2$ to became *locked*. The second event $e2$ corresponds to the detection of an update request. The virtual machine passes to a *pending* status corresponding to SUP searching. The thread T1 continue its execution, the event $e3$ corresponds to the release of the frame F_{12} which corresponds to a restricted method. The thread $T1$ becomes *DSU_locked* since F_{12} was its last restricted frame in order to lead the mechanism to a SUP.

As the illustration shows, the VM status remains pending endless because there is still a restricted frame in the frame list of $T2$ which is locked. The mechanism is unable to lead the VM status to a quiescent state to enter a *Process* status causing a deadlock situation where: Thread $T1$ is *DSU_locked* waiting the end of the update mechanism, Thread $T2$ is locked waiting to be unlocked to continue and get the restricted frame out of the frame list and the VM is waiting for the condition of the quiescent state to enter to *process*.

Tackling Deadlock Situations. In order to avoid deadlock, we thus have to ensure that a thread passes to *DSU_locked* only once we ensure that it does

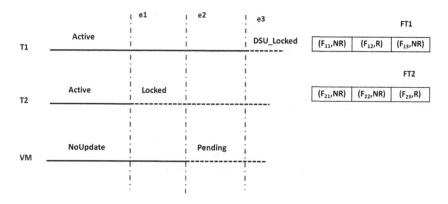

Fig. 4. Illustration of a deadlock scenario

not hold a lock on another thread which still has frames related to restricted methods in its frame list.

This means that an introspection is performed in order to detect the presence of locked threads with frames related to restricted methods. The mechanism is improved with a code that ensures that before each *DSU_locked* instruction, a check is performed over the thread list to detect if the thread owns a lock on another thread. This solution delays *DSU_Locked* instructions until all threads with restricted methods are unlocked. As shown on Fig. 5, this solutions implies to delay the application of *DSU_locked* to a thread. In the considered scenario, thread $T1$ continues executing until the mechanism receives a notification (event $e3'$) that there is no locked threads with restricted frames. In Fig. 5, $e3$ corresponds to release frame from $T1$ and $e4$ corresponds to the execution by $T1$ of an UNLOCK instruction which allows $T2$ to get the *Active* status again. The event $e5$ represents the release of the frame F_{23} which corresponds to the last restricted method. This leads $T2$ to get *DSU_locked* and the VM to *process*.

4.3   Activeness Safety Property

Activeness safety ensures that an update may be performed only if the functions that are impacted by the update are not running (active). In short, this means that there are no restricted methods. The number of restricted methods is used along the process of SUP searching: the process reaches a SUP if the number of restricted methods is null. This criteria allows us to avoid inconsistency: updating a method while it is active leads to the use of different versions of the same method and thus, creates bugs in the system. In LTL, this property is expressed as follows:

$$\square((UpdateSM == Process) \rightarrow (nb\_meth\_stack == 0))$$

This expresses that when the virtual machine enters the process status, the number of restricted methods in the frames is null and thus guarantees the consistency of the update.

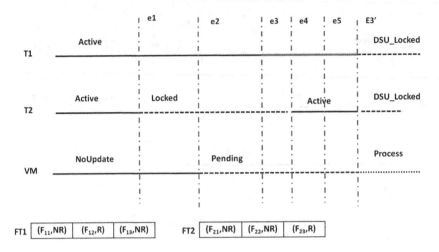

Fig. 5. Illustration of the solution to avoid deadlock

This property is successfully verified on the program by the model checker.

4.4 DSU-Liveness Property

DSU-liveness ensures that once an update request is made, the DSU system brings the application to a safe update point. It is a liveness property. In model checking, liveness properties assert that something good will eventually happen. In the case of SUP detection, this property called DSU-liveness ensures that the system must eventually reach a quiescent state. *DSU-liveness* is formalised as follows:

$$\Box((UpdateSM == Pending) \rightarrow \Diamond(UpdateSM == Process))$$

In the above, Variable $UpdateSM$ is used to express the status of the virtual machine with regard to DSU. The formula expresses that when the virtual machine is in a *Pending* mode, which means that an update request is made and the Virtual Machine (VM) has entered the SUP searching mode, the process will end eventually to a quiscent state which allows to perfom the update (the VM is in *Process* mode).

Thus, this property is successfully verified by SPIN on the improved version of the program.

5   Related Work

Different formal techniques are explored to establish correctness criteria for DSU. In [18], the authors used an algebraic formalism and rewriting techniques to establish type safety, no crash and behavioral properties. The authors used in [19] model checking and theorem proving to ensure deadlock free property. Techniques based on functional formalism and type system are used in [20–22]. In [8], the authors provided a framework using annotation technique to write specifications within the updated code using Hoare logic style. The system computes proof obligations which are discharged by theorem proving.

The definition of safe points to perform DSU is a crucial issue. The problem of defining safe update points is addressed in literature through two major approaches: The first category relies on predictive techniques: In [23], the authors presented a static analysis based on the notion of con-freeness to insert update points in the program. The code is labeled with update expressions at points where the update is possible in addition with the types that must not be updated. In [24,25], the authors proposed algorithms in order to state theorems that ensures correct DSU by determining safe update points and performing update schedules. The formalisation is based on theory built upon a graph-based modelisation (flow graphs and inter-procedural flow graphs) to establish that the correctness of the algorithms. The major inconvenient of this category is that prediction techniques relies generally on the modification of the semantics of the programming language to offer the possibility to insert update points within the code e.g. in [23] and the fact that a new analysis is required after every dynamic update to take changes into account in preparation to the next dynamic update.

In the second category [5,26–28] when the update is detected, introspection mechanisms are activated to lead the system to a quiescent state. A state is quiescent if there is no updated methods in the list of active methods of the application. Studies relying on this techniques proposes techniques to reduces the waiting time which represents the main challenge of this category. The use of formal techniques to ensure correctness is based on bisimulation techniques [5,26] and static analysis [28].

Our contribution belongs to the second category. To the best of our knowledge, this is the first use of formal verification with model checking to establish correctness properties related to safe update point detection in DSU for Java Card applications. In [29], the authors presented a formalism based on model checking to determine safe update points. There is a major difference between their work and ours: our approach is a system approach, the SUP detection is verified with regard to general correctness properties whereas in [29], the verification is based on the semantics of the updated program, the verification process is performed for every single updated program. The novelty of our contribution is the use of model checking to establish three principle correctness criteria related to SUP detection mechanism.

6   Conclusion

To avoid the disruption caused during software updates, DSU consists in updating running programs on-the-fly without any downtime. The use of this feature in critical applications leads to the use of formal methods that offers the high level of guarantee required by such applications. In this paper, we proposed an approach for formal verification using model checking of a SUP search mechanism used in a DSU system dedicated to Java Card applications.

In order to reach SUP, the mechanism implements functions to bring the system to a quiescent state which corresponds to the absence of restricted methods in the execution environment of the updated application. The correctness of this mechanism ensures system consistency. We based the correctness on three criteria: *deadlock free*, *activeness safety* and *DSU_liveness*. We verified these properties using model checking. This technique allowed us to detect deadlock in the first version of a program by returning counter examples. A solution is then proposed in order to improve the program and then successfully verify all the properties and establish the correctness of the SUP detection mechanism. As a future work, we plan to extend our work to verify other parts of the DSU system such as instances update.

References

1. Baumann, A., Kerr, J., Da Silva, D., Krieger, O., Wisniewski, R.W.: Module hot-swapping for dynamic update and reconfiguration in k42. In: 6th Linux.Conf.Au (2005)
2. Arnold, J., Kaashoek, M.F.: Ksplice: automatic rebootless kernel updates. In: Proceedings of the 4th ACM European Conference on Computer Systems, EuroSys 2009, pp. 187–198. ACM, New York (2009)
3. Wahler, M., Oriol, M.: Disruption-free software updates in automation systems. In: Emerging Technology and Factory Automation (ETFA), pp. 1–8. IEEE, September 2014
4. Holmbacka, S., Lund, W., Lafond, S., Lilius, J.: Lightweight framework for runtime updating of c-based software in embedded systems. In: Presented as Part of the 5th Workshop on Hot Topics in Software Upgrades. USENIX, Berkeley (2013)
5. Noubissi, A.C., Iguchi-Cartigny, J., Lanet, J.-L.: Hot updates for Java based smart cards, pp. 168–173, April 2011
6. Liu, J., Tong, W.: A framework for dynamic updating of service pack in the Internet of Things. In: 2011 International Conference on Internet of Things (iThings/CPSCom) and 4th International Conference on Cyber, Physical and Social Computing, pp. 33–42 (2011)
7. Lounas, R., Mezghiche, M., Lanet, J.-L.: An approach for formal verification of updated Java bytecode programs. In: Hedia, B.B., Vladicescu, F.P. (eds.) Proceedings of the 9th Workshop on Verification and Evaluation of Computer and Communication Systems, VECoS, Bucharest, Romania, 10–11 September, vol. 1431. CEUR Workshop Proceedings, pp. 51–64. CEUR-WS.org (2015)
8. Charlton, N., Horsfall, B., Reus, B.: Formal reasoning about runtime code update. In: ICDE Workshops, pp. 134–138. IEEE (2011)
9. Baier, C., Katoen, J.-P.: Principles of Model Checking. Representation and Mind Series. The MIT Press, Cambridge (2008)
10. Common Criteria. https://www.commoncriteriaportal.org/. Accessed 05 June 2016
11. Secrétariat général de la défense et de la sécurité nationale. Security requirements for post-delivery code loading. Agence Nationale de la Sécurité des Systèmes d'Information, Paris (2015)

12. Noubissi, A.C.: Mise á jour dynamique et scurisée de composants systéme dans une carte á puce. Ph.D. thesis, University of Limoges, France (2011)
13. Holzmann, G.: The SPIN Model Checker: Primer and Reference Manual, 1st edn. Addison-Wesley Professional, New York (2003)
14. Holzmann, G.J.: The model checker SPIN. IEEE Trans. Softw. Eng. **23**(5), 279–295 (1997)
15. SPIN model checker. http://spinroot.com/. Accessed 05 June 2016
16. Holzmann, G.J., Smith, M.H.: An automated verification method for distributed systems software based on model extraction. IEEE Trans. Softw. Eng. **28**(4), 364–377 (2002)
17. The modex tool user guide. http://spinroot.com/modex/MANUAL.html. Accessed 05 June 2016
18. Zhang, M., Ogata, K., Futatsugi, K.: An algebraic approach to formal analysis of dynamic software updating mechanisms. In: Leung, K.R.P.H., Muenchaisri, P. (eds.) 19th Asia-Pacific Software Engineering Conference, APSEC, Hong Kong, China, 4–7 December, pp. 664–673. IEEE (2012)
19. Zhang, M., Ogata, K., Futatsugi, K.: Formalization and verification of behavioral correctness of dynamic software updates. Electr. Notes Theor. Comput. Sci. **294**, 12–23 (2013)
20. Neamtiu, I., Hicks, M., Foster, J.S., Pratikakis, P.: Contextual effects for version-consistent dynamic software updating and safe concurrent programming. In: Proceedings of the 35th Annual ACM SIGPLAN-SIGACT Symposium on Principles of Programming Languages, POPL 2008, pp. 37–49. ACM, New York (2008)
21. Anderson, A., Rathke, J.: Migrating protocols in multi-threaded message-passing systems. In: Proceedings of the 2nd International Workshop on Hot Topics in Software Upgrades, HotSWUp 2009, pp. 8:1–8:5. ACM, New York (2011)
22. Bierman, G., Hicks, M., Sewell, P., Stoyle, G.: Formalizing dynamic software updating. In: On-line Proceedings of the Second International Workshop on Unanticipated Software Evolution (USE), Warsaw, Poland (2003)
23. Stoyle, G., Hicks, M., Bierman, G., Sewell, P., Neamtiu, I.: Mutatis mutandis: safe and predictable dynamic software updating. ACM Trans. Program. Lang. Syst. **29**(4), August 2007
24. Murarka, Y.: Online update of concurrent object oriented programs. Ph.D. thesis, Indian Institute of Technology, India (2010)
25. Murarka, Y., Bellur, U.: Correctness of request executions in online updates of concurrent object oriented programs. In: 15th Asia-Pacific Software Engineering Conference, APSEC 2008, pp. 93–100, December 2008
26. Hayden, C.M., Magill, S., Hicks, M., Foster, N., Foster, J.S.: Specifying and verifying the correctness of dynamic software updates. In: Joshi, R., Müller, P., Podelski, A. (eds.) VSTTE 2012. LNCS, vol. 7152, pp. 278–293. Springer, Heidelberg (2012). doi:10.1007/978-3-642-27705-4_22
27. Makris, K., Ryu, K.D.: Dynamic and adaptive updates of non-quiescent subsystems in commodity operating system kernels. SIGOPS Oper. Syst. Rev. **41**(3), 327–340 (2007)
28. Lv, W., Zuo, X., Wang, L.: Dynamic software updating for onboard software. In: Second International Conference on Intelligent System Design and Engineering Application (ISDEA 2012), pp. 251–253, January 2012
29. Zhang, M., Ogata, K., Futatsugi, K.: Towards a formal approach to modeling and verifying the design of dynamic software updates. In: Asia-Pacific Software Engineering Conference (APSEC 2015), pp. 159–166, December 2015

Analyzing the Risk of Authenticity Violation Based on the Structural and Functional Sizes of UML Sequence Diagrams

Hela Hakim[1(✉)], Asma Sellami[1], and Hanêne Ben Abddallah[2]

[1] Computer Science Engineering Department, University of Sfax, Sfax, Tunisia
hakim.hela@yahoo.fr, asma.sellami@isimsf.rnu.tn
[2] King Abdulaziz University, Jeddah, Kingdom of Saudi Arabia
hbenabdallah@kau.edu.sa

Abstract. Paying attention to authenticity, as a security requirement, in the early phases of the software life-cycle (such as requirement and-or design) can save project cost, time, and effort. However, in the ISO 25010 quality model which describes quality sub-characteristics, authenticity measures are not explicitly described, neither are they documented with sufficient details. This paper proposes a clear and precise way of measuring the "authenticity" sub-characteristic based on structural and functional size measurements. This combination can be used to identify the risk of authenticity violation in the design phase. An example of Facebook Web User Authentication is used to illustrate our proposed measurement.

Keywords: ISO 25010 quality model · Security · Authenticity measures · Design phase · Structural Size Measurement · Functional Size Measurement

1 Introduction

Successful software projects produce artifacts that meet functional and non-functional requirements under particular project requirements and constraints. Many researchers focused on the non-functional requirements also called "quality requirements" or "software quality" [2, 10, 11].

Software quality is defined as the "capability of software product to satisfy stated and implied needs when used under specified conditions" [3]. The definition suggested by ISO 25000 [3] implies that stated and implied needs (requirements) are the most important elements for achieving software quality. Software requirements are then classified into software quality characteristics. A number of quality models are proposed to tie together different quality characteristics [10, 14, 22].

According to DeMarco's statement [24], quality requirements that cannot be quantified cannot be controlled. Indeed, without measuring software quality, it becomes difficult to determine its acceptance and to demonstrate whether the quality requirements are satisfied.

The herein presented work focuses on quality requirement in terms of security. More specifically, it tackles the authenticity sub-characteristic of security. According to ISO 25023, authenticity is defined as "the degree to which the identity of a subject or resource

F. Cuppens et al. (Eds.): CRiSIS 2016, LNCS 10158, pp. 46–59, 2017.
DOI: 10.1007/978-3-319-54876-0_4

can be proved to be the one claimed". One main limit of ISO 25023 [8] (Measurement of system and software product quality) is the absence of a detailed measure of authenticity and the interpretation of these measures are yet to be defined. The main objective of this paper is to propose a detailed measurement of the authenticity sub-characteristic at the design phase. That is, we propose to analyze measurements results and classify the related authenticity risk violation. Our main motivation is that software designers can easily measure the authenticity of their work products (software) and thereby predict the risk of authenticity violation. They can also identify authentication issues and initiate corrective action as early as possible in the software life-cycle. As such, the herein proposed measurement can help software designers/quality engineers to detect the risk of violation of authenticity at the design phase.

More specifically, this study provides emphasis on:

- how to measure the authenticity sub-characteristic early at the design phase of the software life-cycle;
- how to analyze/interpret the results of measurement; and
- how to explore these measurement results.

The rest of this paper is organized as follows: in Sect. 2, we present an overview of the ISO 25010 model of software quality, the ISO 19761 COSMIC method (FSM), the Structural Size Measurement method (SSM), and related works. In Sect. 3, we present how a combination of structural and functional sizes can be used as a detailed measure for sizing UML sequence diagram related to the authenticity sub-characteristic. The purpose of using this detailed measure is presented in Sect. 4. In Sect. 5 we illustrate the proposed measurement of authenticity through an example. Section 6 presents conclusion and further works.

2   Background Concepts

2.1   Overview of the ISO 25010 – Quality Model

The ISO 25010 quality model is a "set of characteristics, sub-characteristics, quality measures, quality measure elements and relationships between them" [3]. This model helps to determine which quality characteristics will be taken into account when evaluating the properties of a software product [4]. It describes a two-part model for software product quality:

- A software product quality model is composed of eight characteristics and 31 sub-characteristics that relate to static properties of the software and dynamic properties of the computer system. It is applicable to both computer systems and software products.
- A system quality-in-use model composed of five characteristics (Effectiveness, Efficiency, Satisfaction, Safety, and Usability) that relate to the outcome of interaction when a product is used in a particular context of use. It is applicable to the complete human-computer system, including both computer systems in use and software products in use.

The ISO 25010 quality model distinguishes three views of the software product quality at the highest level: internal, external and quality in use. Internal quality is believed to impact external quality, which in turn impact quality in use.

A. Measuring the ISO 25023 Authenticity Sub-Characteristic

The ISO 25023 offers a consensual set of measures for measuring authenticity as a sub-characteristic of the "security" characteristic. "Authenticity" is considered as the Highly Recommended (HR) quality measure which means "this quality measure is always used" [8].

Table 1 shows the quality measures related to the authenticity sub-characteristic as defined in the ISO 25023 [8].

Table 1. Measures of the security characteristic [8]

Quality characteristic	Quality sub characteristics	Quality measures (Internal I/External E/ Both B)
Security	Authenticity	Authentication protocols (B)
		Establishment of authentication rules (B)

To measure authenticity sub-characteristic according to ISO 25023 [8], it is required to provide Quality Measures (QM) which are the Authentication protocol measures and the Establishment of authentication rules measures.

(1) Authentication protocol measure is calculated by function F,

$$F = A/B \tag{1}$$

where:
A = Number of provided authentication protocols (e.g., User ID/password or IC (Integrated Circuit) card);
B = Number of required authentication protocols in the specification;
A and B are denominated as Quality Measure Elements (QME).

(2) Establishment of authentication rules measure is calculated by function F,

$$F = A/B \tag{2}$$

where:
A = Number of authentication rules implemented for secure data;
B = Number of authentication rules required for secure data;
A and B are denominated as Quality Measure Elements (QME).

2.2   Overview of the ISO/IEC 19761 COSMIC–Functional Size Measurement

ISO international standards recognize a number of Functional Size Measurement (FSM) methods (such as COSMIC ISO/IEC 19761 and others). In COSMIC, a functional process is a set of data movements representing the Functional User Requirements (FUR) for the software to be measured. COSMIC measurement is based on the identification of four types of data movement [25]:

- Entry (E) and Exit (X) data movements of a data group between the functional user of the software and a COSMIC functional process allow data exchange with a functional user across a software boundary.
- Read (R) and Write (W) data movements of a data group between a COSMIC functional process and persistent storage allow data exchange with the persistent storage hardware.

Each data movement is equivalent to 1 CFP. The software functional size is computed by adding all data movements identified for every functional process.

COSMIC method is applied to any type of application in any software life-cycle phase, e.g. software work-product which is modeled in UML diagrams.

2.3 Overview of the Structural Size Measurement Method

The Structural Size Measurement (SSM) is a measurement method proposed by Sellami et al. [13]. It was designed by following the measurement process recommended by Abran [28]. This Structural Size Measurement is applied on the combined fragments of a sequence diagram, to measure its structural size. The SSM of a sequence diagram is defined at a finer level of granularity, i.e. the size of the flow graph of their control structure described through the *alt, opt* and *loop* constructs.

The use of SSM requires the identification of two types of data manipulation depending on the structure type in which it is defined:

- Data manipulation represented in the flow graph of the conditional control structure (*alt, opt* combined fragment)
- Data manipulation represented in the flow graph of the iterative control structure (*loop* combined fragment)

Each data manipulation is equivalent to 1 CSM (Control Structure Manipulation). The sequence structural size is computed by adding all data manipulations identified for every flow graph.

2.4 Related Works

Many researchers focused on software quality models and quality evaluation to overcome certain issues identified in ISO models of software quality [4].

Aiming to make ISO 25010 operational, the authors of [17] proposed a security product quality model. They specified four requirements for the ISO 25010 model: (1) the model shall be applicable for all types of software products; (2) the model shall be applicable from the early development phase; (3) the model shall be lightweight, concrete and repeatable; and (4) the model shall lead to ratings that allow for comparison between software products.

Authors in [16] proposed a metric of authenticity evaluation based on ISO 25010 quality model for android applications to quantify the permission application usage. This metric can be used to classify the malware applications. Its applicability was evaluated through benign and malware applications.

In [9], the authors proposed measurements applied in software design i.e., measurements of the quality characteristic as an *internal* quality measure applied at the code level.

In [20], the authors proposed a set of rules to develop and evaluate software quality models in order to address problems related to the ambiguity of the relationships among elements in the ISO 25010 quality model. They also suggest to evaluate in their future research the quality aggregation (and correspondingly the presentation of the evaluation into a single aggregated number).

In summary, most of these researches focused on different ways to make the quality model practicable. In fact, they proposed different types of measuring quality sub-characteristics. However, none of these works considered measurement at the design phase. Nor have they provided benefits before the implementation (code) phase.

3   Measuring the Authenticity Sub-characteristic

As described by ISO 25023 (see Sect. 2.1.A) the two quality measures (QM), i.e. authentication protocol measure and establishment of authentication rules measure are used for both internal and external quality. They also lack several details for their applicability which hinders their practical use. More specifically, to measure the authentication protocols using Eq. (1), it is unclear how to identify the target entity, how to distinguish whether the entity is internal or external, and in which phase the measure should be applied (requirement, design or source code)? In contrast the herein presented measure resolves these open questions: it is applied during the design phase on the sequence diagram specifically the authentication use case. Similarly to measure the establishment of authentication rules using Eq. (2), the problem of target entity, the related phases (requirement, design or source code), in which we can apply these measures, and the interpretation of these measures should be addressed. Consequently, ISO 25023 [8] does not yet accommodate a clear set of measures for measuring authenticity. It is allowed, if necessary, to refine these proposed measures; in ISO 25023, it is noted that "The set of quality measures in this International Standard are not intended to be exhaustive, and users of this standard are encouraged to refine them if necessary."

We present in the next Sect. 3.1 a more detailed measurement of these QM.

3.1   Measuring Authenticity Based on the Structural Size and Functional Size of Its UML Sequence Diagram

The Structural Size (SS) Measurement is intended to be used in complementary with the Functional Size (FS) Measurement of the sequence diagram. Since non-functional requirements can be transformed into functional requirement through the software lifecycle [24], we will present, in the following sub-Sections, the alignment of the SS and FS to measure respectively the authentication protocols and the establishment of authentication rules.

3.1.1   Measuring the QME of Authenticity Sub-characteristic Using the Structural Size Measurement

QM as proposed by ISO 25023 (Table 1) can be aligned with the UML combined fragments in the sequence diagram of the Authenticity sub-characteristic. In the matrix of Table 2, the rows represent the different quality measures (QM) of Authenticity sub-characteristic and their respective quality measures elements (QME) according to ISO 25023 [8]. The columns represent the combined fragments of a UML sequence diagram (*alt*, *opt* and *loop*) [13].

Table 2. Mapping of the ISO 25023 authenticity QM (and their related QME) with the combined fragments (alt, opt, loop) of UML sequence diagram

		Combined fragments		
QM	QME	*alt*	*opt*	*loop*
Authentication protocols	A	✓	✓	
	B			
Establishment of authentication rules	A			✓
	B			

When an element of UML sequence diagram is deemed or judged to have a strong influence on particular measures (there is a relationship between the UML element and one of the listed QME in the matrix rows), a check mark is drown in the corresponding cellule.

From Table 2, we can deduce that the structural size method (SSM) can be applied to provide the QME (A) of both Authenticity QMs (Authentication protocols and Establishment of authentication rules). The QME of A as the Number of provided authentication protocols (e.g., User ID/password or ICcard) is mapped with the *alt* and *opt* combined fragments. Whereas, the QME of A as the Number of authentication rules implemented for secure data is mapped with the *loop* combined fragment.

Since the authenticity protocol can be represented as an UML sequence diagram (and it describes the controlling access of data), SS measurement can be explored to measure the authenticity sub-characteristic.

3.1.2   Measuring the QME of Authenticity Sub-characteristic Using the Functional Size Measurement

In the same ways, we investigate the use of COSMIC – FSM method to provide the QME (B) of both authenticity QMs (Authentication protocols and Establishment of authentication rules). Instead of counting intuitively the Number of required authentication protocols (B) and the Number of authentication rules required for secure data in the specification document (B), we propose to measure the functional size of the UML sequence diagram describing the authentication functional process in terms of COSMIC Function Point units [25]. Indeed, different data movements describing the authentication functional process (i.e., messages between objects in the authentication sequence diagram) present the number of both required authentication protocols (noted B_p) and authentication rules required for secure data (noted B_r) in the specification.

Figure 1 illustrates the measurement process of applying Structural and Functional Size measurement (SS and FS) on the authenticity sub-characteristic.

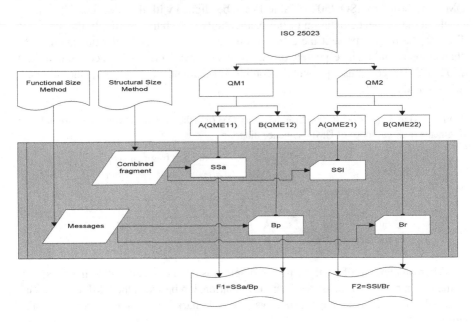

Fig. 1. Measurement process of applying Structural (SS) and Functional Size (FS) measurements on the QME authenticity (QM1 and QM2 refer to the Authenticity QMs)

3.1.3 Function, Qualifiers and QMEs Related to the Proposed Authenticity Sub-characteristic

In this Section, we present a new way for measuring authenticity (including the authentication protocol measures and establishment of authentication rules measures) based on the Structural Size measure and Functional Size measure of its QME. Authenticity measures are then represented by a new function, qualifiers & QMEs related.

Table 3 describes the representation of the quality sub-characteristic measures related to authenticity measures such as mentioned by the ISO 25023 [8] and the new proposed authenticity measures. Figure 2 illustrates the relationship among properties to quantify, measurement method, QME and QM to present the authentication protocols measure as examples of ISO 25021.

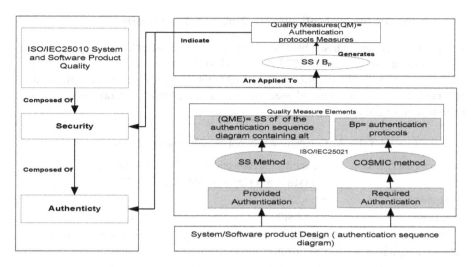

Fig. 2. An example of relationship among property to quantify, measurement method, QME and QM of "Authentication protocols measure"

Table 3. The authenticity measures

Quality subCharacteristic measures: authenticity measures	Qualifiers and QMEs related to the measure in ISO 25023 [8]	Qualifiers and QMEs related to the proposed measure based on SS [13] and FS [25]
Authentication protocols	A = Number of provided authentication protocols (e.g., User ID/password or ICcard)	SSa: Structural size of the authentication sequence diagram containing *alt* combined diagram
	B = Number of required authentication protocols in the specification	Bp: Functional size of sequence diagram describing the authentication functional process
Establishment of authentication rules	A = Number of authentication rules implemented for secure data	SSl: Structural size of the authentication sequence diagram containing *loop* combined diagram
	B = Number of authentication rules required for secure data	Br: Functional size of sequence diagram describing the authentication functional process

SS_a replace the numerator A = Number of provided authentication protocols.

SS_l replace the numerator A = Number of authentication rules implemented for secure data.

3.2 Comparing the Authenticity Sub-characteristic Measures

Table 4 presents a comparison between the new proposed authenticity measures and the authenticity measures in ISO 25023 [8]. Based on the measurement criteria (measurement functions, type of measures, measurement unit, etc.) as described in [25], it can be observed that the new proposed measures of the authenticity is more specific, more comprehensive and even more useful.

Table 4. Comparison between the authenticity measures

Measurement criteria	Measuring the authenticity quality sub-characteristic	
	COSMIC FSM [25] and SSM [13]	ISO 25023 [8]
Measurements	$F1 = SSa/B_p$	$F = A/B$
Functions	$F2 = SSl/B_r$	$F = A/B$
Type of measures	Internal	Internal and external
Measurement unit	CSM/CFP	Numbers
Measurement method	Structural Size Method/COSMIC method	Counting
Phases in the SDLC	Design	Not explicitly described

4 Identifying Risk Violation of Authenticity

Starting from the lowest level of measurement detail (the level of the attribute – see Fig. 3), we clarify the links between the QM and its corresponding characteristic (i.e. the high level of quality model – authenticity characteristic – see Fig. 3). For instance, let M1 be the new authentication protocols measures, and M2 be the new establishment of authentication rules measures. The sum of these two measures (M1 + M2) leads to a single measurement value at a high level (M). The aggregated value can be used as indicator to evaluate the security quality characteristic. In other words, to predict the risk of violation of authenticity by designers and to facilitate an objective communication between software project managers and designers regarding the authenticity quality objective. Figure 3 presents how to aggregate measured values from the lowest level to the highest level of quality model.

4.1 Interpretation of Measurement Values of Authenticity

We assume that the results of these measurements are generally in the range of values 0 and 1 because the SS_a or SSl are always equal or lower than Bp, Br respectively.

Let: $F1 = SSa/Bp$, $F2 = SSl/Br$, M1 is the measure calculated by the function F1; M2 is the measure calculated by the function F2; Ms is the aggregated measure; $Ms = (M1 + M2)/n$ (n is equal to the sum of the measures numbers); $n = 2$; Bp is bigger than SSa; Br is bigger than SSl.

Clearly, the two measures M1 and M2 avoid the misinterpretation. The reference values for M can be as follows:

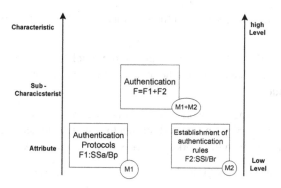

Fig. 3. The hierarchical aggregation measurement

- If the measured value Ms is nearer or equal to the min value (the zero) then we have a weak authentication. In fact, if (M1 + M2 = 0) then SSa and/or SSl is equal to 0. It means that the target entity (i.e. combined fragment) is omitted and then there is no structure control and no control of authentication.
- If the value Ms is nearer or equal to the max value (the one) then we have a strong authentication. The combined fragments exist and are measured correctly.
- If the value Ms is in the medium (between 0 and 1; ±0.5) then we have an acceptable authentication. The combined fragments exist but not all of messages in the sequence diagram are controlled.

4.2 Classification of the Risk of Authentication Violation

In this Section, we tackle to the main question "How the measured value can be explored?"

The above proposed early quality measure of authenticity (Ms) can be used to identify the risk of authentication violation as observed early in the design phase (particularly in the authentication sequence diagram). Once identified, the risk can be classified into different categories.

In fact, violation authentication is defined as "a vulnerability that includes all the vulnerabilities that could lead to impersonation" [23]. These weak points in a software applications can open attackers access to the application features that they do not have the right normally. So it allows them to steal information or damage the operation of the application. Protecting access to the application is generally based on an authentication system. Most of the time, the authentication system is redeveloped for each application, which means that these systems do not benefit from the experience gained in the development of other applications.

We propose to classify the risk violation of authentication based on the interpretations presented in the Sect. 4.1 as following:

- A weak authentication means that the software product can have a very high risk.
- An acceptable authentication means that the software product can have a moderate risk.

- A strong authentication means that the software product is secure and without much risk.

Note that very high risk, moderate risk and without much risk (secure) depends essentially on the range of values in which the numerical value of measurement it belongs. If the numerical value is:

- "0" or nearer to "0" then the work product is not secure and presents a very high risk
- "0.5" or nearer to "0.5" then the work product presents a moderate risk
- "1" or nearer to "1" then the work product is without much risk.

Table 5 resumes this classification of risk.

Table 5. Classification of authenticity risk

Security measurement value	"0" or nearer to "0"	"0.5" or nearer to "0.5"	"1" or nearer to "1
Classification of risk	Very high risk	Moderate risk	Secure and without much risk

5   Illustrative Example: Facebook Web User Authentication [21]

In this Section, we present an illustrative example of UML sequence diagram: the "Facebook Web User Authentication" [21]. We first apply the COSMIC method to measure the functional size of the "authenticity" sequence diagram and then we apply our proposed method [13] to measure the structured size of the same sequence diagram. Then, we evaluate the quality of software application in terms of "authenticity" based on the aggregation of the provided measurement values.

5.1   Description of Facebook Web User Authentication

The UML sequence diagram shown in Fig. 4 shows how a Facebook (FB) user can be authenticated in a Web application to allow access to his/her FB resources.

Facebook uses OAuth 2.0 protocol framework that enables web application (called "client"), to request access to resources controlled by the FB user and hosted by the FB server. The web application is usually not the FB resource owner but is acting on the FB user's behalf, Instead of using the FB user credentials to access to the protected resources; the web application obtains an access token.

Web application should be registered by Facebook to have an application ID (client_id) and secret (client_secret). When request to some protected Facebook resources is received, web browser ("user agent") is redirected to Facebook's authorization server with application ID and the user URL should be redirected back to after the authorization process.

User receives back Request for Permission form. If the user authorizes the application to get his/her data, Facebook authorization server redirects back to the URL that was specified with the authorization code ("verification string"). The authorization code can be exchanged by web application for an OAuth access token.

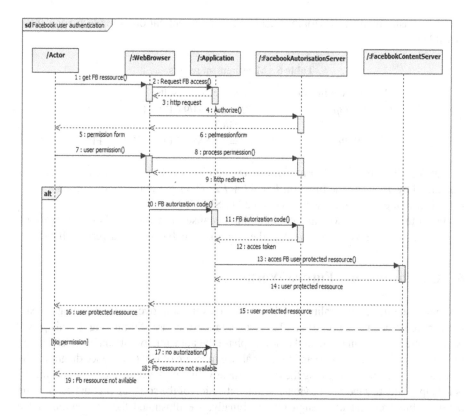

Fig. 4. Facebook user authentication UML sequence diagram [21]

If a web application obtains the access token for a FB user, it can perform authorized requests on behalf of that FB user by including the access token in the Facebook Graph API requests. If the user did not authorize web application, Facebook issues redirect request to the URL specified before, and adds the error_reason parameter to notify the web application that authorization request was denied. Figure 4 illustrates this Facebook Web User Authentication UML sequence diagram.

5.2 Application and Use of FS and SS Measurements

As described in Sect. 3.1.3 – Table 3, we can calculate the measurement functions $F1 = SS_a/B_p$ and $F2 = SS_l/B_r$ by applying the Functional Size Method (COSMIC) and Structural Size Method. Note that: *SSa* is the Structural size of the Facebook Web User Authentication sequence diagram containing *alt* combined fragment and SS_l is the Structural size of the Facebook Web User Authentication sequence diagram containing *loop* combined fragment. But, in this case $SS_l = 0$ since loop does not exist. *Bp* is the number of required authentication protocols in the specification and *Br* is the number of authentication rules required for secure data calculated by COSMIC method (FS).

The measurement results for the Facebook user authentication example are presented in Table 6.

Table 6. Measurement results

Measurement functions	Measurement results
$F1 = SSa/Bp$	$F1 = 2$ CSM/9 CFP $= 0.22$ CSM/CFP
$F2 = SSl/Br$	$F2 = 0$ CSM/9 CFP $= 0$ CSM/CFP

As described in Sect. 4 (Fig. 3), the aggregation of these measurement results is calculated by applying the function $F = F1 + F2$. Then, the authenticity sub-characteristics is provided by the measure Ms = 0.22 (CSM/CFP).

From this measure, we can conclude that because the value of Ms is nearer to the min value (0), then we have a weak authentication which can have a very high risk.

6   Conclusion and Future Works

Although the ISO 25010 quality model has gained several improvements, including a measurement reference model in ISO 25020, detailed measures are still missing. In this paper, we presented how to measure at the design phase the authenticity sub-characteristic based on the Structural Size measure and functional size measure of UML sequence diagram. The measure deduced by aggregating the measurement values of the authenticity sub-characteristic help to identify the risk of violation authentication of the software product early in the software life-cycle (at the design phase). Finally, we illustrated the application of the proposed measurement through an example from the Facebook Web User Authentication sequence diagram.

Our future works involve preparing a survey with industry experts to validate the proposed measure.

References

1. Wagner, S.: Software Product Quality Control, pp. XII–210. Springer, Heidelberg. doi: 10.1007/978-3-642-38571-1, ISSN 978-3-642- 38571-1
2. ISO/IEC 25021:2012 Systems and software engineering – Systems and software Quality Requirements and Evaluation (SQuaRE) – Quality measure elements
3. ISO/IEC 25000:2014 Systems and software engineering – Systems and software Quality Requirements and Evaluation (SQuaRE) – Guide to SQuaRE
4. ISO/IEC 25010:2011 Systems and software engineering – Systems and software Quality Requirements and Evaluation (SQuaRE) – System and software quality models
5. ISO/IEC 9126-1:2001 Software engineering – Product quality – Part 1
6. ISO/IEC 25020:2007 Software engineering – Software product Quality Requirements and Evaluation (SQuaRE) – Measurement reference model and guide
7. ISO/IEC DIS 25022.2 Systems and software engineering – Systems and software quality requirements and evaluation (SQuaRE) – Measurement of quality in use

8. ISO/IEC DIS 25023.2 Systems and software engineering – Systems and software Quality Requirements and Evaluation (SQuaRE) – Measurement of system and software product quality
9. CISQ Specifications for Automated Quality Characteristic Measures Object Management Group, ISO/IEC 2502n – Quality Measurement Division (2012)
10. Karine, M.M., Jannik, L., Stéphane, D.: Modèles de mesure de la qualité des logiciels (2011)
11. Heitlager, I., Kuipers, T., Visser, J.: A practical model for measuring maintainability. In: 6th International Conference on the Quality of Information and Communications Technology (QUATIC 2007), pp. 30–39 (2007)
12. Janusz, Z., Steven, D., Andrew, J.K.: Measuring security: a challenge for the generation. In: Position papers of the Federated Conference on Computer Science and Information Systems, pp. 131–140
13. Asma, S., Hela, H., Alain, A., Hanene, B-A.: A measurement method for sizing the structure of UML sequence diagrams. Inf. Softw. Technol. **59**, 222–232 (2015). http://dx.doi.org/ 10.1016/j.infsof.2014.11.002. IST-Elsevier
14. Al-Qutaish, R.E: An investigation of the weaknesses of the ISO 9126 International Standard. In: Second International Conference on Computer and Electrical Engineering
15. Software Engineering - Software Product Quality Requirements and Evaluation (SQuaRE) Guide to SQuaRE (ISO/IEC 25000). International Organization for Standardization, Geneva (2005)
16. Won, Sh., Jin-Lee, L., Doo-Ho, P., Chun-Hyon, C.: Design of authenticity evaluation metric for android applications. In: 2014 Fourth International Conference on Digital Information and Communication Technology and it's Applications (DICTAP), pp. 275–278, 6–8 May 2014
17. Haiyun, X., Jeroen, H., Joost, V.: A practical model for rating software security. In: 2013 IEEE 7th International Conference on Software Security and Reliability-Companion (SERE-C), pp. 231–232, 18–20 June 2013
18. Jean-Marc, D.: Software Measurement. In: Analysis of ISO/IEC 9126 and 25010
19. ISO/IEC 14598-1:1999 Information technology – Software product evaluation – Part 1: General overview
20. Al-Badareen, A.B., Desharnais, J.-M., Abran, A.: A suite of rules for developing and evaluating software quality models. In: Kobyliński, A., Czarnacka-Chrobot, B., Świerczek, J. (eds.) IWSM/Mensura-2015. LNBIP, vol. 230, pp. 1–13. Springer, Heidelberg (2015). doi: 10.1007/978-3-319-24285-9_1
21. http://www.uml-diagrams.org/
22. Al-Badareen, A.B., Selamat, M.H., Jabar, M.A., Din, J., Turaev, S.: Software quality models: a comparative study. In: Mohamad Zain, J., Wan Mohd, W.M., El-Qawasmeh, E. (eds.) ICSECS 2011. CCIS, vol. 179, pp. 46–55. Springer, Heidelberg (2011). doi:10.1007/978-3-642-22170-5_4
23. Guillaume, H.: Failles de sécurité des applications web principes. parades et bonnes pratiques de développement, 03 April 2012
24. Alain, A., Jean-Marc, D., Barbara, K., Dylan, R., Charles, S., Steve, W.: Guideline on Non-Functional & Project Requirements, November 2015
25. http://cosmic-sizing.org/cosmic-fsm/
26. Alain, A.: Software Metrics and Software Metrology. Wiley, IEEE Computer Society Press, Hoboken (2010)

Towards the Weaving of the Characteristics of Good Security Requirements

Sravani Teja Bulusu[(⊠)], Romain Laborde, Ahmad Samer Wazan,
Francois Barrère, and Abdelmalek Benzekri

IRIT/Université Paul Sabatier, 118 Route de Narbonne, Toulouse, France
{Sravani-Teja.Bulusu,laborde,ahmad-samer.wazan,
Francois.Barrere,Abdelmalek.Benzekri}@irit.fr

Abstract. Over the past two decades, there has been a significant emphasis on the research work towards the amelioration within the discipline of security requirements engineering. Many researchers, international standards and organizations have come up with various methodologies to facilitate the elicitation and evaluation of security requirements. However, the task of deriving good quality requirements still remains challenging. One of the main reasons is that there is no consensus in defining what is a good and a bad requirement. The purpose of this paper is to provide with a survey of various quality characteristics of requirements proposed by various authors from different perspectives. Our survey analysis shows that there are a total of 20 distinctive characteristics that are defined in order to evaluate the quality aspects of requirements.

Keywords: Security requirements engineering · Requirement analysis · Requirement errors · Quality characteristics of security requirements

1 Introduction

Since early 90's many researchers and organizations have contributed their work towards the discipline of security requirements engineering. Security mainly subsumes to the three properties: availability, confidentiality and integrity. Typically, security requirements are derived on the basis of these ACI properties. From a broader perspective, all their contribution can be viewed as two parallel streams of research. One stream is towards eliciting, cataloging, evaluating and reusing of security requirements. In this context, numerous security concepts [1–3], security requirements engineering methodologies, modelling notations and security enhancements [4–7] were proposed. The second stream of research concerns with defining quality characteristics such as completeness, consistency, correctness, etc. [8]. These characteristics are used to evaluate the way requirements are derived; if they are good or bad. However, despite the research advancements, deriving good requirements still remain demanding and challenging till date. Yet many derived requirements are identified as poor requirements. The conspiracy lies within the term *good*. And ambiguity appears in answering basic questions like, what is the definition of a *good security requirement*? How can one measure a *security requirement*? How to identify a *bad security requirement*? One

© Springer International Publishing AG 2017
F. Cuppens et al. (Eds.): CRiSIS 2016, LNCS 10158, pp. 60–74, 2017.
DOI: 10.1007/978-3-319-54876-0_5

of the reasons behind these ambiguities is there lacks a generic consensus or agreement in defining what are good and bad requirements.

In this context, we have made a study on the existing quality characteristics of requirements cited by different authors. We have developed a weaving strategy that allows us to provide with consolidated view of the existing characteristic definitions and their indifferences. This initiative work intends to highlight the necessity of consensus of quality characteristics for efficient and effective establishment of quality requirements.

The rest of the article is structured as follows. Section 2 of this paper briefly discusses on requirement errors. Section 3 surveys the proposed quality characteristics collected from eight sources. Our proposal is developed in Sect. 4. Finally, we conclude our work in Sect. 5.

2   Causes Behind Requirements Errors

Requirement errors are acknowledged as the most expensive errors compared to others within the whole system engineering process. Boehm [9] has stated that late correction of requirement errors could cost up to 200 times as much as correction during early stages of requirements engineering. For clear understanding of the problem, let us consider an example some requirements derived in a context to provide secure email service in an organization:

- **Req1** – Data flow between device1 and device2 shall be encrypted by a strong algorithm.
- **Req2** – Email transfers must be analysed
- **Req3** – The password recovery system must not disturb users.
- **Req4** – Analyse internal attackers not leave them

All these four requirements are prone to errors that could eventually impact the security design and implementation of the email service. To start with, first *Req1* is not clear. What is a strong encryption algorithm? Next, *Req2* has the same issue. It is not clear on what to analyze for. Here, analyzing the emails can be either detecting virus or detecting the disclosure of sensitive information. In addition, if the emails transfer data flow is encrypted because of *Req1* then it might not be possible to perform any analysis. And next *Req3* employs in terms of the negative form '*must not*', which indicates what not to do instead of what to do. In addition it includes one more snag: how to evaluate if users are disturbed or not? Finally, *Req4* holds an ambiguity due to bad semantics. Imaginary interpretations can be made based on where a comma is placed. If interpreted like *"Analyse internal attackers, not leave them"* this demands an inspection of the internal attackers within the organization. In other hand, if we move a little bit the comma to the right of the statement, our interpretation can change completely. Indeed, *"Analyse internal attackers not, leave them"* means to ignore the internal attackers and do nothing about them. Improper verification of such requirement errors could create trouble at requirement implementation phases. However, identification of such requirement errors, particularly in the earlier stages of requirement engineering process, is known to be one of the hardest and tedious tasks. This is because, most of the information during the earlier stages will be in the form of either abstract ideas or discussions or some rough drafts of old documents with some defi- nitions etc.

GS Walia *et al.* [10] have classified the causing factors which could lead to requirement errors into three types, see Fig. 1. Human based errors correspond to shortcomings in the knowledge acquisition on domain environment, or stakeholder needs, and improper communication. Process based errors correspond to inadequate planning and implementation of requirements engineering process. Finally, docu- mentation errors correspond to bad documentation of the elicited stakeholder needs or objectives that could lead to either missing or misrepresentation of requirements.

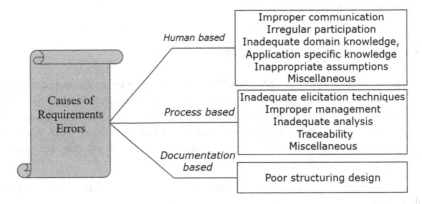

Fig. 1. Requirement errors: causing factors [10]

Although it is not only sufficient to analyse security requirements at the early stages, explicitly defining requirements errors is also mandatory. We need to charac- terize good requirements to minimize risks pertaining to bad quality requirements. And from security engineering perspective, these characteristics help to measure the quality of security requirements.

3   Characteristics of Good Requirements

This section provides the literature on the various quality characteristics gathered from related works. We have projected below the characteristics proposed by each of them. Different sources have listed different set of criteria defining different characteristics of good requirements. However, some of their criterion definitions share similar meaning with similar characteristic name. In such cases, to avoid reputation and to reduce space, we have included the definition only once. In all other cases we have included the respective definitions as given in the respective sources.

3.1 ISO29148

The international standard for requirements engineering [1] has defined a total of 12 characteristics to measure the quality of requirements. The definitions as per the standard are as follows:

1. **Complete:** for a singular requirement, complete means that the requirement needs no further amplification because it is measurable and meets stakeholder needs. For a set of requirements, it means that the selected requirements contain everything pertinent to the system to be built.
2. **Consistent:** The stated requirement must be free of conflicts with other requirements.
3. **Feasible:** The stated requirement must be technically achievable within the technological constraints of the system (e.g., cost, schedule, legal, regulatory, etc.) with acceptable risks.
4. **Affordable:** The set of defined requirements must be feasible within a given system life cycle constraints.
5. **Traceable:** The stated requirement is traceable upward to specific documented stakeholder needs. And also must traceable to downward to low end requirement specifications or design artefacts.
6. **Implementation Free:** The requirement must state only what is required when exhibiting the necessary characteristic and not how the requirement is met or achieved.
7. **Unambiguous:** The requirement must be stated that it does not lead to more than one interpretation of the same.
8. **Necessary:** a requirement is considered necessary when in cases it is removed; it will raise a deficiency in the system to be built.
9. **Bounded:** The set of requirements must maintain the identified scope for the intended solution without increasing beyond what is required.
10. **Singular:** The stated requirement must define only one need at a time with no use of conjunctions (i.e. atomic).
11. **Verifiable:** The requirement must possess means to prove that the system satisfies the specific requirement. This is enhanced when the requirement is measurable.
12. **Requirement language criteria:** vague and general terms used for the description of requirements are to avoid such as superlatives, subjective language, and vague pronouns.
13. **Attributes:** Requirements should have descriptive attributes defined to help in understanding and managing requirements. Requirement attributes may include stakeholder priority, requirement identification, risk related information etc.

3.2 Axel Van Lamsweerde

This source [4] has proposed 11 characteristics of requirements. In this work, there is no explicit mentioning of the applicability of those characteristics to a singular or to a set of requirements. However, new conceptual elements are considered in characteristic definitions are domain properties (e.g. physical laws) and assumptions. The characteristics *completeness, consistency, unambiguity, traceability* and *feasibility* share same meaning as the ISO29148, we list the remaining characteristics in below:

1. **Adequacy:** The requirements translation to specifications must ensure that the actual needs of the new system are completely satisfied.
2. **Measurability:** The requirements must be formulated at a level of precision that enables people such as analysts, developers, users to verify and evaluate if the requirements really meets what is needed.
3. **Pertinence:** The requirements and assumptions must at least contribute to the satisfaction of one or several objectives.
4. **Comprehensibility:** The stated requirements must be comprehensible to the respective people who need to use them.
5. **Good Structuring:** The requirements document should be organized in a structured manner for clear understanding. For example: the definition of a term must precede its use.
6. **Modifiability:** The requirements document should be flexible to revise and adapt to any changes or modifications.

3.3   Donald Firesmith

This source [8] has mentioned a total of 15 characteristics. In this list, *completeness, consistency, feasibility,* and *lack of ambiguity* are similar to aforementioned works. The remaining characteristics are as follows:

1. **Metadata:** Individual requirements should have metadata (i.e., attributes or annotations) that characterizes them. This metadata can include (but is not limited to) acceptance criteria, allocation, assumptions, identification, prioritization, rationale, schedule, status, and tracing information.
2. **Cohesiveness:** Individual requirement should be cohesive. The requirements are considered cohesive if all its parts (data, interface, functions and quality) belong together.
3. **Validatability:** Individual requirements must actually fulfil the needs and desires of their primary stakeholders.
4. **Customer/User Orientation**: Individual requirements should be defined in a way that they are understandable and validatable around the customers and users. They should not include any technical jargon of the development team.
5. **Usability:** Stated individual requirements must be understandable and reusable by numerous stakeholders.
6. **Mandatory:** Individual requirements should be necessary and required to fulfil the organizational objectives.
7. **Relevance:** Some identified and specified "requirements" actually turn out to be outside of the scope of the current endeavour. Thus, it is important to ensure that individual requirements are relevant.

8. **Correctness:** Individual requirements should be semantically and syntactically correct. It should be the accurate elaboration of high level goal or high level requirement.
9. **Currency:** The requirements document should be updated when in need of changes or modifications
10. **Verifiability:** Requirements always have sources, and it is important that requirements are consistent with them. Similarly, requirements need to be consistent with the standards, guidelines, and templates that are used in their preparation. Thus, individual requirements should be verifiable.
11. **External Observability:** Requirements should not unnecessarily specify the internal architecture and design of an application or component. Thus, individual requirements should only specify behaviour or characteristics that are externally observable.

It should be noted that the characteristics of *cohesiveness* and *relevance* are ambiguous. Additionally, some characteristics encompass other characteristics, such as *completeness* that refers to *traceability* and *language criteria*.

3.4   Ian Sommerville

This source [11] has defined a list of 7 characteristics. Among them *completeness, consistency, verifiability, traceability, comprehensibility, adaptability (modifiability) and realism (feasibility)* are similar to aforementioned works. The remaining characteristic is as follows:

1. **Validity** – The requirements should provide the functions which *best* support the customer's needs.

It should be noted that, this characteristic definition is complex and ambiguous. The author uses an ambiguous term *"best support"* which can be interpreted in different ways.

3.5   R R Young

The author [12] has proposed a list of 15 characteristics. Among them *complete, consistent, feasible, traceable, unambiguous, necessary, written using standard construct* and *devoid of escape clauses (language criteria), design independent (implementation free)* and *verifiable* are similar to aforementioned works. The remaining characteristics are as follows:

1. **Allocated:** The requirement is assigned to a component of the designed system.
2. **Non-redundant:** The stated requirement is not a duplicate one.
3. **Assigned a unique identifier:** Each requirement should be identified uniquely.
4. **Concise:** The stated requirement must be simple.
5. **Correct:** The facts related to requirement are accurate, and it is technically and legally possible.

Again in this work, some of the defined characteristics are not clear. The author has used the term *simple* and *accurate* to describe the characteristics.

3.6 E Hull *et al.*

The authors [13] have proposed a list of 14 characteristics. Among them *complete, consistent, feasible* and *verifiable, structured, unique, legal, abstract* (implementation free) and *non-redundant* are similar to aforementioned works. The remaining characteristics are as follows:

1. **Atomic:** The stated requirement must carry a single traceable element,
2. **Clear:** The stated requirement must be clearly understandable,
3. **Precise:** The requirement statement must be precise and concise.
4. **Modular:** The set of requirements must belong together or close to one another.
5. **Satisfied/qualified:** The requirements document must achieve the appropriate degree of traceability coverage.

3.7 Karl *et al.*

The authors [14] have proposed a list of 10 characteristics. Among them *complete, consistent, feasible, traceable, unambiguous, necessary,* and *verifiable, modifiable* and *correct* are similar to aforementioned works. The remaining characteristic is as follows:

1. **Prioritize:** The requirement stated must be assigned with an implementation priority

4 Towards the Weaving of the Characteristics of Good Security Requirements

In our study on the existing characteristics of good requirements, we have identified a total of 20 distinctive criteria definitions. However, we have observed many variations in their corresponding definitions. Our objective is to define an exhaustive list of the existing characteristics that can be integrated to any security requirement engineering process. This entails defining a weaving strategy that we present in the next section.

4.1 Weaving Methodology

To avoid confusions and misinterpretations, we have decided to:

1. Give a unique reference to each characteristic of good requirements. In previous section, we noticed that different authors, for similar criteria, have defined different names. We use the term criterion to refer to each characteristic name. As result, we have named 20 criteria and referred to them as C1 to C20.

Table 1. Survey on quality characteristics of requirements

No	Abstract criterion definition	Characteristics fetched from the works of different authors							Applic ability	Credibi lity
		ISO29148 (3.1)	Lamsweerde (3.2)	Firesmith (3.3)	Sommerville (3.4)	R R Young (3.5)	Hull et al (3.6)	Karl et al (3.7)		
C1	All requirements are included and meet the stakeholder needs	Complete	Complete	Complete	Complete	Complete	Complete	Complete	All	High
C2	Compatible, non-contradictory requirements	Consistent	Consistent	Consistent	Consistent	Consistent	Consistent	Consistent	All	High
C3	Accomplishable within the given financial, time, legal, technological constraints	Feasible/ Affordable	Feasible	Feasible	Realism	Feasible	Feasible/legal	Feasible	All	High
C4	Requirements needs to be well documente	--	Well Structured	--	--	--	Structured	--	All	Low
C5	Requirement should be able to refer back to its objective. Dependency or reference links between requirements should be explicitly defined.	Traceable	Traceable	Cohesiveness	Traceable	Traceable/ Allocated	Satisfied/ Qualified, Modular	Traceable	All	High
C6	Requirements should state what is needed but not how it is met	Implementation Free	--	External Observability	--	Design Independent	Abstract	--	All	Medium
C7	Documented requirements must be easily adaptable to new changes	--	Modifiable	--	Adaptability	--	--	Modifiable	All	Medium
C8	No redundant requirements	--	--	--	--	Non-redundant	Non-redundant	--	All	low
C9	Every requirement is uniquely identified	--	--	--	--	Unique	Unique	--	All	low
C10	Stakeholders needs are sufficiently expressed	--	Adequacy	Validatability	Validity	--	--	--	Each	Medium

Table 1. Continued

No	Abstract criterion definition	Characteristics fetched from the works of different authors							Applic ability	Credibi lity
		ISO29148 (3.1)	Lamsweerde (3.2)	Firesmith (3.3)	Sommerville (3.4)	R R Young (3.5)	Hull et al (3.6)	Karl et al (3.7)		
C11	Requirements defined are simple using common terminology and non-technical jargon.	--	Comprehensbility	Customer / User Orientation	Comprehensility	Concise	Clear	--	Each	Medium
C12	Requirements are defined precisely not leading to multiple interpretations	Unambiguou	Unambiguou	Lack of Ambiguity	--	Unambiguou	Precise	Unambiguou s	Each	High
C13	Requirements defined allows evaluation - quantifiable values	--	Measurable	--	--	--	--	--	Each	low
C14	Every requirement has a purpose	Necessary/B ounded	Pertinence	Mandatory Relevance	--	Necessary	--	Necessary	Each	Medium
C15	Requirement should correctly represent the facts and needs. Syntactically and semantically	--	--	Correctnes s/ Currency	--	Correct	--	Correct	Each	Medium
C16	Non conjunctive requirements	Singular	--	--	--	--	Atomic	--	Each	low
C17	Should define some means to prove the compliance or satisfaction of requirement with stakeholder needs, standards and constraints.	Verifiable	--	Verifiability	Verifiability	Verifiable	Verifiable	Verifiable	Each	high
C18	Formulation of Requirement statements must follow specific criteria	Requirement language criteria	--	--	--	Devoid of escape clauses/ Standard Construct	--	--	Each	low
C19	Requirements must be reusable by numerous stakeholders	--	--	Usability	--	--	--	--	Each	low
C20	Individual requirements should be defined with some attributes or annotations that characterizes them	Attributes	--	Metadata	--	--	--	--	Each	low

2. Colour different notable special cases. Same author has defined different characteristic names for similar criterion definition for which we have highlighted the characteristic name in orange colour. Another interesting case is to show the list criteria proposed by all the authors. This list is highlighted in bold. Furthermore, similar criterion definitions are named differently by different authors for which we have projected the variation in italic. And finally, we have used the blue colour to indicate the case where a criterion is proposed by only one author.

3. Give one-line definition to each criterion. If the characteristic is defined in ISO29148, we give their definition. Otherwise, we give the definition of the respective authors if the characteristic description is clear. Finally, when the characteristics description is ambiguous, we give our own interpretation. In this way, we link the different characteristics to each other and thereby address the ambiguities.

4. Distinguish the applicability of each characteristic to one requirement or to a set of requirements or to a requirements specification document as a whole. We have projected this difference in the *Applicability column* in the Table 1.

5. Define credibility scores in terms of the frequency of mentions of each criterion. Credibility *high* corresponds to criterion proposed by at least six authors; medium corresponds to criterion proposed by at least three authors; low corresponds to criteria proposed by less than three authors.

4.2   Weaving Results

We have highlighted our observations of the aforementioned variations in Table 1.

(a) **Criteria**: Criteria used by all the authors [C1, C2, C3 and C5]
(b) Criteria: Single criterion defined by only one author – [C13 and C19]
(c) *Characteristic name:* Different names used for same criterion definition by different authors [C3, C5, C6, C7, C10, C11, C12, C14, C16, C17, C18, C20]
(d) Characteristic Name: Different names defined by single author maps to single criterion [C3, C5, C11, C14, C15 and C17]
(e) Applicability – **All**: Applies to whole set of requirements or to Requirement specification document
(f) Applicability – **Each**: Single or set of requirements corresponding to a particular stakeholder needs

4.3   Discussion

The essence of requirements engineering deals with managing the evolution of business objectives, from abstract ideas in to an aggregated set of requirement specifications. The resulting requirement specifications document serves as a baselined source which fills the communication gap between stakeholders and system developers. Here comes the role of quality characterises which are used to evaluate the integrity and reliability of these specified requirements in terms of expression. In Table 1 significant amount of contribution can be observed from eight different authors. Many interesting aspects and arguments were discussed in the respective criterion definitions from multiple perspectives. In below, we briefly discuss some notable propositions as well as notable indifferences within the characteristics definitions.

Criterion C1 ensures that final set requirement specifications sufficiently express all the needs of stakeholders, respecting all the considerable aspects and scenarios. In a way, this criterion insists on efficient requirements elicitation and risk analysis process. The difficulty in fulfilling this criterion lies in identifying all considerable aspects such as stakeholder security and risk management objectives. The common keyword (characteristic name) used to represent this criterion is *complete* with credibility *high*.

Criterion C2 ensures that all requirements are compatible and consistent with one another. Accordingly, this criterion **C2** insists on verifying if there exist any conflicts in terms of contradicting requirement statements, improper representation of viewpoints, or possibility of incompatible interpretations of a statement, etc. The difficulty in fulfilling this criterion corresponds to establishment of right level of trade-off as highlighted in related works [15–17]. This criterion indirectly contributes to the fulfilment of requirement completeness. The common keyword used is *consistent* with credibility as *high*.

Criterion C3 ensures that all those derived requirements are accomplishable within the given constrains. Constraints can be viewed in two ways, one as they are imposed by stakeholders and the other based on operational context. On a whole, this criterion insists on identifying and acquiring all the possible constraints in terms of financial or technological implementations. ISO defines some of the considerable constraints such as time, cost, and process control, financial, technical, legal, and regulatory. In addition, dependency constrains and domain constraints [4] can also be considered. The common keyword used is *feasible* with credibility *high*. And other keywords used are *affordable* (3.1), *realism* (3.4) and *legal* (3.6).

Criterion C4 ensures that all requirements within the document are well categorized and well documented in a structured manner so that it is maintainable with fewer changes. Credibility of this criterion is *low* and common keyword used is *structured*.

Criterion C4 ensures that all requirements within the document are prioritized and well documented in a structured manner. Credibility of this criterion is *low* and common keyword used is *structured*.

Criterion C5 ensures that specified within the document are traceable in both forward and backward ways. Credibility of this criterion is *high* and common keyword used is *traceable*. Some sources have highlighted different aspects in the same context; hence different keywords were used accordingly. The keywords are *cohesiveness* (3.3), *allocated* (3.5), *satisfied/qualified* (3.6).

Criterion C6 ensures requirements derived do not specify the implementation details of the solution instead it specifies what is needed. Credibility of this criterion is *medium* and the keywords used are *implementation free* (3.1), *external observability* (3.2), *design independent* (3.5) and *abstract* (3.6).

Criterion C7 ensures that the document containing all set of derived requirements is modifiable and adaptable to changes. It is to note that this is like a Meta characteristic to criterion C4 (well structured). Credibility of this criterion is *medium* and the keywords used are *modifiable* (3.2 and 3.7), *adaptability* (3.4).

Criterion C8 ensures that there is no redundancy of information corresponding requirement needs. It insists during the requirements elicitation process, one must clearly be able to distinguish between redundant stakeholder needs and non-redundant stakeholder needs. Credibility of this criterion is *low* and the common keyword used is *non-redundant*.

Criterion 9 ensures that all the requirements in the document are uniquely identifiable. This criterion helps to achieve the traceability feature (C5). Credibility of this criterion is *low* and the common keyword used is *unique*.

Criterion C10 ensures that completeness feature of an individual requirement. In a way it insists on verifying if the stakeholder need is sufficiently elicited. Credibility of this criterion is *low* and the keywords used are *adequacy* (3.2) and *validatability* (3.3).

Criterion C11 ensures that requirements are derived using simple terminology without usage of technical jargon. Technical jargon corresponds to terminology used by different teams working in different areas of business operational environments. For example, terminology used in software development environment is difficult to be understood by individuals belonging to organizational environment. Hence, this criterion enforces that the derived requirement must be comprehensible to all the readers of the document with in the business environment. Credibility of this criterion is *medium* and the common keyword used is *comprehensibility*. Some sources have highlighted different aspects in the same context; hence accordingly different keywords used. They are *customer or user orientation* (3.3) and *clear* (3.6).

Criterion C12 ensures that the derived requirements are precise enough and does not lead to any misinterpretations. It is to note that this criterion is different from the previous one C11 (comprehensibility). C11 insists on the aspect that there is no difficulty in the comprehension of the text (phrase or sentence), in the way it was written (focus on terminology). And C12 insists on the aspect that the content of the text maintains careful precision while expressing the idea so that it does not lead to misinterpretation of the idea. In end, this criterion emphasizes on the verification that comprehension of the text is not wrong. It focuses on punctuation and meaning of terminology or vocabulary used. In a way, this criterion can be viewed as a meta-characteristic of the criterion C11. Credibility of this criterion is *high* and the common keyword used is *unambiguous*. Another keyword used is *precise* (3.6).

Criterion C13 it ensures that requirements derived can be measured with some quantifiable values. For example, consider a requirement need *"a service must be available to all the customers"*. This need cannot be measured and while eliciting such needs, it is important to elicit measurable information. For this derived requirement for this need can say *"a service must be available on an average to 'x' number of customers at 't' units of time"*. This way, the requirements can be measured. Credibility of this criterion is *low* and the common keyword used is *measurable* (3.2).

Criterion C14 ensures that the derived requirement specifies what is needed and it has not got any unnecessary information. It is to note that this criterion complements the criterion C10 (adequacy). Credibility of this criterion is *medium* and the common keywords used are *necessary* and *mandatory*. Some sources have highlighted different aspects in the same context; hence accordingly different keywords used. They are *bounded* (3.1), *pertinence* (3.2) and *relevance* (3.3).

Criterion C15 ensures that requirement must possess accurate and up to date information. Credibility of this criterion is *medium* and the common keyword used is *correct*. Firesmith [8] has highlighted another aspect within the same context with a key word *currency* (3.3).

Criterion C16 ensures that one requirement derives one need. For example, if a requirement need says *"entrance to aircraft allowed to customers with boarding pass and special emergency pass"*. This is not singular or atomic in nature. It is speaking allowing customers of two different types. One can split this into two as: *"entrance to aircraft allowed to customers with boarding pass"* and *"entrance to aircraft allowed to customer's special emergency pass"*. This way it helps to defined more precisely what does it mean by saying special or emergency. Accordingly, we can say that this criterion C16 contributes towards C13 (measured). Credibility of this criterion is *low* and the keywords used are *singular* (3.1) and *atomic* (3.6).

Criterion C17 it ensures that each of the requirements is verifiable against the constraints, standards and regulations to ensure the correctness of the requirements. This criterion somewhere again falls between C10 (adequacy) and C15 (Accurate). Credibility of this criterion is *high* and the common keyword used is *verifiability*.

Criterion C18 it ensures the formulation of requirement must follow some standard so that they are understandable globally. Credibility of this criterion is *low* and the common keywords used are *requirement language criteria* (3.1) and *devoid of escape clauses* (3.5).

Criterion C19 it ensures that requirements must be formulated in such a way that they are reusable. This criterion emphasizes on the using some common pattern for similar type of requirement needs. Credibility of this criterion is *rare* and the common keyword is *usability* (3.3).

Criterion C20 it ensures that every requirement should be identified with some metadata such as attributes, acceptance criteria. This way, it facilitates in their validation and evaluation. Credibility of this criterion is *rare* and the keyword used is *Metadata* (3.3).

In our survey we have identified that criteria *complete, consistency, feasibility, traceability, verifiability and unambiguous* holds high credibility. However, apart from the credibility factor, the respective criterion definitions are ad hoc and they lack consensus. Inharmonious proposition of various aspects, concerning a characteristic definition, could result in missing or inadequate knowledge acquisition, vague comprehension or misinterpretation, etc. Quality criteria definitions in general are written in natural language and it is generally difficult to identify how failing of one criterion could impact the fulfilment of other criteria. Therefore, it is required to first obtain consensus in order to define what a good requirement is.

5   Conclusion

The importance of eliciting and evaluating requirements is largely recognized now. Different approaches, inspired by the domain of requirement engineering, have proposed methods to express and analyse requirements. These methods can help to structure the early phases of requirements specification. However, what makes a requirement good is still an open question. Many quality characteristics have been proposed to describe the good quality of requirements. Nonetheless, there is no one complete and consistent list of quality characteristics. In this article, we have proposed a comprehensive survey on these characteristics showing that if some characteristics are common, other have the same name but different meanings or conversely different names for the same meaning, etc. Based on this analysis, we built a unified list of characteristics for good quality requirements.

In practice, it may seem not always possible that security requirements fulfill all these quality criteria; for instance achieving both anonymity and accountability security objectives. If there is no revocable anonymity scheme available, then it is not possible to identify the malicious users in case of any misuse (such as in case of preventing double spending of anonymous eCash [18]). Therefore, some trade-offs between the anonymity and accountability objectives need to be found in such a way that the final set of security requirements derived to address both security objectives should be non-conflicting. Therefore, although the link between quality criteria and security requirement engineering is not commonly seen, it is indeed important to consider the quality characteristics in order to derive good quality security requirements.

For future works, we plan to integrate these quality characteristics in the process of security requirements engineering. This will encompass providing a meta-model of security requirements including the quality characteristics. Also, we will have to link the meta-model to the risk management process as well as the processes of verification and validation of security requirements.

Acknowledgement. This work is part of project IREHDO2 funded by DGA/DGAC. The authors thank M. Michalski and Eric Lacombe, security experts at Airbus, for their useful comments. Finally, we would like to thanks the anonymous reviewers for their valuable inputs.

References

1. ISO, I., IEC, IEEE: ISO/IEC/IEEE 29148:2011 Systems and software engineering – Life cycle processes – Requirements engineering. International Organization for Standardization (2011)
2. Pohl, K.: Requirements Engineering: Fundamentals, Principles, and Techniques. Springer Publishing Company, Incorporated (2010)
3. Wieringa, R., Maiden, N., Mead, N., Rolland, C.: Requirements engineering paper classification and evaluation criteria: a proposal and a discussion. Requirements Eng. **11**, 102–107 (2006)
4. Van Lamsweerde, A.: Requirements engineering: from system goals to UML models to software specifications (2009)
5. Mouratidis, H., Giorgini, P.: Secure tropos: a security-oriented extension of the tropos methodology. Int. J. Softw. Eng. Knowl. Eng. **17**, 285–309 (2007)
6. Hatebur, D., Heisel, M., Schmidt, H.: A pattern system for security requirements engineering. In: The Second International Conference on Availability, Reliability and Security, 2007, ARES 2007, pp. 356–365. IEEE (2007)

7. Graa, M., Cuppens-Boulahia, N., Autrel, F., Azkia, H., Cuppens, F., Coatrieux, G., Cavalli, A., Mammar, A.: Using requirements engineering in an automatic security policy derivation process. In: Data Privacy Management and Autonomous Spontaneous Security, pp. 155–172. Springer, Heidelberg (2012)
8. Firesmith, D.: Specifying good requirements. J. Object Technol. **2**, 77–87 (2003)
9. Mills, H.D.: Software Engineering Economics by Barry W. Boehm (1982). Comments on
10. Walia, G.S., Carver, J.C.: A systematic literature review to identify and classify software requirement errors. Inf. Softw. Technol. **51**, 1087–1109 (2009)
11. Sommerville, I., Sawyer, P.: Requirements Engineering: A Good Practice Guide. Wiley, Hoboken (1997)
12. Young, R.R.: The Requirements Engineering Handbook. Artech House (2004)
13. Hull, E., Jackson, K., Dick, J.: Requirements Engineering. Springer Science & Business Media (2010)
14. Wiegers, K.E.: Writing quality requirements. Softw. Develop. **7**, 44–48 (1999)
15. Egyed, A., Grunbacher, P.: Identifying requirements conflicts and cooperation: how quality attributes and automated traceability can help. IEEE Softw. **21**, 50–58 (2004)
16. Ciechanowicz, Z.: Risk analysis: requirements, conflicts and problems. Comput. Secur. **16**, 223–232 (1997)
17. Massacci, F., Zannone, N.: Detecting Conflicts between Functional and Security Requirements with Secure Tropos: John Rusnak and the Allied Irish Bank. MIT Press, Cambridge (2008). Social modeling for requirements engineering
18. Miers, I., Garman, C., Green, M., Rubin, A.D.: Zerocoin: Anonymous distributed e-cash from bitcoin. In: 2013 IEEE Symposium on Security and Privacy (SP), pp. 397–411. IEEE (2013)

Methodology for Security

Towards Empirical Evaluation of Automated Risk Assessment Methods

Olga Gadyatskaya[1]([⊠]), Katsiaryna Labunets[2], and Federica Paci[3]

[1] SnT, University of Luxembourg, Esch-sur-Alzette, Luxembourg
`olga.gadyatskaya@uni.lu`
[2] DISI, University of Trento, Trento, Italy
`katsiaryna.labunets@unitn.it`
[3] ECS, University of Southampton, Southampton, UK
`f.m.paci@soton.ac.uk`

Abstract. Security risk assessment methods are numerous, and it might be confusing for organizations to select one. Researchers have conducted empirical studies with established methods in order to find factors that influence their effectiveness and ease of use. In this paper we evaluate the recent TREsPASS semi-automated risk assessment method with respect to the factors identified as critical in several controlled experiments. We also argue that automation of risk assessment raises new research questions that need to be thoroughly investigated in future empirical studies.

Keywords: Security risk assessment · Empirical studies · TREsPASS · CORAS

1 Introduction

Security risk assessment (SRA) is an integral part of operations in many companies. A recent report by PWC states that as many as 91% of surveyed companies have adopted a risk-based cybersecurity framework, often based on guidelines provided in ISO 27001 and NIST Cybersecurity Framework [25]. Risk assessment methodologies are the core part of such risk-based cybersecurity frameworks, as they allow to identify, prioritize, mitigate and communicate security risks. Yet, the sheer variety of existing security risk assessment methodologies makes it difficult for organizations to understand which methodology is more beneficial in their context. Thus, the security community recently started to pay more attention to empirical studies of risk assessment methodologies, in order to discover what are the benefits and drawbacks of existing methods, and to provide guidelines to CISOs on what kinds of approaches provide better results. Typically, these empirical studies take the form of controlled experiments,

This work was partially supported by the European Commission under grant agreement No. 318003 (TREsPASS) and by the SESAR JU WPE under contract 12-120610-C12 (EMFASE).

© Springer International Publishing AG 2017
F. Cuppens et al. (Eds.): CRiSIS 2016, LNCS 10158, pp. 77–86, 2017.
DOI: 10.1007/978-3-319-54876-0_6

in which participants apply the investigated methods, or their aspects, to realistic scenarios, and researchers observe these exercises and evaluate the outcomes [2,12,14–18,21,27,28,30].

The body of knowledge already accumulated from these experiments can, and should, be considered when new methods are designed. Furthermore, emerging SRA methods can be immediately evaluated based on the criteria identified as important in empirical studies. Moreover, recent advances in automation bring about new types of SRA methods that aim to identify, prioritize and treat security risks in (semi-) automated manner. We argue that these next-generation approaches pose new challenges to method designers, which should be empirically investigated in controlled experiments.

In this paper we benchmark[1] the recent TREsPASS socio-technical risk assessment method [29] with the established CORAS method [1] based on the criteria identified in previous empirical studies [15,18]. Furthermore, we outline the challenges that the emerging type of automated risk assessment methods poses, and ponder about research questions that can be investigated in future empirical studies with these new methods.

2   Criteria for Security Risk Assessment Methodologies

Labunets et al. [2,15,17,18] have conducted a series of controlled experiments to investigate which are the main features of SRA methods that are behind the method's success. Success of a method is typically measured according to its *actual efficacy* in identifying threats and security controls and the *perceived efficacy* that participants have of the method, e.g. if they find the method easy to use or useful [22]. To identify the features, Labunets et al. have applied qualitative analysis techniques from grounded theory to the interviews conducted with participants during the experiments. Four main features were identified that can determine the actual success of an SRA method.

Clear process. Clear process means that the steps to identify assets, threats and security controls are well-defined and guidelines on how to apply the steps are provided to the analysts. If an SRA method has clear process, this positively affects the actual effectiveness of the method and the perception that the analysts have of the method. On the contrary, if the analysts do not know how a step of the process should be executed, the method will not be effective and will not be perceived as easy to use.

Visualization of risk models. Risk model visualization gives an overview of results of SRA, and thus may have a positive impact on an SRA methods success. However, if the visual notation does not scale for complex scenarios, it no longer provides a big picture of the risks threatening the target of analysis, and therefore it negatively affects the methods' effectiveness and perception.

---

[1] Notice that in this paper the evaluation was performed by the authors. No controlled experiments with the TREsPASS method were executed yet.

Catalogues of threats and security controls. Catalogues can facilitate the identification of threats and controls especially for the analysts with limited security knowledge. As reported in [2], domain experts without security expertise using domain-specific catalogues achieve better results than domain and security experts. Finding, sharing and validating threats and controls with catalogues is more efficient and effective, and, thus, the actual and perceived efficacy of an SRA method is higher.

Tool support. Tool can automatize the execution of an SRA process (e.g., computation of risk level) or can facilitate reporting of the results using an appropriate format (e.g. provide a set of tables that match methods steps). A well-designed tool can thus have a positive effect on methods success. In contrast, a primitive or buggy tool can only have a negative impact on the analysts perception of the method.

In addition to these main features, other important factors identified were:

Help in identifying threats and controls. Even if catalogues may not be included by default, the analysts appreciate if the methodology supports brainstorming and communication, and helps to elicit relevant threats and controls.

Change management and evolution support for SRA elements. The analysts appreciate if the method helps to ensure consistency across SRA elements (e.g. via traceability) when changes are introduced or the system evolves. This is especially important when dealing with large or evolving systems.

Scalability. For visual methods, such as CORAS and TREsPASS, scalability of diagrams becomes a challenge that, if not handled, can worsen method's effectiveness and perception.

3   CORAS Evaluation Findings

CORAS is an established model-driven risk analysis approach based on the ISO 31000 standard on risk management [1,20]. It offers a customised language for threat and risk modelling and guidelines on how to use the language. Furthermore, CORAS provides a software tool to be used together with the CORAS method [1]. The CORAS process consists of eight different steps, where the first four steps focus on context establishment and the last four steps are about risk identification, estimation, evaluation and possible risk treatments. The CORAS modelling language defines four kinds of diagrams (asset, threat, risk and treatment diagrams) as part of its model-based approach to support visualisation in all steps of the process. A detailed description of the CORAS steps can be found in [1,20, Chap. 3].

With respect to the criteria listed in the previous section, controlled experiments with CORAS have resulted in the following conclusions [15,18].

Clear process. The participants found the CORAS process to be clear and easy to use: "good methodology, not difficult to use. It is much clear to understand the security case there" in [15]. CORAS provides different types of diagrams that help practitioners to model the system and possible attack scenarios. However, some participants regarded that CORAS has redundant steps: "I think CORAS has some duplications" in [18].

Visualization of risk models. CORAS enables a visual overview of the assets, possible sources of threats, threat scenarios and security controls, and helps the analysts to check that nothing has been overlooked: "diagrams are useful. You have an overview of the possible threat scenarios and you can find links among the scenarios" in [15].

Catalogues of threats and security controls. CORAS does not include catalogues of threats and security controls. However, it can be used together with existing catalogues, e.g., BSI IT-Grundschutz or NIST-800-53.

Tool support. CORAS is supported by a diagram editor that helps to draw CORAS diagrams. However, the participants reported that the tool had low usability and was poorly developed. Thus, some of the participants acknowledged that they switched to an alternative solution for diagram drawing due to issues in using the tool [18].

Help in identifying threats and controls. CORAS threat and treatment diagrams support the analysts in brainstorming threats and security controls.

Change management and evolution support for SRA elements. Once the analysis with CORAS is over, it can be hard for the analyst to update created diagrams. There is no traceability between diagrams in the tool. The participants in [18] reported that in the CORAS tool "objects have no references between the diagrams. Changes on an object in a diagram are not reflected on the same object in other diagrams". Manual changes are time consuming and should be done carefully as it may affect many different diagrams.

Scalability. The participants of studies [15,18] found the scalability issue to be relevant for CORAS: "these diagrams are getting soon very huge and very complex" in [18].

4   Evaluation of TREsPASS

TREsPASS. We start by briefly introducing the TREsPASS approach, which has recently emerged as a more automated methodology for risk assessment. The TREsPASS toolset assists a security analyst in finding attacks and ranking them [24,29]. The core phases of the TREsPASS approach are preparation, analysis, and assessment [24,29]. In the **preparation** phase the analyst gathers company- and sector specific data, and populates the knowledge base with relevant information (e.g. probability of employees to fall victim of a phishing attack) and attack scenarios (for example, a social-engineering attack on an employee expressed as an attack tree). She may also perform exploratory sessions with the stakeholders to understand their most pressing needs and the context (TREsPASS offers exploratory modelling sessions using Lego [24]). In the **analysis** phase, which takes advantage of the automatization, the analyst together with stakeholders designs a socio-technical model of the company, which could be at several layers of granularity: from a satellite view (only core infrastructure elements and assets) to a detailed view comprising employees, servers, virtual machines, relevant files, etc. The analyst and the stakeholders will then identify relevant abstract attack scenarios (expected attacker profiles and assets that could be compromized). Afterwards, the TREsPASS toolset generates a set of concrete threat scenarios represented as attack trees [5,11], which are then extended and annotated with data using a knowledge base populated at the preparation phase. The extended and annotated trees are then analyzed to identify critical attack scenarios [7,8], which are traced back to socio-technical model elements affected and visualized to the stakeholders [19]. Finally, in the **assessment** phase, the analyst with the stakeholders can brainstorm on risk treatment elements (which security controls can be implemented to eliminate the threats) or decide to repeat the analysis with another set of scenarios or with a redesigned model.

Evaluation. We now evaluate the TREsPASS methodology based on the criteria listed in Sect. 2 and identify research questions to be investigated in follow-up experiments.

Clear process. The studies [15,17,18] mainly included novices in particular SRA methods (but not in information security), thus, the requirement of method and process clarity refers more to the question whether it is easy to master the method, than to whether a seasoned professional is able to achieve with it better results than with another method also familiar to him. For TREsPASS it is currently not known how steep is its learning curve or how easy it is to apply the method in the field.

Recommendation. We recommend to conduct controlled experiments to evaluate how comprehensible is the TREsPASS process to novices in the method.

Visualization of risk models. The TREsPASS toolset supports hierarchical visualization of the system model and advanced visualization of attack scenarios (as paths on the system model, as well as attack trees) [19].

Recommendation. There are ongoing efforts to evaluate the TREsPASS visualization capabilities with security practitioners [9]. These can be further strengthened by conducting ethnological studies with security analysts using the TREsPASS method for actual SRA tasks and capturing their reflections on the visualizations.

Catalogues of threats and security controls. In TREsPASS the role of catalogues is played by the knowledge base incorporating databases with relevant data, attacker profiles, and attack pattern library (tree banks). Thus, TREsPASS provides (limited) support for using existing knowledge in risk assessment.

Recommendation. Established catalogues of threats and controls (e.g., BSI IT-Grundschutz or NIST-800-53 catalogues) can be incorporated in the TREsPASS tool, as a part of the knowledge base. Introduction of catalogues and established industry taxonomies can be also useful for automating controls selection and attack scenarios suggestion [4,6].

Tool support. The TREsPASS methodology is supported by the TREsPASS toolset that provides great support to the security analyst, as it automates some steps in risk assessment, as well as visualizes attack scenarios and the organization model. Yet, as studies [15,17,18] reported, tools should not hinder the work of the analyst, and a buggy or unreliable tools may worsen the risk assessment results. Quality of the TREsPASS toolset has not yet been independently evaluated.

Recommendation. The TREsPASS toolset can be empirically evaluated.

Help in identifying threats and controls. One of the main features of TREsPASS is to automatically find attack scenarios based on the system model. This is of great value to the practitioners, as their workload is significantly reduced [6]. However, currently TREsPASS does not yet include automated selection of security controls, or automated attack scenario identification.

Recommendation. The TREsPASS method can be further improved by introducing automated suggestions for preferable security controls and relevant scenarios (assets, high-level attack goals and attacker profiles).

Change management and evolution support for SRA elements. Risk assessment artifacts, such as threat diagrams in case of CORAS or system models in case of TREsPASS, are not stable but often need to be modified, e.g., when some earlier mistake or wrong assumption is identified. As both CORAS and TREsPASS are model-based, and they rely on model transformations as a part of their processes, change management is crucial. In this respect, TREsPASS includes some evolution support, but not very advanced. Since the attack generation part is automatic, if the organization model is changed or the considered attack scenario is revised, the discovered attack paths and analysis of those will be automatically re-computed. The identified critical attack paths will be mapped back to the organization model. Therefore, minor changes can be accommodated in the TREsPASS process seamlessly to the analyst. Yet, evolution support can still be improved by maintaining more explicit traceability links among different underlying models and by improving the change management, e.g., via maintaining logs of changes.

Recommendation. The TREsPASS toolset can be enhanced by improving the change management capabilities following, for instance, the suggestions outlined in [3] for security modelling artifacts.

Scalability. The TREsPASS tool adopts a scalable visualization approach, as it is able to zoom in and out the organization model. Moreover, the visualization of attacks is also scalable, as the analyst is presented with not a full generated attack tree, but with only the most important its parts (the zoom out feature for attack trees), or even only the critical attack paths, which are laid down in the organization model. Thus, the TREsPASS methodology, in principle, is able to deal with large use cases. The only critical point still to investigate is design of fine-grained organization models, when the analyst together with the stakeholders need to introduce many intricate details of the organization, while being able to keep track of all different bits and pieces.

Recommendation. The TREsPASS toolset and methodology need to be empirically evaluated on large case studies, in order to understand whether design of fine-grained socio-technical models is scalable.

Summary. Both CORAS and TREsPASS are visual methods and they have comparable processes, therefore it is possible to compare them based on the listed criteria. Following the results of studies with CORAS [15,17,18], and the evaluation of TREsPASS done above, we can summarize that the automation introduced in TREsPASS contributes to improvement of such features as *scalability, help in identifying threats and controls*, and *change management*. Furthermore, TREsPASS seems to provide better support for *catalogues of threats and controls*, because it incorporates the knowledge base comprising threat-relevant information. However, TREsPASS could be further improved by ensuring integration with established catalogues in order to support controls selection.

TREsPASS and CORAS are comparable in their support for *visualization of risk models*. A comparative study can be organized to assess which visualization approach is better comprehensible and thus more suitable for communication with the client. For the other important factors, i.e., *clear process* and *tool support*, they can be evaluated for TREsPASS only in practical setting (by running case studies, or, better, controlled experiments). Thus, for these two factors, it is currently not possible to compare TREsPASS with CORAS.

5 Discussion

The emerging class of automated and assisted risk assessment methods calls for new types of research questions to be posed about these approaches. Evidently, the usability dimension needs to be explored more in deep. *Tool quality* becomes of the utmost importance for the success of a new automated method. We can propose to apply extended approaches of usability studies from the Human-Computer Interaction domain [10], especially usability studies focused on systems security in this domain [26]. These approaches will allow to evaluate how usable are the different components responsible for various steps in the risk assessment process, how well-balanced is their interplay, and what particular features are exemplary or can be further improved.

At the same time, one important question to answer now is *What is the ideal balance of human expertise and tool support?* in a risk assessment method. *Would well-thought and automated security catalogues or patterns be able to compensate for involvement of domain experts, or analyst's lack of security knowledge?* is an immediate question. Controlled experiments involving experts performing risk assessment manually versus students exercising elaborate tools will not be able to answer this question. We need first to perform exploratory studies of currently established risk assessment techniques and best practices (e.g., interviews with security managers as in [23]), in order to evaluate what can and cannot be successfully automated without new breakthroughs in artificial intelligence.

Another dimension that needs to be taken into account by new studies is comprehensibility and usefulness of the risk assessment results. *Do the stakeholders understand and trust the outcomes and recommendations presented by an automated tool?* Indeed, risk assessment methods are considered to be an important communication means among security managers and the decision makers [25]. Interaction among different stakeholder groups in the process ensures that everybody shares the same view and has better situational awareness. Thus, automating risk assessment should not remove this communication channel, and the recommendations proposed by the tool should be justified and explained *in context*. Therefore, to have a better view on this dimension, we call for new empirical studies on comprehensibility of risk models and risk treatment recommendations. Our own ongoing work is focused on comprehensibility of different risk modelling approaches [13].

6   Conclusions

In this paper we have reviewed the results of empirical studies with SRA methodologies [15,18] and we have evaluated the recent TREsPASS risk assessment method on these criteria. Our main conclusions from comparison with the results for CORAS obtained in controlled experiments is that automation directly improves such important factors as *help in identifying threats* by including a knowledge base, and *scalability of visual risk models*. To understand better how TREsPASS fares in the *clear process* and *tool support* factors we need to have more results from practical exercises with this methodology.

Automation in risk assessment raises new research questions, which can be answered by conducting empirical studies with the emerging methodologies, by applying user study techniques from the Human-Computer Interaction domain, and by conducting ethnographical studies in the security risk assessment community. We hope that we can start a discussion on this topic that will result in better awareness in the security research community, and ultimately in better security posture of organizations through more thorough security risk assessment.

References

1. CORAS: http://coras.sourceforge.net/ (2016)
2. Gramatica, M., Labunets, K., Massacci, F., Paci, F., Tedeschi, A.: The role of catalogues of threats and security controls in security risk assessment: an empirical study with ATM professionals. In: Fricker, S.A., Schneider, K. (eds.) REFSQ 2015. LNCS, vol. 9013, pp. 98–114. Springer, Heidelberg (2015). doi:10.1007/978-3-319-16101-3_7
3. Felderer, M., Katt, B., Kalb, P., Jurjens, J., Ochoa, M., Paci, F., Tran, L.M.S., Tun, T.T., Yskout, K., Scandariato, R., Piessens, F., Vanoverberghe, D., Fourneret, E., Gander, M., Solhaug, B., Breu, R.: Evolution of security engineering artifacts: a state of the art survey. Int. J. Secure Soft. Eng. 5(4), 48–98 (2014)
4. Fraile, M., Ford, M., Gadyatskaya, O., Kumar, R., Stoelinga, M., Trujillo-Rasua, R.: Using attack-defense trees to analyze threats and countermeasures in an ATM: a case study. In: Horkoff, J., Jeusfeld, M.A., Persson, A. (eds.) PoEM 2016. LNBIP, vol. 267, pp. 326–334. Springer, Heidelberg (2016). doi:10.1007/978-3-319-48393-1_24

5. Gadyatskaya, O.: How to generate security cameras: towards defence generation for socio-technical systems. In: Mauw, S., Kordy, B., Jajodia, S. (eds.) GraMSec 2015. LNCS, vol. 9390, pp. 50–65. Springer, Heidelberg (2016). doi:10.1007/978-3-319-29968-6_4

6. Gadyatskaya, O., Harpes, C., Mauw, S., Muller, C., Muller, S.: Bridging two worlds: reconciling practical risk assessment methodologies with theory of attack trees. In: Kordy, B., Ekstedt, M., Kim, D.S. (eds.) GraMSec 2016. LNCS, vol. 9987, pp. 80–93. Springer, Heidelberg (2016). doi:10.1007/978-3-319-46263-9_5

7. Gadyatskaya, O., Jhawar, R., Kordy, P., Lounis, K., Mauw, S., Trujillo-Rasua, R.: Attack trees for practical security assessment: ranking of attack scenarios with ADTool 2.0. In: Agha, G., Houdt, B. (eds.) QEST 2016. LNCS, vol. 9826, pp. 159–162. Springer, Heidelberg (2016). doi:10.1007/978-3-319-43425-4_10

8. Gadyatskaya, O., Hansen, R.R., Larsen, K.G., Legay, A., Olesen, M.C., Poulsen, D.B.: Modelling attack-defense trees using timed automata. In: Fränzle, M., Markey, N. (eds.) FORMATS 2016. LNCS, vol. 9884, pp. 35–50. Springer, Heidelberg (2016). doi:10.1007/978-3-319-44878-7_3

9. Hall, P., Coles-Kemp, L., Heath, C.: Visualisation in cyber-security: Towards a critical practice. In: Proceedings of EVAA (2016)

10. Helander, M.G.: Handbook of Human-computer Interaction. Elsevier, Amsterdam (2014)

11. Ivanova, M.G., Probst, C.W., Hansen, R.R., Kammüller, F.: Transforming graphical system models to graphical attack models. In: Mauw, S., Kordy, B., Jajodia, S. (eds.) GraMSec 2015. LNCS, vol. 9390, pp. 82–96. Springer, Heidelberg (2016). doi:10.1007/978-3-319-29968-6_6

12. Karpati, P., Redda, Y., Opdahl, A.L., Sindre, G.: Comparing attack trees and misuse cases in an industrial setting. Inf. Softw. Tech. **56**(3), 294–308 (2014)

13. Labunets, K., Li, Y., Massacci, F., Paci, F., Ragosta, M., Solhaug, B., Stølen, K., Tedeschi, A.: Preliminary experiments on the relative comprehensibility of tabular and graphical risk models. In: SESAR Innovation Days (2015)

14. Labunets, K., Massacci, F., Paci, F.: On the equivalence between graphical and tabular representations for security risk assessment. In: Proceedings of REFSQ. Springer, New York (2017, to appear)

15. Labunets, K., Massacci, F., Paci, F., et al.: An experimental comparison of two risk-based security methods. In: Proceedings of ESEM, pp. 163–172. IEEE (2013)

16. Labunets, K., Paci, F., Massacci, F.: Which security catalogue is better for novices? In: Proceedings of EmpiRE, pp. 25–32 (2015)

17. Labunets, K., Paci, F., Massacci, F., Ragosta, M., Solhaug, B.: A first empirical evaluation framework for security risk assessment methods in the ATM domain. In: SESAR Innovation Days (2014)

18. Labunets, K., Paci, F., Massacci, F., Ruprai, R.: An experiment on comparing textual vs. visual industrial methods for security risk assessment. In: Proceedings of EmpiRE, pp. 28–35. IEEE (2014)

19. Li, E., Barendse, J., Brodbeck, F., Tanner, A.: From A to Z: developing a visual vocabulary for information security threat visualisation. In: Kordy, B., Ekstedt, M., Kim, D.S. (eds.) GraMSec 2016. LNCS, vol. 9987, pp. 102–118. Springer, Heidelberg (2016). doi:10.1007/978-3-319-46263-9_7

20. Lund, M.S., Solhaug, B., Stølen, K.: Model-Driven Risk Analysis - The CORAS Approach. Springer, Heidelberg (2011)

21. Massacci, F., Paci, F.: How to select a security requirements method? a comparative study with students and practitioners. In: Jøsang, A., Carlsson, B. (eds.) NordSec 2012. LNCS, vol. 7617, pp. 89–104. Springer, Heidelberg (2012). doi:10. 1007/978-3-642-34210-3_7

22. Moody, D.L.: The method evaluation model: a theoretical model for validating information systems design methods. In: Proceedings of ECIS, pp. 1327–1336 (2003)

23. Pettigrew, J.A., Ryan, J.J.: Making successful security decisions: a qualitative evaluation. IEEE Secur. Priv. **10**(1), 60–68 (2012)

24. Probst, C.W., Willemson, J., Pieters, W.: The attack navigator. In: Mauw, S., Kordy, B., Jajodia, S. (eds.) GraMSec 2015. LNCS, vol. 9390, pp. 1–17. Springer, Heidelberg (2016). doi:10.1007/978-3-319-29968-6_1

25. PWC: The global state of information security survey. http://www.pwc.com/gx/en/issues/cyber-security/information-security-survey.html (2016)

26. Sasse, M.A., Brostoff, S., Weirich, D.: Transforming the weakest link – a human/computer interaction approach to usable and effective security. BT Technol. J. **19**(3), 122–131 (2001)

27. Scandariato, R., Wuyts, K., Joosen, W.: A descriptive study of microsofts threat modeling technique. Requirements Eng. **20**(2), 163–180 (2015)

28. Stålhane, T., Sindre, G.: Identifying safety hazards: an experimental comparison of system diagrams and textual use cases. In: Bider, I., Halpin, T., Krogstie, J., Nurcan, S., Proper, E., Schmidt, R., Soffer, P., Wrycza, S. (eds.) BPMDS/EMMSAD -2012. LNBIP, vol. 113, pp. 378–392. Springer, Heidelberg (2012). doi:10.1007/978-3-642-31072-0_26

29. The TREsPASS Project: Technology-supported Risk Estimation by Predictive Assessment of Socio-technical Security. http://www.trespass-project.eu/ (2016)

30. Wuyts, K., Scandariato, R., Joosen, W.: Empirical evaluation of a privacy-focused threat modeling methodology. J. Syst. Soft. **96**, 122–138 (2014)

An n-Sided Polygonal Model to Calculate the Impact of Cyber Security Events

Gustavo Gonzalez-Granadillo[✉], Joaquin Garcia-Alfaro, and Hervé Debar

Institut Mines-Télécom, Télécom SudParis, CNRS UMR 5157 SAMOVAR,
9 rue Charles Fourier, 91011 Evry, France
{gustavo.gonzalez-granadillo,joaquin.garcia-alfaro,
herve.debar}@telecom-sudparis.eu

Abstract. This paper presents a model to represent graphically the impact of cyber events (e.g., attacks, countermeasures) in a polygonal systems of n-sides. The approach considers information about all entities composing an information system (e.g., users, IP addresses, communication protocols, physical and logical resources, etc.). Every axis is composed of entities that contribute to the execution of the security event. Each entity has an associated weighting factor that measures its contribution using a multi-criteria methodology named CARVER. The graphical representation of cyber events is depicted as straight lines (one dimension) or polygons (two or more dimensions). Geometrical operations are used to compute the size (i.e., length, perimeter, surface area) and thus the impact of each event. As a result, it is possible to identify and compare the magnitude of cyber events. A case study with multiple security events is presented as an illustration on how the model is built and computed.

Keywords: Polygonal model · Multiple cyber events · Impact representation · CARVER · Response actions

1 Introduction

A range of difficult issues confront the assessment of the impact of cyber security events [22]. A set of individual actions performed either by the attacker (e.g., malicious actions executed in order to exploit a system's vulnerability) or by the target system (benign actions executed as a response to an adversary) is hereinafter referred to as a cyber security event.

Computing the economic impact of cyber security events is an open research in the ICT domain. Specialized information security organizations e.g., Computer Emergency Response Team (CERT) [25], Ponemon Institute [13], Verizon [23], etc., perform annual reports on such estimations based on real-world experiences and in-depth interviews with thousands of security professionals around the world. The research is designated to help organizations make the most cost-effective decisions possible in minimizing the greatest risk to their organizations.

© Springer International Publishing AG 2017
F. Cuppens et al. (Eds.): CRiSIS 2016, LNCS 10158, pp. 87–102, 2017.
DOI: 10.1007/978-3-319-54876-0_7

Previous researches propose simulation models [4,5] and geometrical models [8,9] to estimate and analyze the impact of cyber events. Geometrical models have been the core topic of a variety of research in many disciplines [6,16]. However, most of the proposed solutions are limited to three dimensions, making it difficult to provide a graphical representation of geometrical instances in four or more dimensions.

In this paper, we propose a geometrical model to calculate the impact of cyber events in an n-sided polygonal system. The approach considers information about all entities composing an information system (e.g., users, IP addresses, communication protocols, physical and logical resources, etc.), as well as contextual information (e.g., temporal, spacial, historical conditions) to plot cyber attacks and countermeasures as instances of n sides, in a polygonal system.

In addition, we are able to perform geometrical operations (e.g., length, perimeter, area) over the polygonal instances, which allows us to compare the impact of multiple cyber events. Such comparison provides the means to determine the coverage level i.e., the portion of the incident that is covered by a given security countermeasure and the portion that is left as a residual risk.

The rest of the paper is structured as follows: Sect. 2 presents our proposed polygonal model and discusses about its construction. Section 3 details the main polygonal instances that result from our model. Section 4 details the impact measurement of the different geometrical instances. Section 5 presents a case study with multiple events (e.g., attacks and countermeasures) to illustrate the applicability of our approach. Related works are presented in Sect. 6. Finally, conclusions and perspectives for future work are presented in Sect. 7.

The contributions on this paper are summarized as follows:

- A geometrical model that projects the impact of security events (e.g., attacks, countermeasures) in an n-sided polygonal system. The instances resulting from the model are straight lines (mono-axial system) or polygons (multi-axial system).
- A process that performs geometrical operations to calculate the size of the polygonal instances (i.e., length, perimeter, area), which allows us to compare the impact of multiple cyber events.
- The deployment of our model in a case study with multiple events over several dimensions.

2 Proposed Polygonal Model

A polygon is defined as an end to end connected multilateral line which can be expressed as point sequence $(P_0, P_1, P_2,..., P_n)$. The $P_0 P_1$, $P_1 P_2,..., P_{n-1} P_n$ are known as the polygon edges. And the P_0, P_1, $P_2,..., P_N$ are referred to as the apex of the polygon [10].

Considering the characteristics of access control models [14, 15], we identified several entities that contribute directly to the execution of a given attack e.g., User account (subject), Resource (object), and Channel (the way to execute actions, e.g., connect, read, write, etc.). In addition, we used the notion of contexts proposed in the Organization based Access Control (OrBAC) model [2, 3], to extend the approach into an n dimensional system, where every context will be a new dimension, such as information security properties (e.g., confidentiality, integrity, availability); temporal conditions. (e.g., granted privileges only during working hours), spatial conditions (e.g., granted privileges when connected within the company premises), and historical conditions (e.g., granted privileges only if previous instances of the same equivalent events were already conducted).

Our polygonal model is proposed to represent services, attacks and countermeasures as an n-sided polygon, n being the number of entities (e.g., user account, channel, resource, etc.). Each entity is projected in one axis of the polygonal system. There is no limit in the number of axes composing our model. It can be mono-axial (considering only one entity), or multi-axial (considering two or more entities).

Our proposed geometrical model has the following characteristics:

- There is at least one entity represented in the geometrical instance;
- The contribution of each entity is represented in one axis of the polygonal system;
- The contribution of each axis must be greater than zero and no more than one hundred percent;
- The end points of the instance axes are connected to form a polygon;
- The union of two end points represents one side of the polygon;
- Polygons can be regular, irregular, and/or convex;
- Concave polygons are excluded from our model since it is not possible to plot instances in which one or more interior angles are greater than 180°;
- Polygons are closed with no holes inside;
- Polygons are not self-intersecting;

The remaining of this section gives examples of the possible entities that can be used to calculate the impact of cyber events and details the contribution calculation of each side of our polygonal model.

2.1 Entities of the Polygonal Model

An entity is an instance that exists either physically or logically. Entities regroup elements with similar characteristics or properties. An entity may be a physical object such as a house or a car (they exist physically), an event, such as a house sale or a car service, or a concept such as a customer transaction or order (they exist logically as a concept). Examples of entities used in our polygonal model are given as follows:

2.1.1   User Account

It considers all active user accounts from the system. A user account is the equivalent of a subject in an access control policy. User accounts are associated to a given status in the system, from which their privileges and rights are derived (e.g., system administrator, standard user, guest, internal user, nobody).

2.1.2   Resource

It considers physical components (e.g., host, server, printer) and logical components (e.g., files, records, database) of limited availability within a computer system. A resource is the equivalent of an object in an access control policy.

2.1.3   Channel

In order to have access to a particular resource, a user must use a given channel. A channel is the equivalent to an action in an access control policy. We consider the IP address and the port number to represent channels in TCP/IP connections. However, each organization must define the way its users connect to the system and have access to the organization's resources.

Other entities can consider temporal conditions (e.g., connection time, detection time, time to react, time to completely mitigate the attack, recovery time, etc.), spatial conditions (e.g., user's location, security areas, specific buildings, a country, a network or sub-network, etc.).

In addition, an event can be associated to a particular issue compromising the system's confidentiality (e.g., unauthorized access to sensitive information, disclosure resources, etc.), integrity (e.g., unauthorized change of the data contents or properties, etc.), or availability (e.g., unavailable resources, denial of service, etc.).

Every organization must define their own entities based on their historical data, expert knowledge and assessments they perform on their systems.

2.2   Dimension Contribution

Each side contributes differently in the impact calculation of the polygon. This contribution represents the affectation of a given element in the execution of an event. Following the CARVER methodology [20,21], which considers six criteria (i.e., criticality, accessibility, recuperability, vulnerability, effect, recognizability), we assign numerical values on a scale of 1 to 10 to each type of element within the axis. As a result, we obtain a weighting factor (WF) that is associated to each type of element. Examples of the practical implementation of this methodology in real case scenarios can be seen in [8,9].

The contribution Co of each side D in the execution of an event E is a value than ranges from zero (when there is no element of the dimension affected to a given event), to one (when all elements of the dimension are affected to a given event). The contribution of a side D is calculated using Eq. 1.

$$Co(D, E) = \frac{\sum_{j=1}^{n} Y_j \times WF(Y_j) \quad \forall j \in Y}{\sum_{i=1}^{n} X_i \times WF(X_i) \quad \forall i \in X} \tag{1}$$

Where
X = total number of elements
Y = affected elements
WF = Weighting Factor

In order to apply Eq. 1 in a practical case, let us consider the axis defined in the previous section. The contribution for the user account dimension, for instance, can be evaluated as the number of users affected by a given attack over the total number of active users from the system. Similarly, the contribution of the confidentiality dimension can be evaluated as the number of alerts indicating a confidentiality issue over the total number of alerts in a given period of time. For spacial contexts we can evaluate the number of incidents occurring in a given location over the total number of reported incidents within a period of time.

3   Resulting Polygonal Instances

A variety of geometrical instances (e.g., regular and irregular polygons such as: line segments, triangles, squares, pentagons, etc.) results from the analysis of the entities' information included in a system, attack and/or countermeasure. By definition, polygons are not allowed to have holes in them [22]. The remaining of this section details the different polygonal instances.

3.1   One Dimension

Plotting the contribution of one dimension into our polygonal system results into a line segment. Let us consider, for instance, an attack A_1 that compromises standard users $U1 : U5$ ($WF = 2$) and admin $U11 : U20$ ($WF = 5$), from a list of 30 users (users $U1 : U10$ with $WF = 2$ and users $U11 : U30$ with $WF = 5$). The contribution of this dimension will be equal to $Co(Dim1) = \frac{(5 \times 2) + (10 \times 5)}{(10 \times 2) + (20 \times 5)}$ $= 0.5$. Figure 1(a) shows the graphical representation of the impact contribution of attack A_1 over the user dimension (Dim_1).

3.2   Two Dimensions

When we have information of two dimensions of our polygonal system (e.g., resources and channels, or users and location), we plot the information to obtain polygons in two dimensions (i.e., right triangles). For instance, an attack that compromises 70% of resources (Dim_1), using 70% of the system's channels (Dim_2), will be represented as a right isosceles triangle[1] Fig. 1(b); the same attack that compromises 40% of resources (Dim_1), using 70% of the system's channels (Dim_2) will be represented as a right scalene triangle[2].

---

[1] Triangle with a right angle and two equal sides and angles.
[2] Triangle with a right angle and all sides of different lengths.

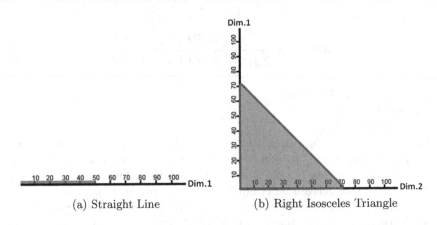

(a) Straight Line   (b) Right Isosceles Triangle

Fig. 1. Impact graphical representation in one and two dimensions

3.3   Three Dimensions

The representation of the impact contribution in three dimensions results into any type of triangles except for right triangles. For instance, an attack with 70% of resources, users and channels contribution will be represented as an equilateral triangle[3]; the same attack with 40% of resource contribution, 70% of user contribution, and 60% of channel contribution will be graphically represented as a scalene triangle[4] (Fig. 2(a)).

3.4   Four Dimensions

Four-dimensional geometry is Euclidean geometry extended into one additional dimension. The graphical representation of the impact contribution of a given event in four dimensions results into a quadrilateral[5]. We discard rectangles, since it is not possible to represent instances that have both: two equal alternate sides and right angles. In addition, we discard rhombus from our graphical representation, since it is not possible to represent instances that have both: equal lengths and non-right angles.

Let us consider, for instance, an attack with 40% of contribution in four dimensions: resources (Dim_1) users (Dim_2), channels (Dim_3), and recovery time (Dim_4) will be represented as a square. The same attack compromising 40% of resources (Dim_1) and channels (Dim_3), 10% of users (Dim_2), and 70% of the recovery time (Dim_4) will be graphically represented as a kite[6]. Similarly, the same attack compromising 40% of resources (Dim_1) and channels (Dim_3),

---

[3] Triangle in which all three sides are equal and all three internal angles are congruent to each other.

[4] Triangle with all sides and angles unequal.

[5] Polygon with four sides and vertices (e.g., square, rhombus, kite, etc.).

[6] Quadrilateral whose four sides can be grouped into two pairs of equal-length sides that are adjacent to each other.

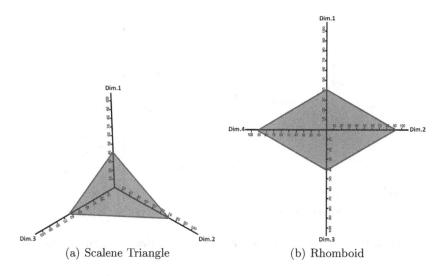

(a) Scalene Triangle   (b) Rhomboid

Fig. 2. Impact graphical representation in three and four dimensions

and 90% of users (Dim_2) and recovery time (Dim_4) will be represented as a rombhoid[7], as shown in Fig. 2(b).

3.5   N Dimensions

Following the same approach as in previous examples, we propose to represent the impact of each dimension composing our polygonal system as segments, and to connect them to form a 2D (regular or irregular) closed polygon (e.g. pentagon, hexagon, octagon, etc.).

For instance, let us assume that we have information of attack A_1 affecting five dimensions: $Co(Dim_1) = 50\%$, $Co(Dim_2) = 80\%$, $Co(Dim_3) = 60\%$, $Co(Dim_4) = 65\%$, and $Co(Dim_5) = 90\%$. The contribution impact of attack A_1 is graphically represented as an irregular pentagon, as depicted in Fig. 3(a).

The model selects all elements affected in each dimension to represent it as a continuous segment that indicates the impact of such dimension for that particular event. We connect them all in order to form an n-polygon (n being the number of dimensions of the polygonal system).

In addition, Fig. 3(b) depicts the graphical representation of an irregular octagon, where the contribution of the odd dimensions is 30%, and the contribution of the even dimensions is 100%. A variant of this case will be if the contribution to an event on one or more dimensions is zero. In such a case, the dimension will be discarded from the graphical representation.

---

[7] Parallelogram in which adjacent sides are of unequal lengths and angles are non-right angled.

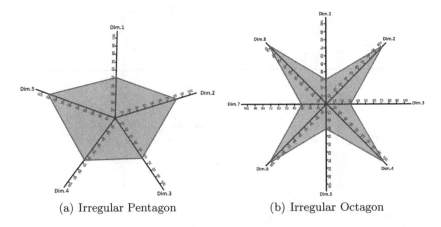

(a) Irregular Pentagon   (b) Irregular Octagon

Fig. 3. Impact graphical representation in more than four dimensions

4   Geometrical Operations

This section details the measurements of the different geometrical figures described in the previous section. Such measurement allows the mathematical computation of the impact of multiple events in the system.

4.1   Length of Polygons

The length of a straight line corresponds to the distance from its origin to its endpoint. In a mono-axial polygonal system, the length is computed as the impact contribution of such dimension over the event. Results are expressed in units, using Eq. 1. In a bi-axial or multi-axial polygonal system, the length is the equivalent of the perimeter of a polygon.

The perimeter of a regular polygon equals the sum of the lengths of its edges. A regular polygon may be defined by the number of its sides n and by its radius R, that is to say, the constant distance between its center and each of its vertex. The perimeter of a regular polygon is computed using Eq. 2.

$$P(Regular\,Polygon) = 2 \times n \times R \times sin(\frac{180}{n}) \qquad (2)$$

Particular cases can be defined. In a bi-axial polygonal system, for instance, the perimeter (P) of an event is calculated as the sum of the impact contribution of each dimension to the event and the length of the connecting side of the two axes, as shown in Eq. 1. For equilateral polygons (e.g., hexagon, heptagon,...) whose edge's length is known, we calculate the perimeter using Eq. 2, whereas for irregular polygons, we use Eq. 3 to calculate their perimeter.

$$P(RightTriangle) = Co(Dim_1) + Co(Dim_2) + L(X) \qquad (3)$$

$$P(EquilateralPolygon) = n \times L(X) \qquad (4)$$

$$P(IrregularPolygon) = \sum_{i=1}^{n} L_i(X) \qquad (5)$$

Where

$L, L_1, L_2, ..., L_n$ = length of the edges of the polygon

n = Number of sides of a regular polygon.

Let us consider, for instance, a regular polygon of five sides (i.e., pentagon), with each dimension contribution equals to 10%. The perimeter of the pentagon is calculated as $P(Regular\,Pentagon) = 2 \times 5 \times 10 \times \sin(45) = 58.78\,units$. For irregular polygons, the perimeter is calculated as the sum of the length of each edge (Eq. 3), considering the same pentagon, whose edges measure (10, 25, 10, 45, 20), the perimeter of such polygon is equal to $P(Iregular\,Pentagon) = 110\,units$.

4.2   Area of Polygons

The area (A) of a given event measures the amount of space inside the boundary of a flat (2-dimensional) object such as a triangle or square.

For regular polygons, the area equals the product of the perimeter and the apothem[8] divided by two. Results are expressed in $units^2$, using Eq. 6.

$$A(Regular\,Polygon) = \frac{Perimeter \times Apothem}{2} \tag{6}$$

For irregular polygons, we compute the area as the sum of the contribution value of Dim_i times the contribution value of Dim_{i+1} divided by two, as shown in Eq. 7.

$$A(Irregular\,Polygon) = \frac{\sum_{i=1}^{n} Co(Dim_i) \times Co(Dim_{i+1})}{2} \tag{7}$$

For the previous Equation, note that in the last term (i.e., $Co(Dim_n)$), the expression must wrap around back to the first term (i.e., $Co(Dim_1)$). This method works correctly for triangles, regular and irregular polygons, as well as convex and concave polygons, but it will produce wrong answers for self-intersecting polygons, where one side crosses over another. However, such cases are excluded from our research.

Let us take an example of an attack A_1 that affects 60% of resources (Dim_1), 60% of channels (Dim_2), 80% of users (Dim_3) and requires 40% of recovery time (Dim_4). Attack A1 will have an area equal to $A(Quadrilateral) = [(60 \times 60) + (60 \times 80) + (80 \times 40) + (40 \times 60)]/2 = 700\,units^2$

5   Case Study

A vulnerability in OpenSSH (i.e., CVE-2015-5600) has been exploited to bypass the maximum number of authentication attempts and launch attack A_1 (brute force attack against a targeted server). The vulnerability is related to the keyboard-interactive authentication mechanism and it can be exploited through

---

[8] The line segment from the center of a regular polygon to the midpoint of a side.

the KbdInteractiveDevices option. The crucial part is that if the attacker requests 10,000 keyboard-interactive devices, OpenSSH will gracefully execute the request and will be inside a loop to accept passwords until the specified devices are exceeded. A remote attacker could therefore try up to 10,000 different passwords and they would only be limited by a login grace time setting, which by default is set to two minutes. Attack A_1 affects a great number of users, channels, resources, and systems where keyboard-interactive authentication is enabled. Three security countermeasures have been proposed to mitigate attack A_1. Table 1 summarizes this information.

Proposed Countermeasures:

C.1 Install an OpenSSH patch
C.2 Limit access to SSH in the firewall,
C.3 Disable password authentication for the root account

Table 1. Events dimensional information

Dimension	Category	Q	WF	A1	C1	C2	C3
Internal	Root	3	5	3	3	3	3
User	Standard user	25	2	25	25	25	-
Channels	Credentials	28	4	28	-	-	3
	IP addresses	30	3	-	-	30	-
Physical	PC	27	2	-	27	-	-
Resources	Server	12	5	5	3	-	12
Logical	Firewall	2	4	2	-	2	-
Resources	Software	10	3	4	4	-	5

The first two columns from Table 1 identify the four main dimensions and categories of each dimensions respectively. The next two columns shows the number of elements (Q) composing each category of the dimension, and their corresponding weighting factor (WF). The rest of the columns show the number of elements affected by attack A_1 and countermeasures C_1, C_2, and C_3.

5.1   Impact Calculation

1. System Dimensions: We compute the system's dimensions using information from Table 1, as follows:

- Internal User (IU) = $(3 \times 5) + (25 \times 2) = 65$ $units$
- Channels (Ch) = $(28 \times 4) + (30 \times 3) = 202$ $units$
- Physical Resources (PR) = $(27 \times 2) + (12 \times 5) = 114$ $units$
- Logical Resources (LR) = $(2 \times 4) + (10 \times 3) = 38$ $units$

2. Dimension Contribution: We calculate the contribution of each dimension on the execution of the events (i.e., A_1, C_1, C_2, and C_3) with respect to the system value, using Eq. 1. For instance, Attack A_1 affects the following dimensions:

- IU $= (3 \times 5) + (25 \times 2) = 65 \ units \rightarrow 100\%$
- Ch $= 28 \times 4 = 112 \ units \rightarrow 55.45\%$
- PR $= 5 \times 5 = 25 \ units \rightarrow 21.93\%$
- LR $= (2 \times 4) + (4 \times 3) = 20 \ units \rightarrow 52.63\%$

3. Impact Calculation: We calculate the geometrical operations of attack A_1 and countermeasures C_1, C_2, and C_3, using Eqs. 5 and 7. For attack A_1, for instance, we compute the perimeter and area as follows:

$$P(A_1) = L(IU - Ch) + L(Ch - PR) + L(PR - LR) + L(LR - IU)$$
$$P(A_1) = 114.34 + 59.62 + 57.02 + 113.00 = 343.99 \ units$$
$$A(A_1) = \frac{(100 \times 55.45) + (55.45 \times 21.93) + (21.93 \times 52.63) + (52.63 \times 100)}{2}$$
$$A(A_1) = 6,588.91 \ units^2$$

Table 2 summarizes the impact values of all events.

Table 2. Event impact evaluation

Event	P(units)	A(units²)
S	565.69	20,000.00
A_1	343.99	6,588.91
C_1	333.66	2,534.63
C_2	277.28	3,280.35
C_3	188.31	1,719.12
$C_1 \cup C_2$	357.77	6,110.71
$C_1 \cup C_3$	340.76	3,645.09
$C_2 \cup C_3$	351.73	6,412.67
$C_1 \cup C_2 \cup C_3$	364.40	6,744.36

As depicted in Table 2, attack A_1 is compared against the system S and countermeasures C_1, C_2, and C_3. Attack A_1 affects 32.94% of the total system area. Applying countermeasures individually will reduce part of the attack impact. However, if multiple countermeasures are implemented, the risk is expected to be reduced substantially. The best solution for this attack scenario is implementing C_2 and C_3, since the application of the three countermeasures will probably increase costs and potential collateral damages with no improvement in the mitigation level of attack A_1.

5.2   Graphical Representation

Figure 4 shows the graphical representation of attack A_1 (in blue) and the individual implementation of countermeasures C_1 (in red), C_2 (in green), and C_3 (in grey).

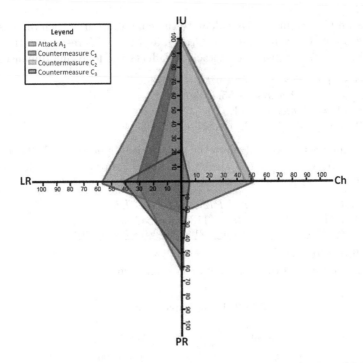

Fig. 4. Impact graphical representation of events - Case by Case Analysis (Color figure online)

The graphical representation shows a case by case implementation of the different security countermeasures. It is important to note that each countermeasure affects a given set of elements in at least one dimension. Countermeasure C_2, for instance, only affects elements that are vulnerable to attack A_1, whereas Countermeasures C_1, and C_3 requires modifications of elements that are not vulnerable to attack A_1 (e.g., physical resources).

The visualization of cyber attacks and countermeasures in the same geometrical space helps security administrators in the analysis, evaluation and selection of security actions as a response to cyber attacks. It is possible to identify priority areas (e.g., those where most attacks are concentrated, or where more elements of the system are vulnerable), and perform reaction strategies accordingly. It is also possible to visualize the portion of the attack (e.g., the area of the polygon) that is being controlled by a security countermeasure, and the portion that is left with no treatment (e.g., residual risk).

Furthermore, it is also possible to plot multiple cyber attacks occurring simultaneously in the system. The same can be performed for multiple countermeasures that need to be implemented simultaneously. The graphical representation of the resulting instance will generally cover a grater area than their individual representations. For instance, the graphical representation of the three countermeasures implemented simultaneously is depicted in Fig. 5, where attack A_1 is

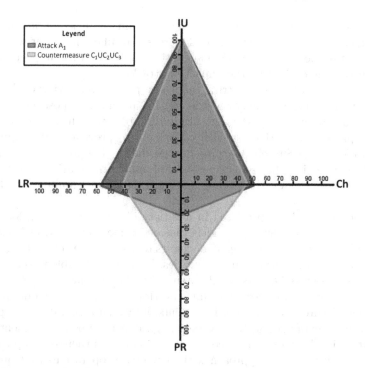

Fig. 5. Impact graphical representation of events - Combined Analysis (Color figure online)

represented by the blue polygon, and the set of countermeasures is represented by the yellow polygon.

For this example, the implementation of multiple countermeasures increases the coverage area of the attack, which in turn reduces the attack impact, making it look more attractive than their individual implementation.

6   Related Work

Determining the impact of cyber security events is an open research in the ICT domain. Several research works rely on metrics to quantitatively measure such impacts. Howard et al., [11,12] and Manadhata et al. [17–19], for instance, propose a model to systematically measure the attack surface of different software. However, the approach presents the following shortcomings: it cannot be applied in the absence of source code; it includes only technical impact; it cannot be used to compare different system environments; and it does not evaluate the impact of multiple attacks occurring simultaneously in the system.

Other researchers rely on simulations to analyze and estimate the impact of cyber events. Dini et al. [4,5], for instance, present a simulative approach to attack impact analysis that allows for evaluating the effects of attacks, ranking them according to their severity, and provides valuable insights on the attack impact since during the design phase. The research differs from our work, since their simulation does not provide quantitative analysis on the impact of countermeasures while evaluating the impact of attacks.

Other approaches use geometrical models to provide a 3D view of the events in a variety of disciplines. Emerson et al. [6], for instance, propose a geometrical 3D model for use within sport injury studies in order to influence the design of sport equipment and surfaces, which could help to prevent sports injuries. In addition, Liebel and Smitch [16], present a geometrical approach for multi-view object class detection that allows performing approximate 3D pose estimation for generic object classes. However, geometrical models are limited to a 3D projection.

2D models have been proposed in a variety of domains [1,7,24,26] as synthetic and generic visualization models that overcome previous drawbacks from 3D representations. 2D models enable viewers to visualize the overall big picture and the interrelationships of various entities. Users may be able to observe how the changes on selected events could potentially affect the overall system to provide understanding on interrelated impacts. However, since the model provides an abstract picture of one or multiple events, its visualization does not provide an accurate value of the impact coverage (e.g., it is not possible to identify the exact mitigation level of a given countermeasures). It is therefore important to combine the visualization approach with geometrical operations that quantitatively indicate the level at which an attack is controlled by a mitigation action.

7   Conclusions

Based on the limitations of the current solutions, we propose a geometrical approach to project the impact of cyber events in an n-dimensional polygonal system. The approach uses geometrical operations to compute the size of the polygon, and thus the impact of the represented event. As a result, we are able to project multiple events (e.g., attacks, countermeasures), in a variety of axes (e.g., users, channels, resources, CIA, time, etc.), which provides the means to propose security countermeasures as a reaction strategy to mitigate the detected attacks.

The main novelty of the approach is the use of multiple criteria to build the n-sided polygon using the dimension contribution Equation discussed in Sect. 2.2 and the use of metrics (i.e., length and area), as discussed in Sect. 4. As such, we overcome previous drawbacks about visualization (e.g., inability to plot the impact of cyber security events in four or more dimensions). Results show that implementing multiple countermeasures simultaneously increases the protection area and thus reduces the impact of a given attack.

Future work will concentrate in quantifying the residual risk and potential collateral damage that result out of the implementation of a set of countermeasures. In addition, we will include other event's related information (e.g., attackers knowledge, capabilities, etc.) in order to explore external dimensions that could influence in the impact calculation of a cyber security event.

Acknowledgment. The research in this paper has received funding from PANOPTESEC project, as part of the Seventh Framework Programme (FP7) of the European Commission (GA 610416).

References

1. Ansari, A.-N., Mahoor, M.H., Abdel-Mottaleb, M.: Normalized 3D to 2D model-based facial image synthesis for 2D model-based face recognition. In: Conference and Exhibition (GCC), pp. 178–181 (2011)
2. Cuppens, F., Cuppens-Boulahia, N.: Modeling contextual security policies. Int. J. Inf. Secur. **7**, 285–305 (2008)
3. Cuppens, F., Cuppens-Boulahia, N., Miege, A.: Modelling contexts in the Or-BAC model. In: 19th Annual Computer Security Applications Conference (2003)
4. Dini, G., Tiloca, M.: On simulative analysis of attack impact in Wireless Sensor Networks. In: 18th Conference on Emerging Technologies & Factory Automation (ETFA). IEEE (2013)
5. Dini, G., Tiloca, M.: A simulation tool for evaluating attack impact in cyber physical systems. In: Hodicky, J. (ed.) MESAS 2014. LNCS, vol. 8906, pp. 77–94. Springer, Cham (2014). doi:10.1007/978-3-319-13823-7_8
6. Emerson, N.J., Carrea, M.J., Reilly, G.C., Offiah, A.C.: Geometrically accurate 3D FE models from medical scans created to analyse the causes of sports injuries. In: 5th Asia-Pacific Congress on Sports Technology (APCST), pp. 422–427 (2011)
7. Gao, X., Tangney, M., Tabirca, S.: 2D simulation and visualization of tumour growth based on discrete mathematical models. In: International Conference on Bioinformatics and Biomedical Technology (ICBBT), pp. 35–41 (2010)
8. Gonzalez-Granadillo, G., Garcia-Alfaro, J., Debar, H.: Using a 3D geometrical model to improve accuracy in the evaluation and selection of countermeasures against complex cyber attacks. In: Thuraisingham, B., Wang, X.F., Yegneswaran, V. (eds.) SecureComm 2015. LNICSSITE, vol. 164, pp. 538–555. Springer, Cham (2015). doi:10.1007/978-3-319-28865-9_29
9. Gonzalez-Granadillo, G., Jacob, G., Debar, H.: Attack volume model: geometrical approach and application. In: Lambrinoudakis, C., Gabillon, A. (eds.) CRiSIS 2015. LNCS, vol. 9572, pp. 242–257. Springer, Cham (2015). doi:10.1007/978-3-319-31811-0_15
10. Hai-Ying, S., Liang, M.: A new triangulation algorithm based on the determination of the polygon's diagonals. In: International Conference on Computational Intelligence and Software Engineering (2009)
11. Howard, M.: Mitigate security risks by minimizing the code you expose to untrusted users. In: MSDN Magazine (2004)
12. Howard, M., Wing, J.: Measuring relative attack surfaces. In: Computer Security in the 21st Century, pp. 109–137 (2005)
13. Ponemon Institute: State of the endpoint report: user-centric risk. Technical report, Technical Paper (2015)
14. Kalam, A.A.E., Baida, R.E., Balbiani, P., Benferhat, S., Cuppens, F., Deswarte, Y., Miege, A., Saurel, C., Trouessin, G.: Organization based access control. In: International Workshop on Policies for Distributed Systems and Networks (2003)
15. Li, N., Tripunitara, M.: Security analysis in role-based access control. ACM Trans. Inf. Syst. Secur. **9**, 391–420 (2006)

16. Liebelt, J., Schmid, C.: Multi-view object class detection with a 3D geometric model. In: Conference on Computer Vision and Pattern Recognition (CVPR), pp. 1688–1695. IEEE (2010)
17. Manadhata, P., Karabulut, Y., Wing, J.: Measuring the attack surfaces of SAP business applications. In: IEEE International Symposium on Software Reliability Engineering (2008)
18. Manadhata, P., Wing, J.: An attack surface metric. IEEE Trans. Softw. Eng. **37**, 371–386 (2010)
19. Manadhata, P., Wing, J., Flynn, M., McQueen, M.: Measuring the attack surfaces of two FTP daemons. In: 2nd ACM Workshop on Quality of Protection (2006)
20. Norman, T.L.: Risk Analysis and Security Countermeasure Selection. CRC Press, Taylor & Francis Group, Boca Raton (2010)
21. Federation of American Scientists: Special operations forces intelligence, electronic warfare operations, appendix d: target analysis process (1991)
22. Roberts, B.: The macroeconomic impacts of the 9/11 attack: evidence from real-time forecasting. Working Paper, Homeland Security, Office of Immigration Statistics (2009)
23. Verizon Enterprise Solutions: 2015 data breach investigations report. Technical report, Research report (2015)
24. Sommer, B., Wang, S.J., Xu, L., Chen, M., Schreiber, F.: Big Data Visual Analytics (BDVA). In: Hybrid-Dimensional Visualization and Interaction - Integrating 2D and 3D Visualization with Semi-Immersive Navigation Techniques, pp. 1–8 (2015)
25. Cyber Emergency Response Team: Common cyber attacks: reducing the impact. Technical report, White Paper, CERT UK (2015)
26. Zhang, J., Huang, M.L.: 2D approach measuring multidimensional data pattern in big data visualization. In: IEEE International Conference on Big Data Analysis (ICBDA), pp. 1–6 (2016)

Security and Formal Methods

SPTool – Equivalence Checker
for SAND Attack Trees

Barbara Kordy[1,2(✉)], Piotr Kordy[3,4], and Yoann van den Boom[5,6]

[1] INSA Rennes, Rennes, France
[2] IRISA, Rennes, France
barbara.kordy@irisa.fr
[3] University of Birmingham, Birmingham, UK
[4] University of Luxembourg, Luxembourg, Luxembourg
[5] University Rennes 1, Rennes, France
[6] INRIA, Rennes, France

Abstract. A SAND attack tree is a graphical model decomposing an attack scenario into basic actions to be executed by the attacker. SAND attack trees extend classical attack trees by including the sequential conjunctive operator (SAND) to the formalism. They thus allow to differentiate actions that need to be executed sequentially from those that can be performed in parallel. Since several structurally different SAND attack trees can represent the same attack scenario, it is important to be able to decide which SAND attack trees are equivalent.

SPTool is free, open source software for checking equivalence of SAND attack trees and computing their canonical forms. It relies on term rewriting techniques and an equational theory axiomatizing SAND attack trees.

Keywords: Attack trees · Sequential operator · Equivalence · Rewriting · Axiomatization · Canonical form · SAND · SPTool · Maude

1 Introduction and Motivation

Attack trees [9] are graphical models aiming to represent and evaluate security vulnerabilities of systems or organizations. An attack tree is a labeled AND-OR tree whose root depicts the ultimate goal of the attacker and the remaining nodes decompose this goal into sub-goals, using disjunctive (OR) and conjunctive (AND) refinements. The leaves of an attack tree represent basic attack steps, i.e., actions that the attacker needs to perform in order to reach his goal. Since attack trees do not only support the representation of security problems, but also help in performing their quantitative analysis [8], the formalism is frequently used in industry as a means to facilitate the risk assessment process [7].

Unfortunately, the simple AND-OR structure is not sufficiently rich to capture all real-life features. One of the main drawbacks of classical attack trees is that they do not distinguish between actions that can be performed in parallel from the ones that need to be executed in a specific order. To overcome this

© Springer International Publishing AG 2017
F. Cuppens et al. (Eds.): CRiSIS 2016, LNCS 10158, pp. 105–113, 2017.
DOI: 10.1007/978-3-319-54876-0_8

limitation, the authors of [5] have formalized SAND *attack trees* which extend classical attack trees with the sequential conjunctive refinement (SAND) in order to allow the modeling of sequences of actions. SAND attack tree depicted in Fig. 1 and described in Example 1 illustrates how to steal money from a bank account.

Example 1. In order to steal money using an ATM machine, the attacker must first get relevant credentials and then withdraw money from the victim's bank account. The root of the tree from Fig. 1 is thus refined using the sequential conjunctive refinement SAND (arc with arrow). To get the necessary credentials, the attacker must steal the victim's card and get the corresponding PIN. The order in which the card and the PIN will be obtained is not relevant, thus the standard conjunctive refinement AND (simple arc) has been used to refine the 'get credentials' node. In order to get the PIN, the attacker has two options: he can either social engineer the victim to convince her to reveal the secret four digits or find a post-it with the PIN written on it. Since each of these options is sufficient to learn the PIN, the 'get PIN' node has been refined using the disjunctive refinement OR (no arc).

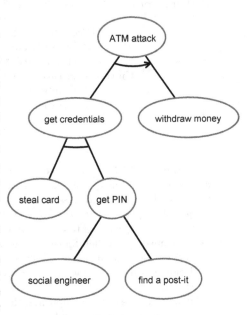

Fig. 1. SAND attack tree for an ATM attack

It is well-known that several structurally different (SAND) attack trees may be equivalent, i.e., represent the same scenario [5, 6, 9]. For instance, the ATM attack described in Example 1 can also be illustrated using the tree from Fig. 2. Both representations are useful and have their strengths. The tree from Fig. 1 is more concise and represents how the attacker will mount his attack. The one from Fig. 2 is in *canonical form* – it enumerates all possible attack vectors explicitly. It thus represents possible executions of the attack.

In order to decide which (SAND) attack trees are equivalent, numerous formal semantics (based on Boolean functions [8], multisets [6,9], series-parallel graphs [5]) have been introduced. The choice of an appropriate semantics is closely related to the type of quantitative analysis to be performed. For instance, if we want to evaluate probability of an attack, we can use the Boolean interpretation of attack trees, as in [8]. However, if the attack time or cost are being evaluated, the multiset-based semantics needs to be used [9]. The relation between formal semantics for the attack tree-like models and their quantitative analysis has been formalized in [6]. It relies on the notion of compatibility which guarantees that the

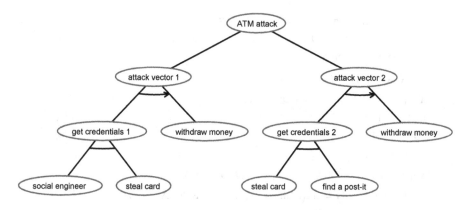

Fig. 2. ATM attack in canonical form

quantification on equivalent trees yields the same value. It is thus important to be able to quickly verify whether two trees are equivalent.

In addition, attack trees used in practice grow quite fast and may reach several thousand of nodes. For instance, in the Galileo risk assessment program attack trees stretching over 40 A4 pages have been considered [10]. Manual handling of such trees becomes infeasible and needs therefore to be automated. However, none of existing tools supporting drawing, automated generation, and quantitative analysis of attack tree-like models, such as [1,3,4,11], can handle semantics preserving transformations of attack trees with sequential conjunction and compare structurally different trees.

To support the use of SAND attack trees, we have implemented a prototype tool, called SPTool, integrating graphical security modeling and term rewriting. SPTool provides the canonical form for SAND attack trees and checks whether two SAND attack trees are equivalent. Since SAND attack trees form a conservative extension of attack trees, as formalized in [9], SPTool can also be employed to reason about classical attack trees which use OR and AND refinements only.

Section 2 gives an overview of the formal foundations for SAND attack trees which are relevant for the understanding of SPTool. The main features of SPTool, its architecture, and implementation characteristics are described in Sect. 3. We evaluate the performance of SPTool in Sect. 4 and conclude in Sect. 5.

2   SAND **Attack Trees Formally**

SAND attack trees are closed terms over the signature $\mathbb{B} \cup \{\text{OR}, \text{AND}, \text{SAND}\}$, generated by the following grammar, where OR, AND, and SAND are unranked operators, $\mathbb{B}$ is the set of terminal symbols, and $b \in \mathbb{B}$:

$$t ::= b \mid \text{OR}(t, \ldots, t) \mid \text{AND}(t, \ldots, t) \mid \text{SAND}(t, \ldots, t).$$

Figure 3 displays the set of equations, introduced in [5] and denoted by $E_{\mathcal{SP}}$, which axiomatize SAND attack trees. These equations express the properties of

$$\texttt{OR}(Y_1, \ldots, Y_\ell) = \texttt{OR}(Y_{\sigma(1)}, \ldots, Y_{\sigma(\ell)}), \quad \forall \sigma \in \mathrm{Sym}_\ell \qquad (E_1)$$

$$\texttt{AND}(Y_1, \ldots, Y_\ell) = \texttt{AND}(Y_{\sigma(1)}, \ldots, Y_{\sigma(\ell)}), \quad \forall \sigma \in \mathrm{Sym}_\ell \qquad (E_2)$$

$$\texttt{OR}\big(\overline{X}, \texttt{OR}(\overline{Y})\big) = \texttt{OR}(\overline{X}, \overline{Y}) \qquad (E_3)$$

$$\texttt{AND}\big(\overline{X}, \texttt{AND}(\overline{Y})\big) = \texttt{AND}(\overline{X}, \overline{Y}) \qquad (E_4)$$

$$\texttt{SAND}\big(\overline{X}, \texttt{SAND}(\overline{Y}), \overline{Z}\big) = \texttt{SAND}(\overline{X}, \overline{Y}, \overline{Z}) \qquad (E_{4'})$$

$$\texttt{OR}(A) = A \qquad (E_5)$$

$$\texttt{AND}(A) = A \qquad (E_6)$$

$$\texttt{SAND}(A) = A \qquad (E_{6'})$$

$$\texttt{AND}\big(\overline{X}, \texttt{OR}(\overline{Y})\big) = \texttt{OR}\big(\texttt{AND}(\overline{X}, Y_1), \ldots, \texttt{AND}(\overline{X}, Y_\ell)\big) \qquad (E_{10})$$

$$\texttt{SAND}\big(\overline{X}, \texttt{OR}(\overline{Y}), \overline{Z}\big) = \texttt{OR}\big(\texttt{SAND}(\overline{X}, Y_1, \overline{Z}), \ldots, \texttt{SAND}(\overline{X}, Y_\ell, \overline{Z})\big) \qquad (E_{10'})$$

$$\texttt{OR}(A, A, \overline{X}) = \texttt{OR}(A, \overline{X}). \qquad (E_{11})$$

Fig. 3. The set $E_{\mathcal{SP}}$ of equations axiomatizing SAND attack trees, where $k, m \geq 0$, $\ell \geq 1$, $\overline{X} = X_1, \ldots, X_k$, $\overline{Y} = Y_1, \ldots, Y_\ell$, and $\overline{Z} = Z_1, \ldots, Z_m$ are sequences of variables and A is a variable. Sym_ℓ denotes the set of all bijections from $\{1, \ldots, \ell\}$ to itself. The numbering of axioms is explained in [5].

the refining operators OR, AND, and SAND and thus encode the transformations that do not change the meaning of a SAND attack tree.

Definition 1. *We say that two SAND attack trees are* equivalent *if they can be obtained from each other by applying a finite number of axioms from* $E_{\mathcal{SP}}$.

In other words, SAND attack trees are equivalent if they are equal modulo the axioms from $E_{\mathcal{SP}}$. For instance, we can easily check by applying axioms $(E_{10}), (E_{10'})$, and (E_2) that the SAND attack trees from Figs. 1 and 2 are equivalent.

The authors of [5] have proven that by orienting axioms (E_3), (E_4), $(E_{4'})$, (E_5), $(E_6), (E_{6'})$, (E_{10}), $(E_{10'})$, and (E_{11}) from left to right, one obtains a terminating and confluent term rewriting system, which we denote by $R_{\mathcal{SP}}$. Using $R_{\mathcal{SP}}$, every SAND attack tree can be transformed into an equivalent one in *canonical form*, i.e., which is in normal form wrt $R_{\mathcal{SP}}$. For instance, the tree from Fig. 2 is a canonical form of the one from Fig. 1. Due to the confluence and the termination of $R_{\mathcal{SP}}$, we obtain the following result.

Proposition 1. *Two SAND attack trees are equivalent if and only if their normal forms with respect to* $R_{\mathcal{SP}}$ *are equal modulo commutativity and associativity of* OR *and* AND *and modulo associativity of* SAND.

Thus, the rewriting system $R_{\mathcal{SP}}$ yields an effective way for handling SAND attack trees and provides formal foundations for SPTool described in the next section.

3   SPTool Software

SPTool is a free and open source tool allowing to reason about SAND attack trees. It offers two main functionalities:

1. Given a SAND attack tree t, SPTool returns the canonical form of t;
2. SPTool checks whether two SAND attack trees are equivalent wrt $E_{\mathcal{SP}}$.

SPTool relies on the term rewriting system $R_{\mathcal{SP}}$, thus we have decided to interface it with Maude – 'a language and system supporting both equational and rewriting logic specification and programming for a wide range of applications' [2]. The choice of Maude was motivated by the fact that it is able to handle rewriting modulo theories (in our case associativity and commutativity). We can thus work with unranked operators OR, AND, and SAND directly. Maude specification file implementing the system $R_{\mathcal{SP}}$ is illustrated in Fig. 4.

```
*** library & type
protecting STRING.
sorts void adterm term.
subsort void adterm < term.

*** operators
op nil : -> void [ctor].
op basic : String -> adterm [ctor].
op OR : adterm adterm -> adterm [ctor assoc comm id: nil].
op AND : adterm adterm -> adterm [ctor assoc comm id: nil].
op SAND : adterm adterm -> adterm [ctor assoc id: nil].

*** variables used
vars x y z : adterm.

*** rewrite rules
eq [e10]  : AND(x,OR(y,z)) = OR(AND(x,y),AND(x,z)).
eq [e101] : SAND(x,OR(y,z)) = OR(SAND(x,y), SAND(x,z)).
eq [e102] : SAND(OR(y,z),x) = OR(SAND(y,x),SAND(z,x)).
eq [e11]  : OR(x,x) = x.
```

Fig. 4. Maude specification for the term rewriting system $R_{\mathcal{SP}}$

A user interacts with SPTool via the GUI shown in Fig. 5. After having provided input SAND attack tree(s) (in windows *Tree 1* and/or *Tree 2*), he selects either to compute the corresponding canonical form (*Find canonical form* button) or to check equivalence between two trees (*Check equivalence* button). In order to find the canonical form of a tree, SPTool uses Maude which is launched in a separate thread for each tree. After having computed the canonical form, the user can switch between seeing the original tree and its canonical form. To distinguish between the two forms easily, the canonical form is displayed on yellow background. The time performance of SPTool is given in the *Message log* window. While calculating a canonical form, two parameters are displayed: *Maude running time* – the time that Maude required to rewrite the input tree to its normal form; and *Total time* – the time SPTool took to interact with Maude, rewrite the tree, parse it, and display the result. In order to check whether two SAND attack trees are equivalent, SPTool first finds their canonical forms and

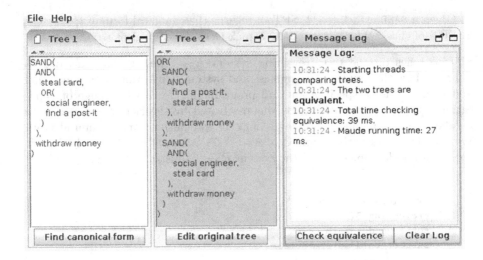

Fig. 5. Graphical user interface of SPTool (Color figure online)

then applies Proposition 1 to draw the conclusion. The answer is displayed in the *Message log* window together with the corresponding time performance.

SPTool offers a possibility of loading SAND attack trees (stored as txt files) and saving the results (i.e., trees in canonical form and the content of the *Message log* window). The format of SPTool files is compatible with ADTool – software allowing to display and quantitatively analyze attack tree-like models [3]. On the one hand, the trees drawn with ADTool can be opened using SPTool to compute their canonical forms. On the other hand, the output trees of SPTool can be graphically visualized and quantitatively analyzed using ADTool.

The architecture of SPTool is presented in Fig. 6. The tool is implemented in Java and requires Java SE 7 or later. It uses Docking Frames library as a docking framework. Due to the use of Maude, SPTool runs on Linux platform.

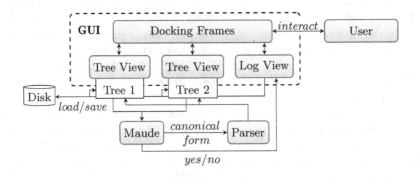

Fig. 6. An overview of the SPTool architecture

Our software is freely available at http://people.irisa.fr/Barbara.Kordy/sptool. It is distributed as a jar package.

4 Experimental Results

For the purpose of testing our software, we have randomly generated SAND attack trees with varying number of nodes. For each of these trees, we have calculated the corresponding canonical form using SPTool. The experiments were performed on a 64-bit Debian Linux machine with Intel i7-4600U processor and 8 GB of memory. Table 1 presents a representative selection of our tests. We notice that the canonical form of a SAND attack tree can be exponentially larger than the input tree. This is especially due to the axioms (E_{10}) and $(E_{10'})$ encoding the distributivity property, which multiply parts of a tree, if applied from left to right. Large size of canonical forms implies that the values of the *Maude running time* and the *Total time* parameters differ substantially. Indeed, in the case of large canonical forms, parsing the tree produced by Maude and displaying it as a formatted string on the screen takes significant time. Our experiments have shown that SPTool handles about 150 k–300 k nodes per second and that it scales linearly.

Table 1. Calculation of canonical form for randomly generated trees

Input tree		Calculation time (ms)		Canonical form	
Non-leaf nodes	Leaves	Maude running time	Total time	Non-leaf nodes	Leaves
73	143	1206	8188	264240	1709520
48	94	880	6921	270000	1045800
39	94	800	2464	80191	971030
42	118	176	529	18430	149848
51	104	81	282	6912	66816
29	71	28	70	381	1696
26	66	29	89	218	1025

We have also employed SPTool to compute canonical forms of manually created SAND attack trees corresponding to real-life scenarios. We have observed that trees produced by humans admit much smaller canonical forms compared to randomly generated trees of similar size. This can be explained by the fact that manually created trees are more structured and their format is close to the canonical form. In consequence, handling of real-life SAND attack trees requires less rewrite steps and is much faster compared to automatically generated trees.

5   Conclusion

SAND attack trees are a popular and practical extension of attack trees allowing to distinguish between actions that need to be performed in a predefined order and those that can be executed in parallel. In this paper, we have presented SPTool – prototype software which makes use of term rewriting to transform a SAND attack tree into its canonical form and to check equivalence between two SAND attack trees. The tool can also be employed to handle classical attack trees which use standard OR and AND refinements only.

The performance tests executed with SPTool have shown that the rewriting theory provides a practical and efficient method to find canonical forms of attack trees and to check their equivalence. These tests allowed us to validate the concept of axiomatization of attack tree-like models, as developed in [6,9].

Our future work will focus on formalization and axiomatization of attack–defense trees with sequential conjunction, a model which augments the expressive power of SAND attack trees by explicitly including countermeasure nodes.

Acknowledgments. The research leading to these results has received funding from the EU Seventh Framework Programme (TREsPASS, grant number 318003) and from FNR Luxembourg (ADT2P, grant number C13/IS/5809105).

References

1. Amenaza: SecurITree. http://www.amenaza.com/SS-what_is.php (2001–2012)
2. Clavel, M., Durán, F., Eker, S., Lincoln, P., Martí-Oliet, N., Meseguer, J., Talcott, C.: All About Maude - A High-performance Logical Framework: How to Specify Program and Verify Systems in Rewriting Logic, vol. 4350. Springer, Heidelberg (2007)
3. Gadyatskaya, O., Jhawar, R., Kordy, P., Lounis, K., Mauw, S., Trujillo-Rasua, R.: Attack trees for practical security assessment: ranking of attack scenarios with ADTool 2.0. In: Agha, G., Houdt, B. (eds.) QEST 2016. LNCS, vol. 9826, pp. 159–162. Springer, Cham (2016). doi:10.1007/978-3-319-43425-4_10
4. Isograph: AttackTree+. http://www.isograph.com/software/attacktree/
5. Jhawar, R., Kordy, B., Mauw, S., Radomirović, S., Trujillo-Rasua, R.: Attack trees with sequential conjunction. In: Federrath, H., Gollmann, D. (eds.) SEC 2015. IAICT, vol. 455, pp. 339–353. Springer, Cham (2015). doi:10.1007/978-3-319-18467-8_23
6. Kordy, B., Mauw, S., Radomirovic, S., Schweitzer, P.: Attack-defense trees. J. Log. Comput. **24**(1), 55–87 (2014)
7. Kordy, B., Piètre-Cambacédès, L., Schweitzer, P.: DAG-based attack and defense modeling: don't miss the forest for the attack trees. Comput. Sci. Rev. **13–14**, 1–38 (2014)
8. Kordy, B., Pouly, M., Schweitzer, P.: Probabilistic reasoning with graphical security models. Inf. Sci. **342**, 111–131 (2016)
9. Mauw, S., Oostdijk, M.: Foundations of attack trees. In: Won, D.H., Kim, S. (eds.) ICISC 2005. LNCS, vol. 3935, pp. 186–198. Springer, Heidelberg (2006). doi:10.1007/11734727_17

10. Paul, S.: Towards automating the construction maintenance of attack trees: a feasibility study. In: Kordy, B., Mauw, S., Pieters, W. (eds.) GraMSec 2014, EPTCS, vol. 148, pp. 31–46 (2014)
11. Pinchinat, S., Acher, M., Vojtisek, D.: ATSyRa: an integrated environment for synthesizing attack trees. In: Mauw, S., Kordy, B., Jajodia, S. (eds.) GraMSec 2015. LNCS, vol. 9390, pp. 97–101. Springer, Cham (2016). doi:10.1007/978-3-319-29968-6_7

Formal Verification of a Memory Allocation Module of Contiki with Frama-C: A Case Study

Frédéric Mangano[1], Simon Duquennoy[2,3], and Nikolai Kosmatov[1(✉)]

[1] CEA, LIST, Software Reliability Laboratory, PC 174, 91191 Gif-sur-Yvette, France
{frederic.mangano,nikolai.kosmatov}@cea.fr
[2] Inria Lille - Nord Europe, Lille, France
simon.duquennoy@inria.fr
[3] SICS Swedish ICT, Kista, Sweden

Abstract. Formal verification is still rarely applied to the IoT (Internet of Things) software, whereas IoT applications tend to become increasingly popular and critical. This short paper promotes the usage of formal verification to ensure safety and security of software in this domain. We present a successful case study on deductive verification of a memory allocation module of Contiki, a popular open-source operating system for IoT. We present the target module, describe how the code has been specified and proven using Frama-C, a software analysis platform for C code, and discuss lessons learned.

Keywords: Deductive verification · Specification · Frama-C · Contiki · Memory allocation

1 Introduction

While formal verification is traditionally applied to embedded software in many critical domains (avionics, energy, rail, etc.), its usage for the Internet of Things (IoT) has not yet become common practice, probably because the first IoT applications were not considered as critical. However, with the emergence of the Internet of Things, embedded devices get massively connected to the Internet. In this context, security concerns become of utmost importance as IoT applications today often deal with sensitive data and act on the physical world. The devices are both constrained and network-facing, thus creating new opportunities for attackers and new challenges for verification. One of these challenges is to verify an embedded yet full-fledged low-power IPv6 stack underlying many potentially critical IoT applications. In this paper we focus on the Contiki OS [1], and in particular on its memory allocation module memb providing a generic mechanism for allocation of a bounded number of blocks of any given type.

Contributions. This experience report paper advocates the use of formal verification for IoT and presents a case study on verification of the memb module performed with Frama-C [2], a rich and powerful toolset for analysis of C code.

© Springer International Publishing AG 2017
F. Cuppens et al. (Eds.): CRiSIS 2016, LNCS 10158, pp. 114–120, 2017.
DOI: 10.1007/978-3-319-54876-0_9

We formally specify memb operations and prove it using the deductive verification tool FRAMA-C/WP. We emphasize two specific issues: the generic nature of the module (resulting in heavier pointer arithmetics and casts) and the need to specify the number of available blocks (requiring an axiomatic definition of occurrence counting). Finally, we describe the verification results and discuss lessons learned.

2   Contiki and Its Memory Allocation Module

Contiki and Formal Verification. Today's IoT software is highly critical because it runs on hardware that is able to sense or even act on physical things. A compromised IoT device may get access to sensitive or private data. Worse, it might become able to take action on the physical world, potentially with safety consequences. Examples of such include reconfiguring an industrial automation process, interfering with alarms or locks in a building, or in the e-health domain, altering a pacemaker or other vital devices.

Contiki is an Operating System for the Internet of Things. It was among the pioneers in advocating IP in the low-power wireless world. In particular, it features a 6LoWPAN stack [3], that is, a compressed IPv6 stack for IEEE 802.15.4 communication. This enables constrained devices to interoperate and connect directly to the Internet. Sensors, actuators or consumer devices can be brought together and create applications in various areas such as home automation or the smart grid.

Contiki is targeted at constrained devices with a 8, 16 or 32-bit MCU and no MMU. The devices usually feature a low-power radio module, some sensors, a few kB RAM and tens of kB ROM. Contiki has a kernel, written in portable C, that is linked to platform-specific drivers at compile-time. At the time of writing, it supports 36 different hardware platforms.

When Contiki started in 2003, the focus was on enabling communication in the most constrained devices, with no particular attention given to security. As it matured and as commercial applications arose, communication security was added at different layers, via standard protocols such as IPsec or DTLS. The security of the software itself, however, did not receive much attention. Although a continuous integration system is in place, it does not include formal verification. While formal verification has already been applied to microkernels and Cloud hypervisors (see [4, Sect. 5] for related work), we are not aware of similar verification projects for IoT software.

Contiki's memb Module. In this case study, we turn our attention to Contiki's main memory management module: memb. To avoid fragmentation in long-lasting systems, Contiki does not use dynamic allocation. Memory is pre-allocated in blocks on a per-feature basis, and the memb module helps the management of such blocks. For instance, the routing module provisions for N entries, which are stored in a static memory area N times the size of a routing entry. Entries are managed by allocating and freeing blocks at runtime.

The module `memb` offers a simple API, enabling to *initialize* a `memb` store, *allocate* a block, *free* a block, *check* if a pointer refers to a block inside the store and *count* the number of allocated blocks. `memb` consists in about 100 lines of code but is one of the most critical elements of Contiki, as the kernel and many modules rely on it. A flaw in `memb` could result in attackers reading or writing arbitrary memory regions, crashing the device, or triggering code execution.

The Contiki code base involves a total of 56 instances of `memb`. Not all are included in a given Contiki firmware, but a subset is included depending on the application and configuration. `memb` is used for instance for HTTP, CoAP (lightweight HTTP), IPv6 routes, CSMA, the MAC protocol TSCH, packet queues, network neighbors, the file system Coffee or the DBMS Antelope.

3   Verification of `memb` with FRAMA-C

3.1   FRAMA-C Platform and Its Deductive Verification Plugin Wp

FRAMA-C [2] is a popular software analysis platform for C programs that offers various static and dynamic analyzers as individual plugins. They include the deductive verification tool WP, abstract interpretation based value analysis, dependency and impact analysis, program slicing, test generation, runtime verification, and many others. FRAMA-C comes with a behavioral specification language ACSL [5]. The user specifies the desired properties of their program by adding ACSL annotations (preconditions, postconditions, loop invariants, assertions, etc.). These annotations are written in special comments `/*@ <annotation>*/` or `//@ <annotation>`. FRAMA-C/WP can be used then to establish a rigorous mathematical proof that the program satisfies its specification. Technically, it relies on automatic provers (SMT solvers) that try to prove the theorems (*verification conditions*, or VCs) automatically generated by WP.

3.2   Declaration of Memory Allocation Data via a Pseudo-Template

A `memb` store is represented by the `struct memb` structure (see Fig. 1a, lines 2–7). Being written in C, it does not allow polymorphism. Instead, it stores as a field of the structure the size of the block type it is meant to store, which enables the implementation to dynamically compute the addresses of the blocks.

The actual blocks are stored in an array (referred to as field `mem`), statically allocated using a global array definition. This is illustrated in Fig. 1b, lines 10–14, for 2 blocks of type `struct point`. Since its length varies, the array cannot be declared directly in the structure, that is why the structure contains a pointer that is initialized to point to the global array. The `count` array is allocated in the same fashion.

All the fields of the `memb` structure are initialized at compile-time and shall not change when the program executes. That is conveniently realized using the `MEMB` macro (whose definition is omitted in Fig. 1a), which relies on the preprocessor in order to

```
 1 /* file memb.h */                        1 /* file demo.c */
 2 struct memb {                            2 #include "memb.h"
 3   unsigned short size; // block size      3 struct point {int x; int y};
 4   unsigned short num;  // number of blocks 4
 5   char *count;         // block statuses  5 // before preprocessing,
 6   void *mem;           // array of blocks  6 // there was the following macro:
 7 };                                        7 // MEMB(pblock, struct point, 2);
 8 #define MEMB(name, btype, num)...         8
 9 // macro used to decrare a memb store for  9 // after preprocessing, it becomes:
10 // allocation of num blocks of type btype 10 static char pblock_count[2];
11                                          11 static struct point pblock_mem[2];
12 void  memb_init(struct memb *m);         12 struct struct memb pblock = {
13 void *memb_alloc(struct memb *m);        13   sizeof(struct point), 2,
14 char  memb_free(struct memb *m, void *p); 14   pblock_count, pblock_mem };
15 ...                                      15 ...
```

Fig. 1. (a) Extract of file memb.h defining a template macro MEMB, and (b) its usage (in file demo.c) to prepare allocation of up to 2 blocks of type struct point

– generate the global array definitions for the count and mem arrays,
– declare an initialized memb store.

Lines 10–14 of Fig. 1b show the result of line 7 after the preprocessing.

3.3 Specifying Operations

First, we specify the functions of memb in ACSL. Let us describe here the contract for the allocation function memb_alloc shown in Fig. 2. Its ACSL contract contains preconditions (requires clauses) that are assumed to be ensured by the caller, and postconditions (ensures clauses) that should be ensured by the function at the end of its execution and thus proved by the verification tool. Lines 2–3 specify that the store respects a global validity property before and after the call. A specific behavior can be expressed in ACSL using a behavior section, which defines additional postconditions whenever the behavior guard given in the assumes clause is satisfied. The contract may stipulate that the given behaviors are disjoint and complete (lines 16–17), the verification tool verifies it as well. The memb_alloc function has two behaviors:

1. If the memb store is full, then it is left intact, and NULL is returned (lines 12–15).
2. If the memb store has at least one free block, then it must be guaranteed that:
   – the returned block is properly aligned in the block array (line 8),
   – the returned block was marked as free, and is now marked as allocated (line 7),
   – the returned block is valid, i.e. points to a valid memory space of a block size that can be safely read or written to (line 10),
   – the states of the other blocks have not changed (line 9),
   – the number of free blocks is decremented (line 11, see also Sect. 3.4).

```
1  /*@
2    requires valid_memb(m);
3    ensures valid_memb(m);
4    assigns m→count[0 .. (m→num - 1)];
5    behavior free_found:
6      assumes ∃ ℤ i; 0 ≤ i < m→num ∧ m→count[i] == 0;
7      ensures ∃ ℤ i; 0 ≤ i < m→num ∧ \old(m→count[i]) == 0 ∧ m→count[i] == 1 ∧
8        \result == (char*) m→mem + (i * m→size) ∧
9        ∀ ℤ j; (0 ≤ j < i ∨ i < j < m→num) ⟹ m→count[j] == \old(m→count[j]);
10     ensures \valid((char*) \result + (0 .. (m→size - 1)));
11     ensures _memb_numfree(m) == \old(_memb_numfree(m)) - 1;
12   behavior full:
13     assumes ∀ ℤ i; 0 ≤ i < m→num ⟹ m→count[i] ≠ 0;
14     ensures ∀ ℤ i; 0 ≤ i < m→num ⟹ m→count[i] == \old(m→count[i]);
15     ensures \result == NULL;
16   complete behaviors;
17   disjoint behaviors;
18 */
19 void *memb_alloc(struct memb *m);
```

Fig. 2. (Simplified) ACSL contract for allocation function `memb_alloc` (file `memb.h`)

3.4 Keeping Track of Free Blocks

When allocating, we may need to ensure the `memb` store is not full, that is, some blocks are available. To this end, we make assumptions on their number that we compute using a logic function named `_memb_numfree`. For instance, requiring that at least n blocks are free ensures that the n subsequent allocations will succeed. The specification states that the number of free blocks is decremented when allocating, and incremented back when a block is freed. Allocation succeeds if and only if the number of free blocks before the allocation is non-zero.

A `memb` store uses its `count` array to determine whether its ith block is free ($count[i] = 0$) or allocated ($count[i] = 1$). In the logic world of ACSL, counting the number of free blocks, or more precisely counting the number of occurrences of 0 in the `count` array, requires an inductive definition using sub-arrays:

- If $to \leq from$, then $count[from \ldots to[$ obviously contains no zeros.
- If $from > to$ and $count[to - 1] = 0$ then $count[from \ldots to[$ contains one more zero than $count[from \ldots to - 1[$.
- If $from > to$ and $count[to - 1] \neq 0$ then $count[from \ldots to[$ contains as many zeros as $count[from \ldots to - 1[$.

In our specification, we use a more general inductive definition from [4], as well as a few auxiliary lemmas proven by induction in the proof assistant Coq (v.8.4pl6).

3.5 Deductive Verification Results

The current specifications of the `memb` modules are fully proven automatically using FRAMA-C/WP Magnesium-20151002, Alt-Ergo 0.99.1, CVC4 1.4 and Z3 4.4.2. The ACSL specification of `memb` is 115 lines of code long, for a total of 259 lines in the header file. To prove it, 32 additional lines of annotations were

```
15  ...
16  /* file demo.c, continued */
17  /*@
18    requires valid_memb(&pblock) ∧ pblock.num == 2;
19    requires pblock.size == sizeof(struct point);
20  */
21  void main() { // all contracts proven with WP except out-of-bounds pointer line 28
22    memb_init(&pblock);
23    /*@ assert _memb_numfree(&pblock) == 2; */
24    void *obj1 = memb_alloc(&pblock), *obj2 = memb_alloc(&pblock);
25    /*@ assert _memb_numfree(&pblock) == 0 ∧ obj1 ≠ NULL ∧ obj2 ≠ NULL; */
26    /*@ assert \valid((char*) obj1 + (0 .. sizeof(struct point)-1)); */
27    /*@ assert \valid((char*) obj2 + (0 .. sizeof(struct point)-1)); */
28    /*@ assert \valid((char*) obj1 + sizeof(struct point)); */ // UNPROVEN - invalid
29    memb_free(&pblock, obj1);  memb_free(&pblock, obj2);
30    /*@ assert _memb_numfree(&pblock) == 2; */
31  }
```

Fig. 3. Example of ACSL-annotated function using memb (file demo.c)

required in the implementation file, summing up to 154 lines. 126 verification conditions are generated.

Figure 3 shows an annotated function using memb that can be automatically proven with FRAMA-C/WP, except for line 28 that contains an out-of-bounds pointer. Thus, out-of-bounds accesses are automatically detected thanks to the provided specification.

This verification case study also allowed to detect a potentially harmful situation. The **memb_free** function used to decrement the count associated to the given block, instead of setting it to 0. An awkward consequence of this is that calling **memb_free** on a block with an unusual count (e.g. greater than 2) would not actually free it. While this should not happen under normal circumstances, we have decided to replace that decrement operation by a set to 0. This choice makes **memb_free** both simpler and more robust, easing the verification process, and we recommend to integrate it into the production code.

4 Conclusion and Future Work

IoT software is becoming more critical and widely used. We argue that formal verification should be more systematically applied in this domain to guarantee that critical software meets the expected level of safety and security.

This paper reports on a case study where deductive verification with FRAMA-C/WP has been applied on the memory allocation module memb, one of the most critical and largely used components of the Contiki OS. We have described the verification methodology and results. In particular, the presented verification *formally guarantees* the absence of out-of-bounds accesses to the block array in the memb module.

We have emphasized two technical aspects. One is related to pointer arithmetics and casts due to the generic implementation of the module for all possible block types. The second one concerns inductive definitions and proofs necessary to count elements in the block status array and to state some properties on the corresponding counting functions. While these aspects could constitute an obstacle for formal verification of real-life C software a few years ago, they can be successfully treated today by modern verification tools like FRAMA-C/WP. This experience report also shows that automatic theorem provers have made significant progress, and that interactive proof, e.g. with Coq proof assistant, can be used in complement on remaining properties that are too complex to be proven automatically.

One future work direction is the verification of memb with a slightly more precise specification, including for example stronger isolation properties between blocks of the same store. This would require a better support of ACSL allocation primitives in WP (such as the frees clause) in order to better trace validity of individual blocks. Secondly, the results of this case study should facilitate the verification of other components of Contiki relying on memb. For some of them (such as list, defining chained lists), this could require further extensions of FRAMA-C and ACSL. Finally, specification and proof of other IoT software modules is another future work direction.

Acknowledgment. Part of the research work leading to these results has received funding for DEWI project (www.dewi-project.eu) from the ARTEMIS Joint Undertaking under grant agreement No. 621353. The second author has also been partially supported by a grant from CPER Nord-Pas-de-Calais/FEDER DATA and the distributed environment Ecare@Home funded by the Swedish Knowledge Foundation 2015–2019. Special thanks to Allan Blanchard, François Bobot and Loïc Correnson for advice, and to the anonymous referees for their helpful comments.

References

1. Dunkels, A., Gronvall, B., Voigt, T.: Contiki - a lightweight and flexible operating system for tiny networked sensors. In: LCN (2014)
2. Kirchner, F., Kosmatov, N., Prevosto, V., Signoles, J., Yakobowski, B.: Frama-C: a software analysis perspective. Formal Asp. Comput. **27**(3), 573–609 (2015)
3. Montenegro, G., Kushalnagar, N., Hui, J., Culler, D.: Transmission of IPv6 packets over IEEE 802.15.4 networks. RFC 4944, September 2007. http://www.rfc-editor.org/rfc/rfc4944.txt
4. Blanchard, A., Kosmatov, N., Lemerre, M., Loulergue, F.: A case study on formal verification of the anaxagoros hypervisor paging system with Frama-C. In: Núñez, M., Güdemann, M. (eds.) FMICS 2015. LNCS, vol. 9128, pp. 15–30. Springer, Cham (2015). doi:10.1007/978-3-319-19458-5_2
5. Baudin, P., Cuoq, P., Filliâtre, J.C., Marché, C., Monate, B., Moy, Y., Prevosto, V.: ACSL: ANSI/ISO C Specification Language. http://frama-c.com/acsl.html

Network Security

A Proactive Stateful Firewall for Software Defined Networking

Salaheddine Zerkane[1(✉)], David Espes[2], Philippe Le Parc[2], and Frederic Cuppens[3]

[1] IRT B<>COM, UBO, Télécom Bretagne, 35510 Cesson-Sévigné, France
Salaheddine.ZERKANE@b-com.com,
Salaheddine.ZERKANE@telecom-bretagne.eu
[2] IRT B<>COM, UBO, 29200 Brest, France
{David.Espes,Philippe.Le-Parc}@univ-brest.fr
[3] IRT B<>COM, Télécom Bretagne, 35510 Cesson-Sévigné, France
Frederic.Cuppens@telecom-bretagne.eu

Abstract. Security solutions in conventional networks are complex and costly because of the lack of abstraction, the rigidity and the heterogeneity of the network architecture. However, in Software Defined Networking (SDN), flexible, reprogrammable, robust and cost effective security solutions can be built over the architecture. In this context, we propose a SDN proactive stateful Firewall. Our solution is completely integrated into the SDN environment and it is compliant with the Open-Flow (OF) protocol. The proposed Firewall is the first implemented stateful SDN Firewall. It uses a proactive logic to mitigate some fingerprinting and DoS attacks. Furthermore, it improves the network performance by steering network communications in order to fulfil network protocol FSM (Finite State Machine). Besides, an Orchestrator layer is integrated in the Firewall in order to manage the deployment of the Firewall applications. This integration empowers the interactions with the administrator and the data plane elements. We conduct two tests to prove the validity of our concept and to show that the proposed Firewall is efficient and performant.

Keywords: Software Defined Networking · Fingerprinting attacks · Stateful Firewall · Network security · Orchestration · TCP · OpenFlow

1 Introduction

Software Defined Networking (SDN) [1] is an emerging paradigm which proposes a programmable and a flexible networking architecture. It is mainly based on two ideas coming from software engineering.

The first idea is the separation of concerns by decoupling the data plane from the control plane. The separation makes the data plane as a simple forwarding layer. The control layer is logically centralized as one or many controllers. The network applications are run on the top of the control layer. They can be integrated into a controller or decoupled into an application plane. The abstraction between these planes enables high level languages to configure network applications, controllers and data plane devices; thus, the latter can be effectively reprogrammed without worrying about hardware and software details constraints

© Springer International Publishing AG 2017
F. Cuppens et al. (Eds.): CRiSIS 2016, LNCS 10158, pp. 123–138, 2017.
DOI: 10.1007/978-3-319-54876-0_10

(heterogeneity, portability, etc.). Besides, Controllers are empowered with a global vision on any part of the SDN network. This holistic knowledge enables them to reinforce network and security policies and improve QoS.

The second idea is the abstraction by the standardization of the different interfaces between data plane devices, *Controllers* and network applications. It defines some protocols to communicate between the SDN planes. An example is the "southbound interface" between the data plane and the control plane such as OpenFlow (OF) [2]. The southbound interface offers a high level of abstraction to enable *Controllers* to reprogram data plane devices by adding OpenFlow rules and collect different information on the traffic by setting counters.

Through these features, the network becomes more flexible, easily reprogrammable and less complex. Network services are effectively and dynamically deployed in the network without worrying about hardware details. As well, network operations and transactions become easily manageable and less error prone.

Security in SDN is two sided [3]; on the one hand, SDN eases the development of efficient, flexible and controllable security solutions. However, on the other hand, it introduces new threats to the network architecture that did not exist before. These vulnerabilities [4] can be in any SDN component with different severities and likelihoods scales.

In this article, we highlight a SDN proactive stateful Firewall and its centralized management interface. Our solution is composed of two components: an *Orchestrator* and a *Firewall Application*. The *Orchestrator* is responsible for the management of the security strategy between the network elements and the administrator. The *Orchestrator*'s main goal is to offer a global view of the network and dynamically deploy the security policies on the data plane when needed. The *Firewall Application* is used to secure networks from unauthorized accesses. Each Instance of the *Firewall Application* is associated with a *Controller* and placed above its northbound interface.

This Firewall is the first SDN stateful Firewall to be compliant with the OpenFlow standard. Our security solution is entirely based on the SDN principles and uses the OpenFlow specification as a way to abstract security policies and install them on the data plane devices.

We think that this solution has many advantages in a SDN environment; it saves the expenditures related to traditional Firewalls, it is reprogrammable without errors and deployable in commodity devices. Our solution induces a stronger scalability comparing with the existent propositions because of the linear relation between the maximum number of installed OpenFlow rules and the number of connections. It requires less memory and processing resources. For example in TCP, it installs up to three OpenFlow rules for each side of the communication.

The remainder of this paper is organized as follow. In Sect. 2, we describe the state of the art of SDN Firewalls. In Sect. 3, we present the fundamental principles and the solution architecture. In Sect. 4, we explain the proactive behavior of the Firewall. We present an example of the Firewall for TCP FSM in Sect. 5. Section 6 provides the details of the Firewall implementation, we also experiment the ability of the Firewall to counter some fingerprinting attacks and we provide some performance results in a virtualized environment based on TCP FSM implementation. Finally, we conclude with some insights and related perspectives.

2   Related Work

A Firewall protects the network from illegal access. It applies a set of filtering rules to the outbound and inbound messages. There are mainly 3 types of Firewalls [5–7]:

- *Stateless Firewalls* filter packets according to rules specified by the administrator. They do not keep track in memory of the connection states. As a consequence, they are unable to manage dynamic network information.
- *Stateful Firewalls* Stateful Firewalls are an evolution of the stateless Firewalls. They use, in addition, elements related to the state of a connection to filter the packets according to the network security policies. They record packets' states and their attributes in memory during the connection lifecycle. However, these Firewalls do not protect the network against the attacks on the application layer.
- *Application Firewalls* were introduced in order to offer more advanced traffic analysis capacities. They use additional attributes related to the application layer protocols to filter the packets in order to handle application problems. In terms of processing, these Firewalls are very memory and CPU consuming.

Some SDN *Controllers* (RYU, Floodlight and POX) propose their own OpenFlow Firewalls [8–10] modules. However, they have many drawbacks and limited capacities because they are stateless, and they lack effectiveness and user graphical interface. In [11] the authors propose a stateless SDN-oriented hardware Firewall based on Open-Flow. The security policies are expressed in OpenFlow rules and stored in flow tables at both the data plane devices and the *Controller* sides. Besides the lack of efficiency, the data plane devices forward unidentified traffic to *Controllers* so an attacker can flood *Controllers* with unknown traffic to overload it. The stateless Firewall proposed in [12] interprets the commands of the Administrator into OpenFlow rules and installs them on the data plane device. [13–15] propose an OpenFlow extension, named FleXam. It adds to OpenFlow a channel that makes it possible to specify flows of filters, sample schemes (parts of packets that will be selected) and actions associated with the filtered sample. FleXam though, forwards all samples to the *Controller* which affects the scalability and the performance of the SDN network.

Some researchers propose a framework to define security applications such as a Firewall. However these frameworks are not appropriated for designing stateful Fire-walls. FRESCO [16, 17] is an OpenFlow development framework. It enables to construct rapidly OF enabled security detection and mitigation applications. It instantiates prede-fined security modules and assembles them together into an OpenFlow security appli-cation such as a Firewall. FRESCO is not appropriated for building stateful Firewalls because it cannot track the states of a packet and handle traffic dynamic information. The framework Flowguard [18, 19] allows building OpenFlow robust stateless Fire-walls. It proposes a mechanism to detect and resolve Firewall policies violations caused by traffic modifications and OpenFlow rules dependencies. But, it does not support stateful Firewalls.

Few authors propose SDN stateful Firewall. In [20] the authors design a SDN stateful Firewall based on OpenFlow. The solution modifies the OpenFlow protocol by adding new tables and new messages in the data plane device. The states of the connection are managed by the data plane device. The controller is only informed about the updates. In [21] the authors integrate a distributed Firewall into the data plane 'Open Virtual Switch (OVS)'. The idea aims to improve the performance of SDN Firewalls and to elevate data plane features by handling layers 4–7 traffic. They incorporate into OVS, the Conntrack tools [22] which are a Linux connection tracking system. Conntrack provides a stateful Firewall with advanced features to perform deep packet inspection. The solution adds a new action to OF in order to send the flows to the Conntrack modules. OpenState [23] is another work belonging to the philosophy of empowering the data plane device with some control functionalities. This solution integrates to the OF switch a state table to enable the data plane to track autonomously from the controller the state of flows. According to the values of the letter, the data plane device executes an action on the flow and updates its state table.

There are many issues with the last 3 propositions; firstly, they are not compatible with the OpenFlow standard since they add their proprietary tables, actions and messages. Secondly, the research trend modifying the design of the OF switch (by integrating to it some control functions) is not aligning with the SDN logic. Finally, these solutions are not yet proven to be better than the standard SDN solutions.

3 Conceptual Foundations

In this section we describe in details all the aspects of our SDN stateful proactive Firewall from the analysis foundations to the design of the general architecture and its algorithm. It is stateful because it tracks the states of the connections and their possible transitions to elaborate security policies into OpenFlow rules. The proactive side of the solution comes from its operational mode. It uses a set of different combinations of OpenFlow rules to prevent the Controller from receiving useless or unauthorized traffic.

3.1 Firewall General Architecture

The solution is entirely integrated into the SDN architecture in three levels (see Fig. 1): the management plane, the control plane and the data plane.

The high level (i.e., the management plane) is composed of one component, the *Orchestrator*. The *Orchestrator* offers a graphical interface to the administrators in order to enable them to deploy the security policies and access to the global view of the SDN network. For this matter, the *Orchestrator* includes a policy security editor and integrates an access to network information such as topology, logs, network configuration, etc. As a federating entity, it collects all the information related to the network topology, SDN events, logs and errors from all the SDN *Controllers* and maintains this information in its data base. Also, it spreads the security policies expressed by the administrator to the *Controllers*.

The mid-level (i.e., the control plane) is composed of two components: the *Controller* and the *Firewall Application*. The *Controller* collects the events coming from the *Orchestrator* and transfers them to the *Firewall Application*. It provides also the *Orchestrator* with the requested network information and guarantees the communication

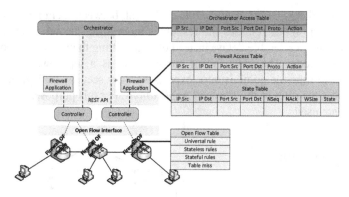

Fig. 1. SDN stateful Firewall general architecture

with the data plane devices. Each *Controller* has an instance of a *Firewall Application*. It is integrated above the *Northbound interface*. The *Firewall Application* behaves according to proactive stateful Firewalling logic. It tracks the connections of the flows and keeps their states for all the network sessions. The integration on the *Controller* ensures a fined-grained Firewalling strategy. The *Firewall Application* is able to install into data plane devices many Firewall rules in order to permit or deny traffic based on physical ports, network nodes, users and other roles.

The communication between the high level (i.e., the *Orchestrator*) and the mid-level (i.e., the *Controllers*) is guaranteed by the *REST API* standard. It allows the *Orchestrator* to interact with any *Controller* solution. The *REST API* is the most common northbound interface. It is supported by a large variety of *Controllers*. Due to the intrinsic heterogeneity of the control plane, the *Orchestrator* can manage any *Controller* through *REST*.

The low level (i.e., the data plane) is composed of the OpenFlow compatible data plane devices. They execute the Firewall *OF Rules* received from the *Controller*. From this moment, each data plane device becomes in part a Firewall like-device.

The communication between the mid-level and the low level is ensured by using the Open Flow protocol. The data plane devices through this protocol send to the Controller many types of events (statistics, errors, packet-in…). The Controller observes all of them and transfers them either to the *Firewall Application* or to the *Orchestrator*.

3.2 Table Management

Specific tables are maintained by the components of our architecture whatever their level. At each layer, one table is in relation with another located in the lower level. The relation between the table of the highest level and the table of the mid-level can operate according to the two following modes (see Fig. 2). The On-demand mode like in the Independent mode:

– On-demand mode: The on-demand mode is a bottom-up synchronous process. The *Firewall Application* queries the Orchestrator periodically to know if new rules have been expressed by the administrator since the last request. In this case, it sends a response containing the new rules. This is useful in an environment where the

Orchestrator, the *Firewall Applications* or the link between them is/are loaded. In this context, the mode releases the resources by sending the set of updates each interval of time (a tolerable delay) instead of transmitting them instantaneously.

– Independent mode: The independent mode works as a top-down asynchronous process. Each time the administrator expresses a new security policy, the *Orchestrator* pushes the rules to the *Firewall Applications*. For this purpose, asynchronous messages are used.

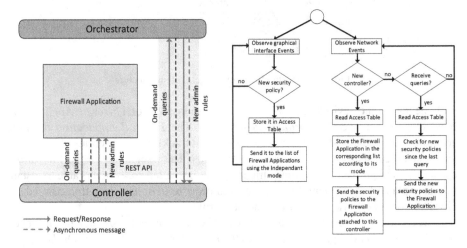

Fig. 2. High level and the mid-level interactions.

Fig. 3. Security policies Orchestration.

In both modes, when a new *Controller* connects to the *Orchestrator*, the latter sends to the former the security policies regarding the part of the network it controls. In the same way, each time the *Firewall Application* receives new rules expressed by the administrator, it sends them to the data plane devices after interpreting them.

3.2.1 Orchestrator Table

The *Orchestrator* proposes a management interface to the administrator. Its security policies are applied to the whole network. They are expressed in the same way as those which are expressed in legacy Firewalls. According to the protocol of the transport layer, the *Firewall Application* is configured by the *Orchestrator to* react as a stateful or stateless Firewall with the security policies.

Once a security policy is entered in the Firewall GUI, it is recorded inside the *Orchestrator Access Table*. The *Firewall Application* gathers the security policies according to two operating modes (i.e., independent or on-demand modes). For that reason, the *Orchestrator* has to react properly to events coming from the administrators.

The algorithm to manage the security policies is given in Fig. 3. It comprises two simultaneous threads. The first one manages the *Firewall Applications* using the independent mode. Each time the administrator expresses new security policies; it sends the policies to the *Firewall Applications*. The second thread manages the connection of new

Controllers and the reception of queries periodically sent by *Firewall Applications* using the on-demand mode.

3.2.2   Firewall Tables

The *Firewall Application* uses two tables: the *Access Table* and the *State Table*. The *Access Table* contains administrator security rules according to a white list approach. It is maintained at two scales. The Orchestrator manages a global *Access Table* that federates all the network security policies. At the *Controller* level, each *Firewall Application* maintains a local *Access Table* in relation with the *Controller*'s network scope. The administrator informs the Orchestrator with only policies expressing authorized routes. When the *Firewall Application* receives them, it interprets them into *Access OF Rules* and installs them on the data plane devices. The Firewall changes the behavior of the data plane devices. The latter executes the received security policies in form of *OF Rules*. The solution produces 3 types of Firewall dedicated *OF Rules*:

–   *Drop all unexpected traffic (Table miss)*.
–   *Access OF Rules* (Administrator's policies).
–   *State OF Rules* (enables to receive only the events triggering the transitions from the actual state of the Active connection).

The Firewall generates *Access OF Rules* by observing the events happening on its *Access Table*. It operates according to one of the two following modes.

Besides, each Firewall Application has a proprietary Table to keep the history of the network connections. The State Table contains all the information to identify and distinguish a connection from another. The Firewall uses it to know the state of the connection, to verify the legitimacy of a packet, to create State OF Rules and to store the states of the active connections with their features.

3.2.3   Open Flow Table

In the data plane a set of OpenFlow rules expresses the security rules according to the OF standard. Each data plane device maintains them in an OpenFlow Table. The *Firewall Applications* install in the tables the interpreted security policies or the stateful decisions. In accordance with these rules, data plane devices change their behavior as following. They block all the network traffic by default. They authorize only the entities allowed by the security policies to communicate. In addition, they force each connection to comply with the legitimate behavior as specified in their standard communication protocol.

3.3   Firewall Generic Algorithm

Our Firewall is compliant with any connection-oriented transport layer protocols. However, before deployment, it is required to design the state transition diagram of the supported protocols. Once the state transition diagram is designed, a generic algorithm is used to send the appropriated *OF Rules* to the data plane devices.

First, the Firewall starts by changing the table-miss entry in the data plane devices. This rule has the most inferior priority, it matches with any packet header and it performs a drop action by default. It allows the *Controller* from the beginning to seal the entire SDN network from any external access.

The sealing mechanism is important in terms of performance because it prevents the *Controller* from receiving any traffic not matching the FSM of the processed network protocols. Also, it eases the tasks of the administrator by preventing it from specifying each time the black listed routes. Also, it mitigates DoS attacks on the Firewall module.

In the second step, the Firewall uses the on-demand mode or the independent mode to interpret the administrator rules to *Access OF Rules* and installs them in the data plane device.

When the *Controller* receives a *packet-in*, it sends it to the *Firewall Application*. In case an active connection does not exist in the *State Table*, the module creates a new active connection in this table (corresponding to the new route) and assigns a state to it. Then, it verifies if the preconditions trigger any of the available transitions from the actual state of the connection. If nothing is found the packet is dropped, else it selects the transition prompted by the preconditions. In this case, it applies the corresponding *Actions*, and it sends messages to the data plane devices to delete the previous *State OF Rules*.

After this step, the module sends the new *State OF Rules* corresponding to the new state of the active connection. For each state, only the corresponding set of preconditions is received. The purpose is to prevent the Firewall from receiving any useless traffic and keep it permanently compliant with the stateful network protocol.

Finally, the *Firewall Application* sets the new state of the active connection corresponding to the processed transition.

4   Main Principle

The stateful Firewall has to be designed efficiently to support three properties:

− It has to be compliant with OpenFlow standard
− It has to forward packets in a proactive way
− It has to be performant

Most networking vendors produce capable SDN data plane devices (compliant with OpenFlow) or propose an update of the data plane device's firmware to support the OpenFlow protocol. As OpenFlow data plane devices are already largely deployed, our stateful Firewall is compliant with this protocol. The OpenFlow standard does not allow storing specific data in a flow table such as the state of a connection. As a consequence, the data plane devices cannot keep track of the state of a connection.

The data plane devices forward the packets to the output port directly. But also, at the same time, they send a copy of the packets to the *Controller* if they trigger a state transition (see Fig. 4). The main reason is to avoid extra delays when delivering packets. Since the version 1.0 of the OpenFlow protocol, it is possible to duplicate packets during the pipeline processing of a flow entry. Each flow entry can have an instruction *Apply-Actions*. The list of actions attached to this instruction is immediately applied to a packet during the processing pipeline. The *packet-in* and the forwarding packet are processed simultaneously. The *packet-in* is processed by the *Firewall Application* before the reply of the destination. During this interval, the *Firewall Application* can install the *State Rules* into the data plane devices.

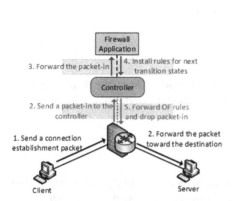

Fig. 4. Firewall forwarding behavior.   **Fig. 5.** Firewall test-bed.

Another important property of the stateful Firewall is its performance. In order to process a large number of connections, it is important to minimize the number of packets received by the *Firewall Application* per connection. During the design phase of the Firewall, we take care to minimize the number of packet-in sent to the *Controller*. The Firewall only receives packets that trigger a change from one state to another. For example in TCP protocol, the Firewall has to process 7 packets per connection (SYN, SYN–ACK, ACK, FINx2, FIN-ACKx2).

5   TCP Example

We have applied the generic algorithm for the Transmission Control Protocol (TCP) [24]. The Firewall enhances the Finite state Machine (FSM) of TCP by including to its conditions and actions OF matching fields and OF rules. Besides, it includes also the Firewalling behavior such as verifying the legitimacy of packet identity.

For example in the Synchronization step, the client sends a SYN packet with a value of the field Flag = SYN. In the FSM of TCP, the SYN flag (the condition of the state) triggers the transition from the initial state LISTENING to the next state *SYN_RCV* of TCP. The TCP machine action is to allow the packet to go to its destination. In the Firewall, firstly, the header of the packet is matched in the data plane device with the available flow rules' matching fields. If the packet header does not match any State and Access *OF Rules*, it is dropped (Universal *OF Rule*). In case it is a legitimate connection initiation, a match with an *Access OF Rule* is found. A copy of the packet is encapsulated in a packet-in message and forwarded to the *Firewall Application*. The packet is also forwarded to its destination. Then, when the *Firewall Application* receives the packet-in, it creates an active connection in the *State Table* with a state value equal to *LISTENING* if there is not an entry for the connection. Moreover, It performs the following actions. It installs a *State OF Rule* to allow the destination to answer with a SYN-ACK Packet. It adds another rule to drop any further connection initiation messages for the same connection in order to mitigate SYN Flooding attacks (the number of connection initiation repetitions can be bounded with a threshold). It installs also, a third *State OF Rule* to allow the client to reset the connection using a RST packet. Finally, it updates the state value to *SYN_RCV*.

6   Test-Bed

To experiment our concept, we have implemented our solution on the Ryu *Controller* [25] using the Python language. Then, we have measured the performance of the implemented solution in a virtual environment.

6.1   Implementation

The *Firewall Application* and the *Orchestrator* are implemented in Python language. The *Orchestrator* allows the network administrator to manage and view the Access *OF Rules*, the logs and the virtual SDN topology. It is composed of a General User Interface (GUI) to manage the *Firewall Applications* and the *Controllers*, and a Web Socket Server to communicate with the *Controllers* through the REST API.

The Firewall Application runs on the top of the Controller as a RYU application. It is able to invoke many RYU classes in order to process SDN events, to parse or serialize packets, and to communicate in OpenFlow 1.3 with the data plane devices.

The *Firewall Application* is composed of the following modules (see Fig. 5): (1) Interpreter module: it translates the Administrator rules into Access OpenFlow rules according to the specification of the OpenFlow protocol. (2) Logger Module: it collects information on the other Firewall modules, connections data and traffic statistics. (3) Sentinel Module: it is responsible for the interaction with the *Controller*. It configures also the Firewall modules according to the information collected from the *Controller*. (4) Engine Module: it expresses the behavior of the Firewall in handling all the phases of a stateful connection and in processing the communication between the client and the server. The actual version of Engine processes TCP communications. The implementation allows building any other Engine modules to handle any FSM protocols. This type of upgrades doesn't affect the design of the firewall. Only a line in Sentinel is added in this case in order to indicate the context related to the instantiation of the Engine threads.

6.2   Test and Results

We deploy a virtual SDN topology using Mininet [26]. It allows the user to emulate a SDN Network. Our test-bed topology is composed of 6 hosts connected to an Open Virtual Switch (OVS) [27]. This latter is managed by a RYU *Controller*. The environment is running under Ubuntu 14, 64 bit, 2 GB of RAM and 2 processors at 2.8 GHz.

We perform two different series of tests. The first one focuses on simulating a fingerprinting attack. The objective is to show that the Firewall prevent this attack from happening. The second one is related to the performances and the scalability of the Firewall. In this test we evaluate the processing times added by the Firewall.

6.2.1   Fingerprinting Attack Experiment

Fingerprinting attacks [28] are generally the first step in mapping out a network; whether, for discovering the vulnerabilities of the system or penetrating the network with more sophisticated threats.

In our experiment we perform a port scanning attack on a host in an SDN network. The objective of this fingerprinting attack is to discover if the host is up and the status of its ports. We use NMAP [29] (a penetration testing tool) to perform the fingerprinting attack. NMAP offers a set of fingerprinting technics such as OS discovery to reveal the OS system of the victim, device discovery and many other advanced scanning technics. Among these methods, we deploy a complex fingerprinting technic called idle scanning. The objective of this attack is to disclose the ports states of a detected node (open, closed or filtered by a Firewall). The attack scenario introduces 3 roles. The victim of the attack is the targeted host. The attacks are directed to it in order to reveal its status and its ports (or services). The zombie machine is another host which the behavior had been deviated by the attacks in order to hide the identity of the attack source. The attacker is the malicious node that prepares and launches the attack.

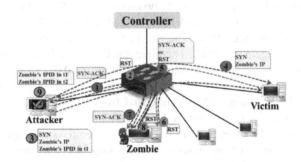

Fig. 6. Idle scan fingerprinting steps.

The steps of the attack are described in the Fig. 6. (1) The attacker sends 6 SYN-ACK packets to a detected node which has been chosen to play the zombie machine. (2) This later replies with consecutive RST packets to the attacker because there are not open TCP connections for the SYN-ACK packets it received. (3) The attacker spoofs the Zombie's IP address and IP identifier (TCP field to identify fragments) in order to forge a fake packet using these data. (4) The attacker sends its fake SYN packet (including the spoofed information) to the victim. (5) The victim answers the zombie with a SYN-ACK packet (if the port is open) because the spoofed SYN contains the information about the zombie. If the victim's port is closed it answers with a RST packet. (6) The zombie answers only the SYN-ACK packet. In this case, it sends to the victim a RST packet since there is not a real open TCP connection. At the same time it increments its IP identifier. (7) The attacker resends a SYN-ACK packet to the zombie. (8) The zombie replies with a RST packet revealing its new IP identifier. (9) The attacker compares this new value with the first zombie's IP identifier.

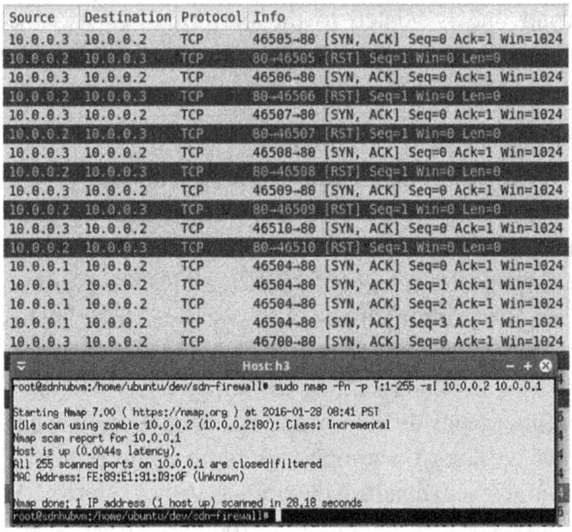

Fig. 7. Fingerprinting results for scenario 1.

If it is incremented at least by 2, the attacker concludes that the targeted port is open. If the increment is less than 2, it means that the port is closed or filtered by a Firewall.

We perform the idle scan according to two scenarios. In the first one we deactivate the SDN Firewall and deploy the attack in the testbed. The *controller* in this case allows all the hosts to talk to each other. Whereas, in the second situation, we activate the Firewall and we run again the attack. Therefore, the Firewall takes the control of all the traffic. In both scenarios, we choose the client H3 (IP = 10.0.0.3) as an attacker, the client H2 (IP = 10.0.0.2) as a zombie and the client (IP = 10.0.0.1) as a target of the attack. We run the following NMAP command from H3: *nmap -Pn -p T:1-255 -sI 10.0.0.2 10.0.0.1* in order to perform the Idle scan.

The results of the first scenario are in the Fig. 7. The data collected in Wireshark during the attack shows that the attacker succeeds to perform the steps of the attacks. The zombie revealed its IP Identifier and responded with the victim to the plan of the attacker by generating the expected reactions. As an outcome, NMAP detects that the ports are closed or filtered. It detects also the victim and zombie as active hosts.

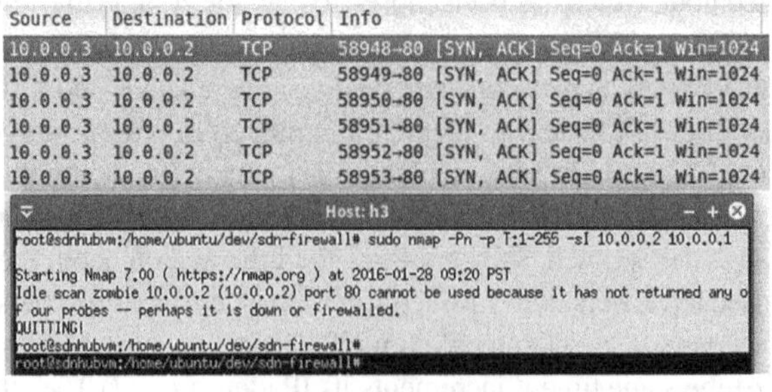

Fig. 8. Fingerprinting results for scenario 2.

The Fig. 8 shows the results of the attack in the case our Firewall is working. By contrast to the previous results, the attacker doesn't succeed to perform all the steps of the attack. It stops at the first step. It doesn't get any zombie's answer to the 6 launched probes. The Firewall rejects them systematically because they don't correspond to a legitimate TCP behavior. Thus, it stopes the attacker from collecting the IP identifier and achieving the attack scheme. NMAP in this case is unable to scan the victim. However, it informs us that the victim is down or Firewalled. The advantage of our solution in this case is as following. In one hand, it can be deployed in any OF switch in a flexible way to prevent any internal fingerprinting attack. In the other hand, if the attacker suspects a Firewall, he cannot locate it exactly since the switch itself behaves partly as a Firewall while hiding the Firewall Application and the Orchestrator.

6.2.2 Performance Experiment

In this experiment (see Fig. 5), we start an apache server on one of the hosts. The 5 others exchange data with this server. The tests have been performed according to two different stages. In the first phase, the Firewall is disabled. The *Controller* acts as a learning switch. It receives the first communication of each connection, learns its route then installs the appropriate OpenFlow rules to allow the clients to communicate directly with the server. Whereas, in the second test, we turned off the *controller*'s learning module and start the SDN Firewall (*Firewall Application* and the *Orchestrator*). In this case, our Firewall handles all the communications between the server and the clients.

In both tests, the clients generate an upward number of TCP connections to download from the server a binary file of 1 MO. We started the tests with 10 connections and ended at 1000 simultaneous connections per second. In each step (number of simultaneous connections), we measure the average processing time of processing packets-in (see Fig. 9) and the average times (see Fig. 10) of processing connections.

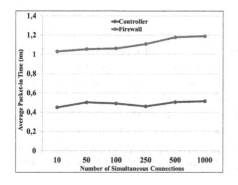

Fig. 9. Packets-in processing times.

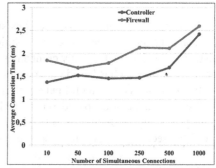

Fig. 10. Connection processing times.

In Fig. 9, we observe in both tests that the average time of processing packets-in is almost steady along the rise of the number of simultaneous connections. In the controller test it is between 0.44 ms and 0.51 ms and in the Firewall test it is between 1.02 ms and 1.18 ms. We observe in both of them a minor increase of the time from 10 simultaneous to 1000 simultaneous connections (0.05 ms for the controller and 0.16 ms for the Firewall).

Furthermore, the Firewall takes 2.5 more times to process packet-in than the learning switch because it performs more operations such as: interpretations of policies to OF rules, State table updates and access, verification of the legitimacy of packets and other tasks available in the previous sections. However, along the increase of the load, the Firewall maintains stable performance. It scales also without reducing the network performance.

In Fig. 10, we observe that the connection processing average time of the Firewall increases slowly from 1.84 ms (10 simultaneous connections) to 2.59 ms (1000 simultaneous connections). In the *controller* test this time increases also from 1.37 ms (10 simultaneous connections) to 2.42 ms (1000 simultaneous connections). We observe that there are two periods of increase in the Firewall, from 50 to 250 simultaneous connections, the average connection time increases with 0.45 ms; however, it is almost stable from 250 to 500 simultaneous connections. After, it increases again with 0.47 ms. Whereas, in the controller test, it is almost stable till 250 simultaneous connections, then it increases with 1 ms (1000 simultaneous connections). These trends are due to 3 factors. The size of the Flow tables in OVS. In the controller test it increases linearly while in the Firewall test it increases and decreases linearly because of the installation uninstallation of the OF rules. The size of the tables reduces the performance when it increases. The second factor is the multithreading behavior of RYU which optimizes the execution of the controller. This mechanism speed the execution of the controller. The last factor is related to our solution, we have introduced a multithreading mechanism in the Firewall in order to optimize its behavior. For this reason, the Firewall doesn't add an extra time while the load increases. The stable periods in both tests represent the best conditions where the 3 factors are optimal. Overall, the Firewall keeps good performances and scale well while the number of the simultaneous connections increases because it doesn't add any extra time to the connections times.

7   Conclusion

In this paper, we present a proactive SDN stateful Firewall. We discuss about the motivation and the interests behind such a solution which can reduce considerably costs and can be an added value for many companies. We describe the conceptual foundations of our proposition which is based on a generic algorithm that mainly transforms the states and the transitions of a stateful network Firewall to OpenFlow rules.

The Firewall is also based on white lists logic and interprets the administrator security policies to OpenFlow rules. It is based on a fine-grained strategy aiming to spread the security policies into the entire network and at different scales. Although it has been specialized for TCP protocol, the generic algorithm can also handle any other stateful protocol.

We then, elaborated the implementation of the solution using Python language. We integrate the Firewall software architecture to RYU based on Python. Finally, we show our proof of concept by experiencing a fingerprinting attack and setting up performance tests in a virtual SDN topology. The results of the experiments are promising.

We plan to undertake two steps to improve our solution and generalize it. The first improvement is to develop an application Firewall for SDN capable to perform deep packet inspection. The other axis of research is about the development of a Meta SDN Firewall using the concepts of model driving engineering. The Meta Firewall will be dynamically instantiated by the *Orchestrator* according to the context of the SDN network and places in any *Controller.*

References

1. Kreutz, D., Ramos, F.M., Verissimo, P.E., Rothenberg, C.E., Azodolmolky, S., Uhlig, S.: Software-Defined Networking: a comprehensive survey. In: Proceedings of the IEEE, pp. 14–76 (2014)
2. The Open Networking Foundation, OpenFlow Switch Specification (2014)
3. Schehlmann, L., Abt, S., Baier, H.: Blessing or curse? Revisiting security aspects of Software-Defined Networking. In: 10th International Conference on Network and Service Management, pp. 382–387 (2014)
4. Kreutz, D., Ramos, F.M.V., Verissimo, P.: Towards secure and dependable software-defined networks, In: Proceedings of the Second ACM SIGCOMM Workshop on Hot Topics in Software Defined Networking, HotSDN 2013, pp. 55–60 (2013)
5. Guo, F., Chiueh, T.: Traffic analysis: from stateful firewall to network intrusion detection system. RPE report, New York (2004)
6. Trabelsi, Z: Teaching stateless and stateful firewall packet filtering: a hands-on approach. In: 16th Colloquium for Information Systems Security Education, pp. 95–102 (2012)
7. Bidgoli, H.: Packet filtering and stateful firewalls. In: Handbook of Information Security, Threats, Vulnerabilities, Prevention, Detection, and Management, pp. 526–536. Wiley, Hooboken (2006)
8. Suh, M., Park, S.H., Lee, B., Yang, S.: Building firewall over the software-defined network controller, In: The 16th International Conference on Advanced Communications Technology, pp. 744–748 (2014)
9. Indiana University: FlowSpaceFirewall. https://github.com/GlobalNOC/FlowSpaceFirewall. Accessed 9 Nov 2015
10. Poxstuff: [On ligne]. https://github.com/hip2b2/poxstuff/blob/master/of_Firewall.py. Accessed 19 Nov 2015
11. Collings, J., Liu, J.: An OpenFlow-based prototype of SDN-oriented stateful hardware firewalls. In: IEEE 22nd International Conference on Network Protocols. Chapel Hill (2014)
12. Pena, J., Yu, W.: Development of a distributed firewall using Software Defined Networking technology. In: 4th IEEE International Conference on Information Science and Technology, pp. 449–452 (2014)
13. Shirali-Shahreza, S., Ganjali, Y.: Efficient implementation of security applications in OpenFlow controller with FleXam. In: 21st Annual Symposium on High-Performance Interconnects, pp. 49–54 (2013)
14. Shirali-Shahreza, S., Ganjali, Y.: Empowering software defined network controller. In: IEEE International Conference on Communication, pp. 1335–1339 (2013)
15. Shirali-Shahreza, S., Ganjali, Y.: FleXam: flexible sampling extension for monitoring and security applications in OpenFlow. In: Proceedings of the Second ACM SIGCOMM Workshop on Hot Topics in Software Defined Networking, pp. 167–168 (2013)
16. Shin, S., Porras, P., Yegneswaran, V., Fong, M, Gu, G., Tyson, M.: FRESCO: modular composable security services for software-defined networks. In: Network and Distributed System Security Symposium, pp. 1–16 (2013)

17. Shin, S., Porras, P., Yegneswaran, V., Gu, G.: A framework for integrating security services into software-defined networks. In: Open Networking Summit (2013)
18. Hu, H., Ahn, G.W., Zhao, Z.: FLOWGUARD: building robust firewalls for software-defined networks. In: Proceedings of the Second ACM SIGCOMM Workshop on Hot Topics in Software Defined Networking, HotSDN 2014 (2014)
19. Hu, H., Ahn, G.W., Zhao, Z.: Towards a reliable SDN firewall. In: Open Networking Summit (2014)
20. Juan, W., Jiang, W., Shiya, C., Hongyang, J., Qianglong, K.: SDN (self-defending network) firewall state detecting method and system based on openflow protocol. China Patent CN 104104561 A (2014)
21. Gross, J.: Open vSwitch with conntrack. In: Netfilter workshop 2014, Montpellier, France (2014)
22. Ayuso, P.N.: Conntrack-tools: connection tracking userspace tools for Linux. http://conntrack-tools.netfilter.org. Accessed 19 Nov 2015
23. Bianchi, G., Bonola, M., Capone, A., Cascone, C.: OpenState: programming platform-independent stateful OpenFlow applications inside the switch. ACM SIGCOMM Comput. Commun. Rev. **44**, 45–51 (2014)
24. RFC 793: Transmission Control Protocol (1981)
25. Natarajan, S.: RYU controller tutorial. http://sdnhub.org/tutorials/ryu/. Accessed 12 Nov 2015
26. Heller, B.: Reproducible network research with high-fidelity emulation. Doctoral thesis, Stanford University (2013)
27. Openvswitch. http://openvswitch.org/. Accessed 12 Nov 2015
28. Allen, J.M.: OS and Application Fingerprinting Techniques, InfoSec Reading Room, SANS Institute (2007)
29. Lyon, G.: NMAP security scanner. https://nmap.org/. Accessed 18 Jan 2016

Protocol Reverse Engineering: Challenges and Obfuscation

J. Duchêne[1,3(✉)], C. Le Guernic[1,2], E. Alata[3], V. Nicomette[3],
and M. Kaâniche[3]

[1] DGA Maîtrise de l'information, Rennes, France
{julien.duchene,colas.le-guernic}@intradef.gouv.fr
[2] Laboratory High Security, INRIA Team TAMIS, Rennes, France
colas.le-guernic@inria.fr
[3] LAAS-CNRS, Univ. de Toulouse, CNRS, INSA, Toulouse, France
{jduchene,ealata,nicomett,kaaniche}@laas.fr

Abstract. Reverse engineering of communication protocols is aimed at providing methods and tools allowing to infer a model of these protocols. It is very relevant for many application domains, such as interoperability or security audits. Recently, several tools have been developed in order to automate, entirely or partially, the protocol inference process. These tools rely on several techniques, that are usually tuned and adapted according to the final goal of the reverse engineering task. The aim of this paper is (1) to present an overview of the main challenges related to reverse engineering, and (2) to introduce the use of obfuscation techniques to make the reverse engineering process more complex and difficult in particular to malicious users.

1 Introduction

Communication protocols allow several components to exchange messages in a consistent way. They are widely used in networks and telecommunications domains. A protocol may be published in an open standard or it may be proprietary and thus hidden from a user of the component. Reverse engineering is mainly useful in this second case, in the context of non documented and non standardised close protocols. Protocol reverse engineering consists in inferring a model of communications established between several components.

Samba project is a popular example of protocol reverse engineering [16]. It offers an open-source implementation of *SMB/CIFS* protocols for Linux clients, enabling Linux and Windows systems to interoperate. At its beginning in 1992, this project was mainly based on manual reverse, a tricky and time consuming work whose success is tightly linked to the skills of the analysts. Moreover, keeping pace with protocol evolutions was a real challenge.

Protocol reverse engineering techniques are most of the time classified into two categories: network traces analysis tools, and application execution traces analysis tools. They can also be differentiated according to their inference type:

© Springer International Publishing AG 2017
F. Cuppens et al. (Eds.): CRiSIS 2016, LNCS 10158, pp. 139–144, 2017.
DOI: 10.1007/978-3-319-54876-0_11

passive or active. While active inference stimulates the system in order to discover or validate information, passive inference is only based on captured data.

During the past decade, several protocol reverse engineering tools have been developed [14]. The main application domains of reverse engineering are presented in Sect. 2. The contribution of this paper is twofold: (i) Section 3 discusses the main open challenges raised in the context of protocol reverse engineering, and (ii) Section 4 presents a proposal to make reverse engineering more difficult to perform for attackers, thanks to the use of obfuscation techniques. Finally, Sect. 5 concludes this paper.

2   Protocol Reverse Application Domains

As presented in the introduction, **interoperability** is one of the domains concerned by reverse engineering. **Network protocols simulation** is another domain, with tools such as *Scriptgen* [13], *RolePlayer* [9], *Replayer* [15] or *Rosetta* [6]. Network simulators are useful to quickly prototype some specific tests of a protocol whereas performing such tests on a real implementation may be tedious or practically impossible. Furthermore, a network simulator may replay communications, in various environments, and possibly adapt them. It is relevant *e.g.*, to analyse a network attack or to develop honeypots that can interact with attackers in order to record and analyse their behaviour.

Software security audits (and associated tools: *Netzob* [3], *Polyglot* [7] or *Tupni* [10]) is another relevant application domain which is closely linked to the previous one. However, its main goal differs: a component is solicited under various scenarios to check whether it correctly handles communications in such scenarios. Thus, a model of the protocol may be used in order to develop smart fuzzers useful for testing robustness of a protocol implementation.

Some tools like *Netzob* [2] again or *Dispatcher* [5,8] enable **Malware protocol analysis**. Indeed, many malwares use protocols to communicate with third parties. The reverse engineering of these protocols is useful to identify some crucial information regarding the localisation of a botnet master, a date, an imminent attack, attack targets, *etc*, and as a consequence, allows to anticipate an attack occurrence and to react accordingly.

Finally, reverse engineering can also be used to support **network protocol conformance testing**. It consists in checking whether a software correctly implements a network protocol whose specification is known. Reverse engineering enables to get a model of the protocol as implemented by an application, then to check whether this model is compliant with its specification or not.

3   Protocol Reverse Engineering Challenges

Protocol reverse engineering raises several challenges. This section presents the different steps of protocols reverse engineering and their associated challenges.

The preliminary phase of protocols reverse engineering should be dedicated to the identification and characterisation of the environment. Based on this knowledge, an analyst can start the observation step, which consists in setting up

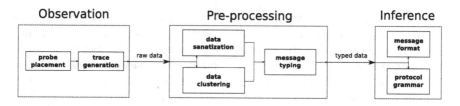

Fig. 1. Protocol reverse engineering steps with associated challenges

some probes for collecting network or application traces. The next step consists in sanitizing these traces in order to obtain relevant messages of the protocol under study. The last step carries out the inference of the message format or of the protocol grammar, from messages obtained at the previous step. These different steps are executed according to an iterative process and the expertise and the intuition of the analyst may largely facilitate some of them. Figure 1 illustrates the steps of the protocol reverse engineering process, and highlights the main challenges associated to each step.

3.1   Observation Step

The inference is based on the gathering of a set of traces thanks to the observation of a communication channel. Two challenges are associated to this observation step: **probe placement** and **traces generation**.

Probe placement is essential to capture different messages required to protocol reverse engineering. This may not be obvious if for instance, applications use several protocols to communicate, each protocol on different channels. Furthermore, a protocol under study may be encapsulated into encrypted channels, thus, it may be necessary to implement the probe in the application itself, at the interface of the cryptographic libraries, in order to be able to decrypt the messages for the sake of the analysis. To our knowledge, this challenge is generally not addressed by any tool, only *Netzob* proposes some generic probes [3].

Collected traces quality also depends on observation duration. A too short observation phase may lead to a poor trace, not containing a set of all the possible message sequences. Such a trace may lead to an incomplete inference. Thus, it is important to identify when the trace is sufficiently rich to be exploitable. This depends on components involved in the protocol as well as their communication frequency. In some cases, to obtain more quickly some appropriate traces, the analyst may adopt an active approach, by stimulating the system, *e.g.* in [3].

3.2   Pre-processing Step

The pre-processing step may be all the more difficult to carry out as an analyst could not place the probes ideally. In this case, collected traces may contain irrelevant information that have to be filtered out. Furthermore, messages relevant to a protocol under reverse engineering may be (1) encapsulated into another protocol; (2) split into several packets transferred in multiple exchanges or (3) observed among messages belonging to other protocols. Thus, a first challenge in this pre-processing step is to correctly sanitize traces in order to reconstruct appropriate messages. This corresponds to **data sanitization**.

When messages are transferred in several packets, another challenge consists in aggregating traces in order to reconstruct messages for the analysis. This challenge concerns both the inference based on network traces, (such as for gathering the TCP segments to obtain a message of an applicative protocol), but also the inference based on application traces, when the analysis of a message is split in several execution traces. Moreover, a trace may contain data related to several messages, thus it is necessary to identify and split corresponding data of each message. These two elements are referred to as **data aggregation**. Data sanitization and aggregation are addressed in [13], but generally left aside.

After their reconstruction, messages are grouped into classes of messages. This clustering phase is required in order to compare the messages that are semantically equivalent. This phase consists in finding a **typing** function allowing, from a message represented as a sequence of bytes, to identify its type. This challenge is addressed by every network based analysis tools except *ReverX* [1], but application based analysis tools generally left it aside.

3.3 Inference Step

Message format inference is aimed, from messages of a same type, at identifying their structure whereas **protocol grammar inference** is aimed at recovering, from sequences of typed messages, rules describing their exchanges. It is also important to identify dependencies between different fields of a message or between messages themselves.

The goal of reverse engineering process is to obtain a specification for message format or protocol grammar. This specification is represented by a model. It is necessary to choose a sufficiently expressive model so that it can faithfully reflect the original specification. For instance, some complex message formats or protocol grammars may have a tree or recursive structure. Such a structure means that a message or value of a field depends on other messages or other fields. This dependency is difficult to express with finite state automata for instance.

4   Obfuscation Techniques

Our current research work focuses on obfuscation techniques aiming at making protocol reverse engineering more difficult to perform in the context of interoperability or network simulation. Such techniques must be easily plugged to existing solutions. Previous work [4,12] has focused on designing protocols similar to widely used protocols to bypass network traffic classification. Thus, our objective is to make it difficult, not to say impossible, for an attacker to entirely reverse the protocol in a reasonable time. The goal is, given a protocol specification, to generate multiple instances of obfuscated protocol, for instance, each one dedicated to a client. This work is orthogonal to cryptographic solutions, generally speaking, it is less robust but faster in its treatment.

To reach our objective, we focus on some challenges presented in the previous section: message typing and the inference itself. Our methodology relies on the following observations: (1) message typing is mostly realized via similarity and (2) inferred models are equivalent to regular languages, e.g., message format only depends on its type. Accordingly, the obfuscated protocols should be more complex than regular protocols. In this case, generalization performed by tools will lead to lots of wrong messages. Moreover, we also propose to ensure that message format depends on the communication context, and to force the dissimilarity between messages originally belonging to the same type.

We plan to adopt algebraic or contextual languages. Most of the time, message format and protocol grammar can both be expressed with formal grammar. Thus, an obfuscation strategy for one of them can be adapted to the second one. For example, the message format "$M \rightarrow$ **<K,V>**;$M|$**<K,V>**", corresponding to a list of (key, value) (for instance **<K$_1$,V$_1$>**;**<K$_2$,V$_2$>**;**<K$_3$,V$_3$>**) is a regular language that can easily be transformed into "$M \rightarrow$ **<KMV>**|,", (i.e., **<K$_1$<K$_2$<K$_3$,V$_3$>V$_2$>V$_1$>**) which corresponds to an algebraic language ($a^n b^n$). The inference of this class of languages is more tricky [11]. Moreover, if modifications injected regularly change, according to the previously exchanged message, this means that we enrich the communication with a context which is difficult to reverse. A same message sent by a component at two different moments will then be obfuscated in two different ways.

We are currently prototyping our solution. It corresponds to a stub added to legitimate communicating components. Each message is processed or generated by this stub, which is itself automatically generated by a framework. Actually, generated code is derived from the original specification, applying some transformations on the message format in order to directly handle obfuscated messages. In other words, the stub is able to directly build and parse obfuscated messages. For developers of the components, using the original stub or the obsfuscated one is transparent as the interfaces of message handling functions are identical.

5 Conclusion

This paper presented the main challenges associated to protocols reverse engineering and our first contribution regarding the use of obfuscation techniques to make reverse a quite complex task. We are currently implementing a prototype of an obfuscation framework, based on a contextual grammar that we have designed for this purpose.

References

1. Antunes, J., Neves, N., Verissimo, P.: Reverse engineering of protocols from network traces. In: 2011 18th Working Conference on Reverse Engineering (WCRE), pp. 169–178. IEEE, New York (2011)

2. Bossert, G., Hiet, G., Henin, T.: Modelling to simulate botnet command and control protocols for the evaluation of network intrusion detection systems. In: 2011 Conference on Network and Information Systems Security (SAR-SSI), pp. 1–8. IEEE, La Rochelle (2011)
3. Bossert, G.: Exploiting semantic for the automatic reverse engineering of communication protocols. Ph.D. Thesis, Suplec December 2014
4. Bridger, H., Rishab, N., Phillipa, G., Rob, J.: Games without frontiers: investigating video games as a covert channel. In: Proceedings of the 2016 IEEE European Symposium on Security and Privacy, IEEE European Symposium on Security and Privacy. IEEE (2015)
5. Caballero, J., Poosankam, P., Kreibich, C., Song, D.: Dispatcher: enabling active botnet infiltration using automatic protocol reverse-engineering. In: Proceedings of the 16th ACM Conference on Computer and Communications Security, CCS 2009, pp. 621–634. ACM, New York (2009)
6. Caballero, J., Song, D.: Rosetta: extracting protocol semantics using binary analysis with applications to protocol replay and NAT rewriting. Technical Report CMU-CyLab-07-014, Carnegie Mellon University, Pittsburgh, USA (2007)
7. Caballero, J., Yin, H., Liang, Z., Song, D.: Polyglot: automatic extraction of protocol message format using dynamic binary analysis. In: Proceedings of the 14th ACM Conference on Computer and Communications Security, CCS 2007, pp. 317–329. ACM, New York (2007)
8. Caballero Bayerri, J.: Grammar and model extraction for security applications using dynamic program binary analysis. Ph.D. Thesis, Carnegie Mellon University, Pittsburgh, PA, USA (2010)
9. Cui, W., Paxson, V., Weaver, N., Katz, R.H.: Protocol-independent adaptive replay of application dialog. In: Proceedings of the 13th Annual Network and Distributed System Security Symposium (NDSS). Internet Society, San Diego, USA, February 2006. http://research.microsoft.com/apps/pubs/default.aspx?id=153197
10. Cui, W., Peinado, M., Chen, K., Wang, H.J., Irun-Briz, L.: Tupni: automatic reverse engineering of input formats. In: Proceedings of the 15th ACM Conference on Computer and Communications Security, CCS 2008, pp. 391–402. ACM, New York (2008)
11. de la Higuera, C.: Grammatical Inference: Learning Automata and Grammars. Cambridge University Press, New York (2010)
12. Hjelmvik, E., John, W.: Breaking and Improving Protocol Obfuscation. Technical Report 2010–05, Chalmers University of Technology, Gothenburg, Sweden (2010). http://publications.lib.chalmers.se/cpl/record/index.xsql?pubid=123751
13. Leita, C., Mermoud, K., Dacier, M.: ScriptGen: an automated script generation tool for Honeyd. In: 21st Annual Computer Security Applications Conference, p. 214. IEEE, Tucson (2005)
14. Li, X., Chen, L.: A survey on methods of automatic protocol reverse engineering. In: 2011 Seventh International Conference on Computational Intelligence and Security (CIS), pp. 685–689. IEEE, Hainan (2011)
15. Newsome, J., Brumley, D., Franklin, J., Song, D.: Replayer: automatic protocol replay by binary analysis. In: Proceedings of the 13th ACM Conference on Computer and Communications Security, CCS 2006, pp. 311–321. ACM, New York (2006)
16. Samba Team: Opening windows to a wider world. http://www.samba.org

Detection and Monitoring

Detection and Elimination

Detecting Anomalous Behavior in DBMS Logs

Muhammad Imran Khan[(✉)] and Simon N. Foley

Insight Centre for Data Analytics, Department of Computer Science,
University College Cork, Cork, Ireland
{imran.khan,simon.foley}@insight-centre.org

Abstract. It is argued that anomaly-based techniques can be used to detect anomalous DBMS queries by insiders. An experiment is described whereby an n-gram model is used to capture normal query patterns in a log of SQL queries from a synthetic banking application system. Preliminary results demonstrate that n-grams do capture the short-term correlations inherent in the application.

Keywords: Anomaly detection · Database intrusion detection · Insider threats · Cybersecurity

1 Introduction

Contemporary enterprise systems rely on Database Management Systems (DBMS) to store and manage access to their application data. While existing security controls such as authentication and role-based access control can help control access to this data, there is the concern of *insider threat* whereby legitimate users of the system abuse the access privileges that they hold. For example, the reported incidents [1,2] whereby hospital staff looked up the medical records of patients in the public-eye. A recent survey [3] reported that 89% of respondent organizations are vulnerable to insider attacks, while its reported [4] that malicious *insiders* are the cause of the costliest cybercrimes.

We are interested in detecting anomalous DBMS queries made by insiders; while the insider may hold the correct access permission to make the query, the particular query is not considered a 'normal' action by the user. Our hypothesis is that intrusion-detection techniques can be used in determining whether a query is anomalous or legitimate. Traditionally, intrusion detection systems can be classified into misuse detection and anomaly detection systems [5]. Misuse detection systems look for well-known attack patterns and detect only previously known attacks. Unlike misuse detection systems, anomaly detection systems [6–9] look for deviation from normal behavior and have the potential to detect previously unknown, or zero-day, attacks [10,11].

In this paper we consider how patterns of normal query behavior can be learnt from DMBS logs, and how these patterns can be in turn used to detect malicious queries made by insiders. The remainder of this paper is organized as follows. Section 2 discusses past research in the area, and our model for anomaly detection

F. Cuppens et al. (Eds.): CRiSIS 2016, LNCS 10158, pp. 147–152, 2017.
DOI: 10.1007/978-3-319-54876-0_12

in DBMS logs is described in Sect. 3. Section 4 describes an initial study based on detecting anomalies in a synthetic banking application and Sect. 5 concludes the paper.

2   Detecting Anomalies

One approach that can be used to detect anomalous queries is to consider queries in isolation, that is, if a given query similar to any past 'normal' query. Prior research on [12,13] has considered the issue of query matching by normalizing queries to a more abstract representation so that, for example, queries involving the same attributes/expression, but with different attribute values might be considered similar. While such approaches can certainly be used to detect individual queries that are entirely different from normal (similar queries) they cannot identify an insider that mimics valid queries. In this case it is insufficient to identify the anomaly by the query alone, we must also correlate it with its surrounding queries/activity.

The Ettu system [14] clusters the queries in the log into intent groups and are classified as safe or unsafe clusters, providing the basis for a similarity index for SQL queries. The DetAnom [15] mechanism correlates an SQL query with the application program code in which it occurs. In the training phase, Concolic testing takes place to explore all possible paths of the application program and for every path that has a query (Q_1), its corresponding constraints (condition, that resulted in this path when satisfied) are tied together with query's (Q_1) signature. In anomaly detection phase, during the execution of application program, when a query is made it is first intercepted, then the constrains are checked and the corresponding signature of the query is matched to detect if the query is anomalous or not.

The approach proposed in this paper is to extend the existing research on query matching by considering anomalies that can arise in query *sequences*. Some of the earliest work [6,7,16,19] considered the problem for sequences of systems calls made by processes as a means of modeling normal behavior of an application. A set of n-grams built from a system log is used to define the normal behavior for the application and models short-range correlation between calls.

3   A Normative Model of SQL Queries

It is assumed that an audit log of SQL statements is available, from which an n-gram based model of normative behavior is constructed. This model is in turn used to monitor/detect anomalies in subsequent queries.

3.1   SQL Query Abstraction

An audit log L is a sequence of SQL statements $\langle Q_1, Q_2, Q_3, \ldots, Q_n \rangle$, where each Q_i can be any SQL statement, including SELECT, UPDATE, INSERT. In building

Q_i	SQL statement	skeleton $abs(Q_i)$
Q_1	`SELECT city FROM dba WHERE id = 2`	`SELECT city FROM dba WHERE id = VAR_VAL`
Q_2	`SELECT city FROM dba WHERE id = 9`	`SELECT city FROM dba WHERE id = VAR_VAL`
Q_3	`SELECT city FROM dba WHERE id = 3`	`SELECT city FROM dba WHERE id = VAR_VAL`
Q_4	`SELECT city FROM dba` `WHERE id = 3 AND Name = "Alice"`	`SELECT city FROM dba` `WHERE id = VAR_VAL AND Name = VAR_VAL`

Fig. 1. SQL log abstraction

the model of normative behavior, some level of abstraction must be chosen for
the SQL statements. In our investigation we found that a naive abstraction
of the log to the SQL operations, such as $\langle$INSERT, SELECT, SELECT$\rangle$, was too
coarse-grained, while considering each statement in its entirety was overly fine
grained; neither revealed any useful normative behavior. Some degree of operation abstraction is required whereby the normative patterns of behavior become
apparent.

Prior research [12,13,17,18] has considered this problem of what is also
referred to as under-summarization and over-summarization, in the comparison of SQL queries. A number of techniques [14,15,17,18] have been proposed
that transform the syntax of an SQL statement into a more abstract fingerprint
that can be used for comparing queries. For example, in [15] the abstraction
of SQL statement Q is characterized in terms of: the SQL statement operation
c (SELECT, UPDATE, INSERT, etc.); the number of relations and attributes for
coarse-grained and relation-identifier and attribute-identifiers for fine-grained
representation, and the number of relation and attributes for coarse-grained
and relation-identifier and attribute-identifiers for fine-grained representation
in selection clause (see [15] for more details). The technique described in [14]
replaces the constant values in a query Q_i with placeholders generating a query
skeleton, which we denote as $abs(Q_i)$ and let $abs(L)$ be the mapping of $abs(Q_i)$
over the elements Q_i of L. We use this query abstraction in the construction of
our model and Fig. 1 provides an illustration of its use. Note that these mappings
are entirely syntactic, and cannot discriminate the semantics of different queries
that have a similar outcome.

3.2   Building a Normative Model of Behavior

We are interested in building normative models from the SQL logs of application
systems, whereby the queries are a result of insider/user interaction as a part of
well-formed transactions that arise from the normal operations and workflows,
both defined and undefined, of an organization. An objective of our work is
to demonstrate that normative behavior can be constructed based on a variety
of perspectives on the SQL log. In this paper we consider *role projection* i.e.
$role(L, R)$, which returns the abstract log $abs(L)$ containing those queries in L
executed on behalf of users in the role R. Note that for reasons of space, the
user/role data are not included in the sample log in Fig. 1. In future work we

plan to use the approach in [8] to determine whether variations in the SQL skeleton/fingerprinting projections used can give rise to other useful views, such as transaction-view.

An n-gram based approach [6] is used in order to investigate a normative model for user roles. N-gram based models are suited to modeling short-range correlations between events in logs. Given a sequence L of SQL query (skeletons), then let $ngram(abs(L), n)$ be the set of all sub-sequences of size n that appear in $abs(L)$. For example, the 2-gram model for the (skeleton) log in Fig. 1 is $\{\langle abs(Q_1), abs(Q_1)\rangle, \langle abs(Q_1), abs(Q_4)\rangle\}$.

4   Anomalous SQL Statement Detection

For our initial study, synthetic datasets were used to evaluate our model. A banking-style application was implemented providing transactions that included, account open and close, withdraw, deposit and transfer. Each transaction is initiated by an employee of the bank (insider/user) and involves the execution of a number of SQL statements. The application system was run with 10,000 random transactions and generating an audit log of around 28,000 SQL statements. This was done twice, once to generate a baseline log of 'normal' behavior Log_N, and on the second run, to generate a test log, initially of normal activity L_A but which is then also perturbed by malicious/attacker activity for the purposes of experimentation as described below.

SQL anomalies can give rise to malicious data observation, malicious data modification or deletion of data from a database. For the purposes of this paper we considered malicious data observation that arises from anomalous SQL queries. An SQL query is malicious if it is not a part of a legitimate transaction; for example, a user carrying out an ad-hoc query to look up a customer's bank account details. Different attack scenarios were considered. For example, in one scenario, the log L_A was perturbed by 50 malicious SQL queries, inserted in groups of 5 statements at 10 locations selected at random, resulting in logs L_{A1}. In other scenario, the log L_A was perturbed by a single malicious SQL query inserted at a random locations i.e. between two transaction, during a transaction and at the end and beginning of the log, resulting in logs L_{A2}, L_{A3}, L_{A4}, and L_{A5} respectively.

In the attack scenarios, the anomalous statements had the same query abstraction/skeleton as the statements in the training log; this ensures that a detected mismatch is not based on the query abstraction alone, but on its correlation (or lack thereof) with other events in the log. An anomalous SQL statement with an SQL abstraction/skeleton that is different to those of the SQL statements in the training log is detected simply against a 1-gram (and therefore not interesting for the purposes of experimentation). It is easy to detect an ad-hoc query of a customer's bank account details if the query skeleton is different from those formed by legitimate transactions; we are interested in detecting ad-hoc queries that mimic these legitimate queries, but cannot be correlated to a legitimate transaction. Lastly, experiments were repeated to take an average.

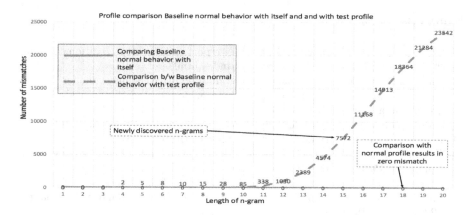

Fig. 2. Discovered number of n-grams when comparing profiles. The zeros on axis shows the comparison of normal profile with itself.

N-gram profiles $ngram(role(Log_N, r), n)$ and $ngram(role(Log_A, r), n)$ were built from the synthetic logs, for different n-gram sizes and roles r. If the baseline normal behavior for the role r is $ngram(role(Log_N, r), n)$, then Fig. 2 depicts the number of mismatches arising when comparing the test (but normal) log $ngram(role(Log_A, r), n)$ against this baseline, for different values of n. This indicates that the number of false positives increases significantly, as the size of n increases, which is to be expected. The reader is reminded that in using a synthetic dataset our characterization of normal behavior, though constrained by the shape of the transactions, is effectively random.

In our experiments, all the attacks were detected and on average an n-gram sizes from 2, 3 and 4 almost detected all the anomalous queries inserted using logs L_{A1}, L_{A2}, L_{A3}, L_{A4}, and L_{A5}.

5   Conclusions and Future Work

This paper described our preliminary experiments to judge the effectiveness of using an n-gram based scheme to detect query anomalies in DBMS logs and thereby identify insider attacks. While limited to a synthetic application, the experiments do show that it is possible to build a useful query abstraction and that n-grams of these queries do capture the short-term correlations inherent in the application. In future work we plan to investigate other query abstractions and to further evaluate the approach using non-synthetic system.

Acknowledgments. This work was supported, in part, by Science Foundation Ireland under grant SFI/12/RC/2289.

References

1. 27 suspended for Clooney file peek, CNN report (2007). http://edition.cnn.com/2007/SHOWBIZ/10/10/clooney.records/index.html?eref=ew
2. Carr, J.: Breach of Britney Spears patient data reported, Sc magazine for IT security professionals (2008). http://www.scmagazine.com/breach-of-britney-spears-patient-data-reported/article/108141/
3. Insider Threat Report, Insider Threat Security Statistics, Vormetric (2015)
4. 2015 Cost of Cyber Crime: Global, Ponemon Institute (2015)
5. Kemmerer, R.A., Vigna, G.: Intrusion detection: a brief history and overview. Computer 35(4), 27–30 (2002)
6. Forrest, S., Hofmeyr, S.A., Somayaji, A., Longstaff, T.A.: A sense of self for Unix processes. In: IEEE Symposium on Security and Privacy, Oakland, California, pp. 120–128, May 1996
7. Forrest, S., Hofmeyr, S., Somayaji, A.: The evolution of system-call monitoring. In: ACSAC 2008, Proceedings of the 2008 Annual Computer Security Applications Conference, pp. 418–430. IEEE Computer Society (2008)
8. Pieczul, O., Foley, S.N.: Discovering emergent norms in security logs. In: IEEE Conference on Communications and Network Security (CNS - SafeConfig), pp. 438–445 (2013)
9. Laszka, A., Abbas, W., Sastry, S.S., Vorobeychik, Y., Koutsoukos, X.: Optimal thresholds for intrusion detection systems. In: Proceedings of the Symposium and Bootcamp on the Science of Security (HotSos 2016), pp. 72–81. ACM, New York (2016)
10. Pieczul, O., Foley, S.: Runtime detection of zero-day vulnerability exploits in contemporary software systems. In: DBSec2016, Trento, 18–21 July 2016
11. Jamrozik, K., von Styp-Rekowsky, P., Zeller, A.: Mining sandboxes. Saarland University, Technical report (2015)
12. Low, W.L., Lee, S.Y., Teoh, P.: DIDAFIT: detecting intrusions in databases through fingerprinting transactions. In: 4th International Conference on Enterprise Information Systems (ICEIS) (2002)
13. Lee, S.Y., Low, W.L., Wong, P.Y.: Learning fingerprints for a database intrusion detection system. In: 7th European Symposium on Research in Computer Security, pp. 264–280 (2002)
14. Kul, G., Luong, D., Xie, T., Coonan, P., Chandola, V., Kennedy, O., Upadhyaya, S.: Ettu: analyzing query intents in corporate databases. In: WWW2016 Workshop on Empirical Research Methods in Information Security (ERMIS 2016) (2016)
15. Hussain, S.R., Sallam, A.M., Bertino, E.: Detanom: detecting anomalous database transactions by insiders. In: Proceedings 5th ACM CODASPY, pp. 25–35. New York, NY, USA (2015)
16. Kosoresow, A.P., Hofmeyr, S.A.: Intrusion detection via system call traces. J. IEEE Softw. 14(5), 35–42 (1997)
17. Kamra, A., Terzi, E., Bertino, E.: Detecting anomalous access patterns in relational databases. J. Very Large Databases (VLDB) 17(5), 1063–1077 (2008)
18. Sallam, A., Bertino, E., Hussain, S.R., Landers, D.: DBSAFE - an anomaly detection system to protect databases from exfiltration attempts. IEEE Syst. J. PP(99), 1–11 (2015)
19. Hofmeyr, S., Forrest, S., Somayaji, A.: Intrusion detection using sequences of system calls. J. Comput. Secur. 6, 151–180 (1998)

Online Link Disclosure Strategies
for Social Networks

Younes Abid[1,2], Abdessamad Imine[1,2], Amedeo Napoli[1,2], Chedy Raïssi[1,2],
and Michaël Rusinowitch[1,2(✉)]

[1] Inria Nancy, Villers-lès-Nancy, France
{younes.abid,abdessamad.imine,amedeo.napoli,
chedy.raissi,michael.rusinowitch}@inria.fr
[2] Lorraine University, Nancy, France

Abstract. While online social networks have become an important channel for social interactions, they also raise ethical and privacy issues. A well known fact is that social networks leak information, that may be sensitive, about users. However, performing accurate real world online privacy attacks in a reasonable time frame remains a challenging task. In this paper we address the problem of rapidly disclosing many friendship links using only legitimate queries (i.e., queries and tools provided by the targeted social network). Our study sheds new light on the intrinsic relation between communities (usually represented as groups) and friendships between individuals. To develop an efficient attack we analyzed group distributions, densities and visibility parameters from a large sample of a social network. By effectively exploring the target group network, our proposed algorithm is able to perform friendship and mutual-friend attacks along a strategy that minimizes the number of queries. The results of attacks performed on active Facebook profiles show that 5 different friendship links are disclosed in average for each single legitimate query in the best case.

Keywords: Online social network (OSN) · Link disclosure attacks · Privacy

1 Introduction

A social network can be defined as a website that allows users to create personal pages in order to share information with their friends and acquaintances. These pages are usually called profiles and contain personal information. Profiles are connected to each other through friendship links that can be either symmetric or asymmetric, depending on the network's policy. Since their appearance at the end of the twentieth century, social networks have known an outstanding success and have become a global phenomenon. For instance, Facebook connects

This work is funded by Fondation MAIF.

F. Cuppens et al. (Eds.): CRiSIS 2016, LNCS 10158, pp. 153–168, 2017.
DOI: 10.1007/978-3-319-54876-0_13

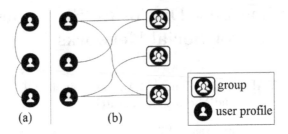

Fig. 1. Social graphs: (a) unipartite friendship graph, (b) bipartite group membership graph.

about 25% of humans in 2016[1] and YouTube served videos to almost one-third of all connected people on the Internet[2]. With this rapid network expansion, new scientific fields have emerged such as online social network analysis [8] creating a common domain of interest from sociology to mathematics and computer science [7]. However, the emergence of social networks is also giving reasons to worry about privacy and ethics issues [11].

In order to mimic real (i.e., non-cybernetical) societal interactions, some social networks such as Facebook, Linkedin and Viadeo support the creation of groups besides the profile creation. Accordingly, social networks can be modeled by two types of graphs – friendship graph and group membership graph – as depicted by Fig. 1.

The friendship graph (a) is unipartite and models the friendship links between users while membership graph (b) is bipartite and models the membership links between users and groups. Some of these links can be masked by users or group administrators. We call a friendship (resp. membership) attack a sequence of actions (e.g., queries) leading to disclose a masked friendship (resp. membership) link. Both kind of attacks are called link disclosure attacks. A mutual-friend attack discloses common friends to a target and other users. We call group uncovering attack a sequence of queries that disclose the membership network of the target and his acquaintances. In this work the attacker is limited to the usage of legitimate and minimal queries provided by the social networks APIs. Therefore the attacker model can be viewed as a passive one. We believe that these constraints are the cornerstones of successful real-world attacks that are difficult to detect because the traffic appears to be legitimate at first.

In [3] researchers propose a Partial Graph Profile Inference (PGPI) algorithm that exploit group memberships to infer profiles attributes. In [10], relational learning approaches and group memberships are used to infer sensitive attribute of users such as locations.

Our experiments over 1,000 active Facebook profiles hiding their friend lists show that in the worst case 2 queries (in average) are sufficient to disclose at

---

[1] http://www.statista.com/statistics/264810/number-of-monthly-active-facebook-users-worldwide/.

[2] https://www.youtube.com/yt/press/en/statistics.html.

least one friendship link and 5 different friendship links are disclosed in average by each query in the best case.

To put the rest of the paper into context, we start by defining problematics and objectives of link disclosure attacks on Online Social Networks in Sect. 2. Then we analyse groups distribution, densities and visibility parameters in Sect. 3. Those properties are then used to perform group uncovering attack as detailed in Sect. 4. In Sect. 5 we depict membership, friendship and mutual-friend attacks steps and we analyse their results. Finally, in Sect. 6 we give more detail about the resulting dataset of the attacks performed online.

2   Problematics and Objectives

Problematics. In online attacks, the attacker is constrained by the network dynamicity and the time needed to scrap it. In fact, the dynamical network structure, with the addition/deletion of new links and nodes will ensure that the sampled graph does not reflect a real online social network at any given time. Therefore, crawling tasks for online attacks must be highly selective to collect only useful profiles and information and be as fast as possible.

For instance, [5] show that homophilic attributes have significant influence on predicting friendship between users of Facebook. Thus, an attacker may be tempted to sweep the network for similar profiles to his target. He can also consider the friends of the target friends as potential friends and check these links. Although these general solutions may seem effective to gather many potential friends, they have major shortcomings. To understand these shortcomings let us recall the "six degrees of separation" phenomenon, that is the possibility to connect any two people in a maximum of six relationship steps. For example, the authors of [1] show that the average degree of separation between Twitter users is 3.43 while the degree of separation on Facebook is between 2.9 and 4.2 for the majority of users [4]. Hence, considering friends of friends as potential friends is equivalent to considering at least tens of thousands users as potential friends for each single target [9]. This is clearly impossible to handle and scale for real-world efficient attacks.

Objectives. Link disclosure attacks in online social networks aim to disclose hidden links by performing authorized requests. The attacks either reveal existing links or potential ones according to the employed method. In this work we aim to improve the accuracy of the attacks. We aim to disclose numerous links without having to verify a huge number of potential friends. In other words, we attempt to gather many potential friends but only those who have high probability to be friend with the target. The best way to achieve our objectives is to disclose the vicinity network of the target. To that end, we analyse groups' properties on online social networks since they reflect the way users are gathering within a network and uncover its structure. To keep our discussion simple, we aim to answer two questions in this work: Which groups leak useful information to meet previously detailed objectives? And how to find and use them?

3   Social Networks Group Properties

In this section we analyse some properties of Facebook groups. This analysis will guide crawling tasks in order to collect only data that leak more information about the target. Exploiting such data will increase the accuracy of link disclosure attacks and maximize the number of disclosed links. We stress that all experiments in this work were carried out online with real Facebook profiles. We have crawled 1,100 Facebook groups and all their members. Then, we have sorted the groups by declared size in sets. Each set contains at least 30 groups. Each group in the first set S_0 gathers between 2 and 10 members. And each group in the set S_i gathers between $10i$ and $10(i + 1)$ members.

3.1   Group Distribution

We first study the distribution of groups in Facebook with regard to their sizes. We notice that the declared group size on this network is often different from the number of users published on the group member list. Moreover, crawling the same group using different IP addresses and accounts can result in slightly different listed members. This technique can reduce the gap between the two sizes by considering the union of all crawled member lists of the same group. However, it adds more complexity to attacks. To study groups distribution we have simulated a simple attack carried out using only one attacker node. All groups are crawled only once and we only rely on the declared group size to build the attack strategy.

Figure 2 shows that there are many more small groups on Facebook than larger ones. However, we notice the curve inflection for groups declaring between 30 and 70 members. By checking these groups members lists we notice huge gaps between declared sizes and the numbers of listed members. Gaps reach 85% for some groups. Some groups are declared to have 60 members or more but they actually display less than 20 members on their members lists. These gaps can be explained by the fact that users unceasingly leave and join the group but size updates are not performed instantaneously. Henceforth, densities of such groups can increase if real sizes decrease since the less connected members are usually the first ones to leave the groups.

The result of our tests carried on 14,517 Facebook profiles shows that the probability of a given Facebook user to join at least one group gathering less than 50 members and publish his membership to it is 0.49. Thus, about half of analysed Facebook profiles are exposed to the danger of friendship link disclosure through groups they join and that gathers less than 50 members.

3.2   Group Densities

In an undirected social graph, a friendship link between two user is considered public if at least one of them publishes it. It is considered hidden only if both users hide it.

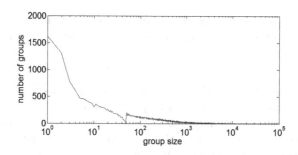

Fig. 2. Group distribution of a sample of 14,517 Facebook users.

In order to guide a strategy for disclosing hidden social links we first try to evaluate the probability that two members of a group are friends. We define three notions of group densities: public density, real density and maximal density, that we will use to estimate the number of friends that can be disclosed through link disclosure attacks. Given a group g, $PD(g)$ stands for its Public Density, $RD(g)$ stands for its Real Density and $MD(g)$ stands for its Maximal Density. The public density of g is the ratio of published friendship links between its members to all possible friendship links between them. It is defined by Eq. (1) where $|g|$ is the number of members of g:

$$PD(g) = \frac{2}{|g|(|g|-1)} \sum_{\{m,m'\} \subseteq g} publicLink(m, m')$$ (1)

The real density of g is the ratio of all (public and hidden) friendship links between its members to all possible friendship links between them. It is greater or equal to the public density. It is defined by Eq. (2)

$$RD(g) = PD(g) + \frac{2}{|g|(|g|-1)} \sum_{\{m,m'\} \subseteq g} hiddenLink(m, m')$$ (2)

The maximal density of g can be met only if all its members who hide their friend lists are friend with each other. It is greater or equal to the real density. It is defined by Eq. (3) where p is the percentage of members who hide their friend lists among the members of g.

$$MD(g) = PD(g) + \frac{p^2|g| - p}{|g| - 1}$$ (3)

Thus we have:

$$PD(g) \leq RD(g) \leq MD(g)$$ (4)

Test results show that among 14,517 crawled Facebook profiles only 6,249 (43%) hide their friend lists or choose to reveal them only to their direct friends, friends of friends or some selected users. The rest (57%) leave the visibility setting by default and publish their friend lists. Hence, p can be considered equal to 0.43 if it is unknown by the attacker. Note that the attacker can easily verify the friend list visibility parameters of other users through the following Facebook request:

$$/<nid\_u>/friends \tag{5}$$

where nid_u is the numeric id[3] of the User u. In fact, this request returns the friend list of the User u if and only if he publishes it.

Figure 3(a) shows that group densities decrease as the declared size of the group increases. It can be noticed that one can even estimate a given group density only from its declared size. This information is precious as it determines the number of links that can be disclosed between group members. In fact, the group real density can be viewed as the probability of the friendship link between a given member and another member from the same group. Hence, if the attacker discloses group membership of his Target t to a Group g, then all other members of g can be considered as potential friends of t with a probability in interval $[PD(g); MD(g)]$. Knowing the declared size of g, $PD(g)$ can be directly deduced from Fig. 3(a) and $MD(g)$ can be deduced from Eq. (3). For instance, the average public density of groups gathering between 10 and 20 members is 0.343. Then, according to Eq. (3) the real density of such groups belongs to interval $[0.343; 0.515]$ for p equal to 0.43. Expressively, the estimated accuracy of link disclosure attack is 0.343 and all the members of corresponding groups can be considered as potential friends with probability in $[0.343; 0.515]$.

Although popular groups gather many members, probabilities of friendship between them are very low. Crawling such groups is fruitful to seek a lot of potential friends of the target but with low probabilities. However, minute groups open small horizon for potential friends but with higher probability of friendship.

The relationship status between two members of a group g is a binary variable. Hence, assuming independence of friendship links in a first approximation, the expected number of published friendship links between a given member and all other members of the same group is the expectation of a binomial distribution of parameters $B(|g|, PD(g))$ which is $|g| \times PD(g)$. For example, Fig. 3(a) shows that the expected public density of groups gathering less than 11 members is greater than 35%. Hence, the expected number of friends of a target within a group he joins and that gather 6 members is 2 (since $0.35 \times 6 = 2.1$). Figure 3(b) shows that the expected number of disclosed links between the target and group members slightly increases as the declared size of groups increases. Note that x-axis unit correspond to 10 members and y-axis unit correspond to 1 friendship link.

3.3   Group Visibility Parameters

Groups and members can independently choose to publish or hide the membership relation. For instance Facebook users can choose to mask some groups from their list of groups. On the other hand, the administrators of groups can independently publish the entire lists of members. With that in mind, an attacker

---

[3] Numeric id can be acquired through http://findmyfbid.in/.

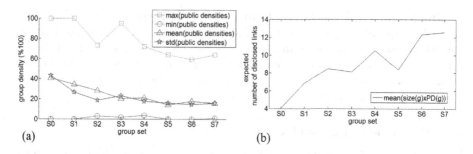

Fig. 3. Results of analysis: (a) Variation of public density with respect to group declared size, (b) Expected number of disclosed links between the target and group members.

can build an attack strategy to disclose the groups that are masked by users or the membership lists of secret groups.

4   Group Uncovering Attacks

In this section we exploit groups properties detailed in previous section to perform group uncovering attacks. To that end, we define real and public n-hop distant groups.

4.1   Real n-Hop Distant Groups

Given a target t that joins Group g, g is considered as a real 1-hop distant group from t (denoted by $g \in RG_1(t)$) and all its members m are considered as real 1-hop distant members from t (denoted by $m \in RM_1(t)$). We define inductively $g \in RG_n(t)$ iff $g \notin RG_{n-1}(t)$ and there is $g' \in RG_{n-1}(t)$ with a non-empty intersection with g. For all m in $g \backslash RM_{n-1}(t)$ we have by definition $m \in RM_n(t)$. We can show the following symmetry rule:

$$u1 \in RM_n(u2) \iff u2 \in RM_n(u1) \tag{6}$$

where $u1$ and $u2$ are two different users. Figure 4 depicts an example of a real 3-hop distant group from the target node t.

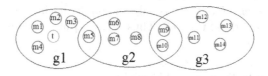

Fig. 4. g3 is a real 3-hop distant group from t.

Group $g1$ is a real 1-hop distant group from t. Consequently, all its members are real 1-hop distant members from t. Members $m6$, $m7$, $m8$, $m9$ and $m10$ are real 2-hop distant members from t since they join the same Group $g2$ as $m5$ who is real 1-hop distant members from t. Finally, $m11$, $m12$, $m13$ and $m14$ are real 3-hop distant members from t as $m9$ and $m10$ join their Group $g3$. Members $m5$, $m10$ and $m9$ act as gateway between groups.

4.2   Public n-Hop Distant Groups

Users can mask their membership to groups and groups can hide their members lists. Consequently, the public n-hop distant relation does not satisfy the symmetry rule.

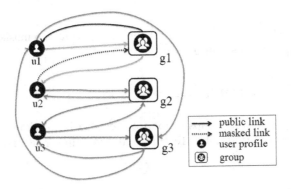

Fig. 5. An example of public n-hop distant groups and members. (Color figure online)

Figure 5 depicts an example of different public n-hop distant groups and members between two users. Arrows from user to groups stand for membership links while arrows on the opposite direction represent group members lists. Dotted lines represent masked links and solid lines represent public links. While both Users $u1$ and $u2$ join the same group $g1$, only $u1$ publishes his membership to $g1$. User $u2$ publishes only his membership to Group $g2$. User $u3$ acts as a gateway between $g2$ and $g3$ and publishes his membership to both of them. All groups $g1$, $g2$ and $g3$ publish their member lists. There are two public paths from User $u1$ to User $u2$. The first one, the green path, goes through $g1$ and is the shortest one with only one hop. The second one, the blue path, is two hops long. It goes through $g3$ then $g2$. Hence, $u2$ is a public 1-hop distant member from $u1$. On the other hand, there is only one public path, the red path, from $u2$ to $u1$ that goes through $g2$ then $g3$. Thus, $u1$ is a public 2-hop distant member from $u2$.

4.3   Social Graph Traversal Algorithm

Let $u2$ be a target user who is friend with both users $u1$ and $u3$ and hides his friend list. Since he publishes his membership to $g2$, the attacker can reach $u3$

through $g2$ member list. And if $u3$ publishes his friend list, the attacker can easily disclose the friendship link between $u3$ and $u2$ by checking the friend list of $u3$. Likewise, the attacker can reach $u1$ through $g3$ member list if $u3$ publishes his membership to that group. And he can search for $u2$ in $u1$ public friend list. Furthermore, next hop lead to $g1$ and hence the attacker can disclose group membership links between $u2$ and $g1$ by checking $g1$ public member list. Algorithm 1 gives more details about the graph traversal steps. The algorithm outputs are two sets of groups and members. And its inputs are the number of hops and a set of seed groups of the target.

Data: gps: set of groups, h: number of hops
Result: d_m: set of distant members, d_g: set of distant groups
1 **Procedure** explore(gps, h, d_g, d_m)
2   **if** ($h > 0$) **then**
3   **for** each $g \in gps$ **do**
4 | $members$.addAll(getMembers(g)) ;
5   **end**
6        $members$.removeAll(d_m);
7   **for** each $m \in members$ **do**
8 | $groups$.addAll(getPublicGroups(m)) ;
9   **end**
10       $groups$.removeAll(d_g);
11   d_g.addAll($groups$);
12   d_m.addAll($members$);
13   explore($groups, h-1, d_g, d_m$);
14   **end**
15 **Return()**

Algorithm 1. Groups uncovering attack through social graph traversal

---

To collect seed groups, the attacker can directly retrieve unmasked groups from his target profile. We note that among 14,517 attacked Facebook profiles 11,446 (78.84%) do not change group visibility parameters and publish their groups membership even to secret groups. Otherwise, if the target masks all his groups and attributes, the attacker can create a fake virgin profile, use it to only visit his target profile, send him friendship request and try to interact with him by liking and commenting his posts or sending him messages. Then, link prediction algorithms of the social network [2] will start suggesting groups and attributes to the attacker that are strongly related to his target. Hence, he can use the suggested groups as seeds or take advantage of network research features and uses suggested attributes to look for seed groups. For instance, one of this paper author hides all his attributes on Facebook. However, the social network suggested his home town and 10% of his friends to a newly created profile that he added as a friend.

By following Algorithm 1 steps the attacker can effectively crawl his target group network and avoid loops. However, some social networks do not allow robots to crawl their network. For instance, Facebook bans robot accounts for a week. To overcome this issue, we used many users accounts. Our robot is able to change IP adresses, simulate human behaviour, switch between accounts, manage connection loss and save data in XML format and SQL database to avoid loops and replay attacks offline.

5   Link Disclosure Attacks

In this section we exploit the group uncovering attack detailed in previous section to perform link disclosure attacks. We aim to disclose two types of link: friendship between users and membership between users and groups.

5.1   Friendship and Membership Attacks

The attacker can explore the group networks of his target then check the member lists of distant groups to disclose group membership links to the masked groups. However, results show that less than 0.1 group membership in average can be disclosed by this attack. This can be explained by the fact that 78.84% of attacked profiles do not change group visibility parameters and even publish their memberships to secret groups. On the other hand, by exploring groups networks of 14,517 profiles we disclosed 430 different secret groups and 756 of their members. Secret groups can help to disclose communities if their member lists are disclosed. Moreover, their members can be taken into consideration to compute the probability of friendship between two users who hide their friend lists.

In this work we aim to disclose friendship links with certainty. In undirected social networks it is sufficient but not necessary that one of the two friends publishes his friend list to disclose the friendship link between them with certainty. In this perspective, an attacker can query all friend lists of the distant groups members of the target and check if he is listed in public ones. Opportunely, some social networks afford features that can be used to rapidly check friendships between users. For instance, friendship between two users of Facebook can be easily checked through the following PHP request (7):

$$/friendship/<nid_1>/<nid_2> \tag{7}$$

Where $<nid_1>$ and $<nid_2>$ are numeric IDs of two different users. In fact, the request (7) returns the date of the link creation between two users if and only if there is a friendship link between them and at least one of them publishes his friend list. Taking advantage of this feature, attacker can easily follow Algorithm 2 to disclose both friendship and group membership links of his target. Algorithm inputs are the profile of the target, the number of hops and the minimum number of links to disclose.

We have attacked more than 100 active Facebook profiles that hide their friend lists from each set detailed in Sect. 3. For each attack we only checked the

Data: t: target profile, h: number of hops, th: disclosed link threshold
Result: d_f: set of disclosed friends, di_g: set of disclosed groups

```
1  seedGroups ← getSeedGroups(t);
2  sizeSort(seedGroups);                            ▷ list of set of groups sorted by size
3  while d_f.size() < th & seedGroups.length()>0 do
4  │  d_m2.addAll(d_m);                             ▷ d_m2 contains all tested profiles
5  │  d_g.clear(); d_m.clear();
6  │  explore(seedGroups.pop(), h, d_g, d_m);                      ▷ see Algorithm 1
7  │  d_m.removeAll(d_m2);                          ▷ remove already tested profiles
8  │  for each m ∈ d_m do
9  │  │   if friendship(m, t) then
10 │  │   │   d_f.add(m);
11 │  │   end
12 │  end
                                          ▷ all newly explored groups are not tested yet
13 │  for each g ∈ d_g do
14 │  │   if getMembers(g).contains(t) then
15 │  │   │   di_g.add(g);
16 │  │   end
17 │  end
18 end
```

Algorithm 2. Friendships and group membership attacks based on k-hop group graph traversal

groups belonging to the same set to disclose friendship links between the target and those groups members. Note that users can be members of many groups from the same set. Since tiny groups densities are higher than large ones, fewer requests are required to disclose friendship links with certainty between the former members than between the latter members. 1-hop attack results (Fig. 9(a), blue curve) show that the average number of required requests to disclose one link with certainty increases as the size of groups increases. Only 6 requests in average are sufficient to disclose a friendship link with certainty of a target joining groups gathering less than 40 members against more than 7 requests in average for larger groups. However, the average number of requests to disclose one friendship link decreases if attacks involve 2-hop distant groups from the target. This does not mean that the ratio of published friendship links (PFLs), between the target and 2-hop distant groups members from him, is higher than the ratio of PFLs between the target and 1-hop distant groups members from him. But, the ratio of PFLs between the target and the union of both 1-hop and 2-hop distant groups members from him is higher than any of the two ratios.

Observations. Figure 6 gives an illustration of an observed social phenomena. Users within the same network tend to crowd in small and highly overlapping groups. Thereby, small networks pop up within big networks. To put it in another way, some members joining the same group (e.g., $g1$) decide to create a new group (e.g., $g2$) of similar size and to add some of their acquaintances to it.

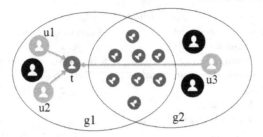

Fig. 6. 2-hop friendship disclosure attack.

And so they act as gateways between both groups (inclined nodes in Fig. 6). Some newly added members to the latter group (e.g., $u3$) publish their friendship links to the former group members. Therefore, the ratio of published friendship links between the target t and all members of the two merged groups (e.g., $3/14$ for $g1 \cup g2$) is greater than the ratio of published friendship links between him and any of the two groups taken alone (e.g., $2/11$ for $g1$ and $1/11$ for $g2$). And consequently, the average number of requests to disclose one friendship link decreases as well as the number of disclosed links increases.

However, Fig. 9(a) shows that 3-hop attacks are less effective than 2-hop attacks. This result can be explained by the fact that the ratio of members publishing their friendship to the target among 3-hop distant groups is low. On the one hand, crawling those groups may orient the attack toward adjacent networks and dramatically increase the number of requests to disclose one link in average. On the other hand, it may disclose masked groups of the target. With this in mind, attackers can perform 3-hop or above attacks to only disclose masked groups of the target by checking public member lists then perform 2-hop attacks to disclose friendship links. Moreover, they can reduce the size of attacked groups after each hop to avoid crawling adjacent networks. Thus, they can effectively uncover the group network of the target and minimize the number of requests to disclose friendship links.

5.2   Mutual-Friend Attacks

The term 'mutual friends' stands for friends in common between two users. Mutual-friend attacks are performed between the target who hides his friend list and another user to disclose a list of friends in common between them. In this section we exploit group uncovering attacks to perform mutual-friend attacks [6] between two members of the same network. Attacker can take advantage of the features afforded by social networks in order to list public mutual friends of two users. For instance, mutual friends of two Facebook users can be rapidly listed through the following Facebook request (8):

$$/browse/mutual\_friends/?uid = <nid_1>\&node = <nid_2> \qquad (8)$$

Where $<nid_1>$ and $<nid_2>$ are the numeric IDs of two different users. Thus, the attacker can follow Algorithm 2 steps while replacing lines from 8 to 17 by the function described by Algorithm 3 to disclose mutual-friend links between his target and other users. Similarly to Algorithm 2, this algorithm inputs are the target profile, the number of hops and the minimum number of links to disclose. But it discloses mutual friends between the target and the groupe members rather than friendships between them.

1 **for** *each* $m \in d_m$ **do**
2 $\quad | \quad d_f$.addAll($mutualFriends(m, t)$);
3 **end**

Algorithm 3. Mutual friend attack

In fact, a mutual-friend request (8) between two users returns the list of their mutual friends that publish their friend list if and only if at least one of the two given users publishes his friend list as well. Starting from the hypothesis that a mutual-friend attack is performed between the target who hides his friend list and another user, it is only successful if both the latter and the mutual friend publish their friend list. Moreover, it is not effective in the case of sparse networks since it does not disclose friendship link between two users that do not have mutual friends even if one of them publishes his friend list. The example depicted by Fig. 7 shows that despite the fact that User $u1$ publishes his friend list, mutual-friend requests cannot disclose the friendship link between him and the target t. Dotted arrows represent masked links and solid ones represent public links. In this example only User $u1$ publishes his friend list and both User $u2$ and the target t hide theirs. Hence, the results of all possible mutual-friend requests between Users $u1$, $u2$ and t are empty since two of them hide their friend list. However, friendship requests can disclose the friendship links between the target t and User $u1$ and between Users $u1$ and $u2$. Figure 8 depicts the average number of undisclosed links by a mutual-friend attack but disclosed by a friendship attack. We notice that this number increases with the number of hops.

Fig. 7. Undisclosed links by mutual-friend attack.

Having said that, mutual-friend attacks can disclose more friends than friendship attacks if the target shares many mutual friends with his distant members. Figure 9(b) shows that the number of mutual-friend requests to disclose one friendship link is quite similar for 1-hop and 2-hop attacks and increases for

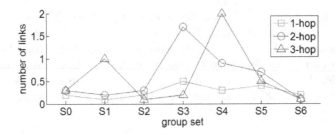

Fig. 8. The average number of undisclosed links by mutual-friend attack but disclosed by friendship attack.

3-hop attacks. However, it is far lower than the number of friendship requests depicted by Fig. 9(a) as mutual-friend request returns a list of friends.

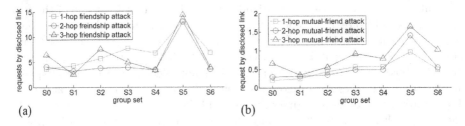

Fig. 9. Results of attacks: (a) The average number of friendship request to disclose one friendship link, (b) The average number of mutual-friend request to disclose one friendship link (Color figure online)

To get better results the attacker can combine both attacks. For instance to maximize the number of disclosed links, he can sequentially perform a friendship attack after a mutual-friend attack. Hence, the number of attack requests will be equal to $2n - d$ where n is the number of distant groups members and d is the number of disclosed links between the target and them by mutual-friend attacks. Besides, he can alternatively perform both attacks to disclose friendship links between the target and his distant groups members. He can then follow Algorithm 2 steps while replacing lines from 8 to 17 by Algorithm 4 in order to focus his attack on distant groups members. Thus, the number of attack requests will belong to interval $[2; 2n]$. In fact, if mutual-friend requests do not disclose any friendship links between the target and his distant groups members then the number of attack requests will be equal to $2n$, by adding n friendship requests and n mutual-friend requests. On the other hand, if the target network is highly connected and the first mutual-friend request between the target and one of his distant groups members returns the rest of distant groups members then the number of attack requests will be 2, namely one friendship request and only one mutual-friend request.

```
 1  for each m ∈ dₘ do
 2  │   if (!d_f.contains(m)) then
 3  │   │   if (friendship(m, t)) then
 4  │   │   │   d_f.add(m);
 5  │   │   end
 6  │   end
 7  │   d_f.addAll(mutualFriends(m, t));
 8  │   if (d_f.containsAll(dₘ)) then
 9  │   │   break;
10  │   end
11  end
```

Algorithm 4. Mutual friend and friendship attacks

6 Dataset

We have performed online attacks on Facebook. We have crawled 14,517 profiles, 22,855 groups and 76,772 mutual-friend lists. The resulting graph contains 4,153,379 user nodes, 131,410 group nodes, 5,720,973 friendship links and 1,225,533 group membership links. We noticed that 78.84% of crawled profiles do not mask their groups 56.95% publish their friend lists and 47.77% publish both. Among users who publish their friend list, the number of friends for a user in average is 530. And among all crawled profiles the number of unmasked groups for a user in average is 14.17. Figure 10 depicts the frequencies of published groups per user (a) and number of friends (b).

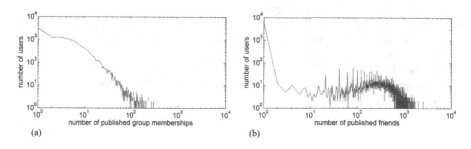

(a)   (b)

Fig. 10. Sample of 14,517 facebook profiles: (a) Frequency of published group membership, (b) Frequency of list of friends size.

7 Conclusion

Friendship links on social networks hold sensitive information about the community structure and affinity between users. Disclosing them can expose users to the highest danger of leaking personal sensitive information such as political orientation. In this paper we have tackled the problem of link disclosure with certainty. We have performed online attacks on active Facebook profiles and proved that attackers can easily and rapidly disclose many hidden links with certainty taking advantage of social network APIs.

References

1. Bakhshandeh, R., Samadi, M., Azimifar, Z., Schaeffer, J.: Degrees of separation in social networks. In: Proceedings of the Fourth Annual Symposium on Combinatorial Search, SOCS, Castell de Cardona, Barcelona, Spain, 15–16 July 2011
2. Barbieri, N., Bonchi, F., Manco, G.: Who to follow and why: link prediction with explanations. In: The 20th ACM SIGKDD, New York, USA, pp. 1266–1275 (2014)
3. Dougnon, R.Y., Fournier-Viger, P., Nkambou, R.: Inferring user profiles in online social networks using a partial social graph. In: Barbosa, D., Milios, E. (eds.) CANADIAN AI 2015. LNCS (LNAI), vol. 9091, pp. 84–99. Springer, Cham (2015). doi:10.1007/978-3-319-18356-5_8
4. Edunov, S., Diuk, C., Filiz, I.O., Bhagat, S., Burke, M.: Three and a half degrees of separation. In: Research at Facebook (2016)
5. Elkabani, I., Khachfeh, R.A.A.: Homophily-based link prediction in the Facebook online social network: a rough sets approach. J. Intell. Syst. 24(4), 491–503 (2015)
6. Jin, L., Joshi, J.B.D., Anwar, M.: Mutual-friend based attacks in social network systems. Comput. Secur. 37, 15–30 (2013)
7. Memon, N., Alhajj, R.: Social networks: a powerful model for serving a wide range of domains. In: Memon, N., Alhajj, R. (eds.) From Sociology to Computing in Social Networks - Theory, Foundations and Applications, pp. 1–19. Springer, Vienna (2010)
8. Scott, J.: Social Network Analysis, 3rd edn. SAGE Publications, London (2013)
9. Ugander, J., Karrer, B., Backstrom, L., Marlow, C.: The anatomy of the Facebook social graph. CoRR, abs/1111.4503 (2011)
10. Zheleva, E., Getoor, L.: To join or not to join: the illusion of privacy in social networks with mixed public and private user proles. In: Proceedings of the 18th WWW 2009, Madrid, Spain, pp. 531–540 (2009)
11. Zheleva, E., Terzi, E., Getoor, L.: Privacy in social networks. Synth. Lect. Data Min. Knowl. Disc. 3, 1–85 (2012). Morgan & Claypool Publishers

A Framework to Reduce the Cost of Monitoring and Diagnosis Using Game Theory

Rui Abreu[1], César Andrés[2], and Ana R. Cavalli[2,3(✉)]

[1] Department of Informatics Engineering, Porto, Portugal
rui@computer.org
[2] TELECOM & Management SudParis, CNRS UMR Samovar, Evry, France
c.andres@fdi.ucm.es, ana.cavalli@it-sudparis.eu
[3] Montimage, 39 rue Bob illot, 75013 Paris, France

Abstract. In this paper, we present the framework MONGT, to aid administrators to manage monitoring properties in an automated fashion in order to detect and define defense strategies against possible networking attacks.

In particular, we propose a novel game theory based approach to reason whether the system is behaving as expected (based on the notion of Nash equilibrium). The framework requires input from KPI deployed in the system (i.e., CPU load), and may dynamically decide to add more monitors to the system in order to diagnose any eventual problem.

This dynamic deployment of monitors takes place when the equilibrium is broken. Furthermore, after diagnosing the problem, the framework has a set of strategies to restore the equilibrium for the system under test. In addition to introduce the MONGT, we present a case study to show the applicability and usefulness of our framework.

1 Introduction

One of the most important ways to improve the availability, performance, and trustworthiness of today's complex software systems is to increase their robustness in the face of run-time deviations from intended behavior [10]. While design-time methods are useful in improving confidence in software, they cannot by themselves eliminate the possibility of run-time breakdowns. Such problems are induced by a variety of factors largely outside the control of the organization producing that software: unpredictable loads, variable resources, and malicious attempts to break a system [13]. Consequently, systems must have an active role in detecting potential problems so that proper corrective measures are taken as quick as possible.

Recognition of this problem has given rise over the past few years to a number of significant advances, including improved techniques for monitoring systems' run-time behavior, new mechanisms for detecting the presence of faults, and novel architectures for selfrepair [5,8]. Such advances have led to a new discipline

---

Research partially supported by the H2020 CLARUS Project.

F. Cuppens et al. (Eds.): CRiSIS 2016, LNCS 10158, pp. 169–182, 2017.
DOI: 10.1007/978-3-319-54876-0_14

of "autonomic computing" which aims to provide systematic techniques for run-time monitoring, analysis, repair planning, and execution [7]. Monitoring and checking these vulnerabilities at runtime is an expensive task [6]. Therefore to use metrics or heuristics to approximate the cost of this task is an industrial necessity.

Game theory [4] allows to model different strategies to recover from a problem. In the last few years these techniques have been applied in the field of vulnerabilities, error and intrusion detections in networks protocols [9,11], to model the attackers and the defenders, in order to automatically decide which strategy to take for each scenario. The application of game theory techniques to define strategies for the systems requires to identify its relevant aspects, that is, those characteristics that will make a player to change his behavior in order to apply an action. While the relevant aspects of some players only concern what they are able to obtain from another computer, in some other players it is equally relevant how can they manage the computational resources of all the network, raising deny of services whenever and wherever, or how can they combine their efforts in order to obtains their best payoffs.

Even though work on game theory applied to different vulnerability scenarios has been carried on for several years, the study of the cost of monitoring using this approach, and to study different strategies that allow to reduce this cost does not receive enough attention. Therefore, in this paper, we propose MONGT, a framework to aid administrators to manage complex systems in order to increase availability, performance, and trustworthiness. We aim at automating as much as possible the problem isolation, diagnosis and repair cycle. To achieve the total automation of this cycle, we propose a novel game theory-based approach to reason whether the system is executed normally. Essentially, the administrator has to define in the framework the equilibrium criteria of the system (based on the notion of Nash equilibrium). The equilibrium is verified by monitoring important aspects of the system such as CPU load or memory consumption. If needed, for example for diagnosis, the framework may decide to dynamically add more monitors to the system (for example, the equilibrium criteria is not met but the deployed monitors do not give enough information for diagnosing the current problem). Furthermore, after diagnosing the problem, the framework applies a strategy to the system (from the set of available corrective ones) to restore the equilibrium for the system under test. When the equilibrium is met, the monitoring is reduced to the information strictly needed to check it. The contributions of this paper are twofold.

- First, we present an automated framework to improve the robustness of today's complex systems by providing the system with a mechanism to isolate, diagnose and recover from eventual run-time problems. An advantage of our framework is that it reduces the monitoring cost to the minimum necessary to detect and diagnose a problem;
- Second, we present several scenarios in which our framework would be of added value to the running system.

The rest of the paper is structured as follows. In Sect. 2 we introduce some preliminaries concepts regarding Game Theory. In Sect. 3 our framework to specify some monitoring rules are presented. Next, in Sect. 4 we model the task of monitoring with a game theory approach, and study those aspects that allow us to reduce the cost of monitoring in this approach. In addition to the theoretical work in Sect. 5 we present a load balancing scenario where MONGT is used to model and to define different strategies. Finally, in Sect. 6 we present the conclusions and some lines of future work.

2   Game Theory

We define a strategic game as a model where different decision makers, also known as players, can interact. Each player will have his own input alphabet denoting the player's set of valid actions. This model also captures the interactions among different players, where each one will have a strategy to choose the action to perform each time. It is frequently used the notion of payoff functions to represent the preferences of the users in this kind of games.

Definition 1. We denote by $\mathcal{U}$ the set of all possible users of a strategic game, and by A the set of all possible actions that these players can apply.

A strategic game is a tuple (U, f, P) where $U \subseteq \mathcal{U}$ is a finite set of players, $f : U \rightarrow \wp(A)$ is the function that associates the input alphabet for each user, and P is a set of payoff functions that returns the preferences over the set of action profiles.

A payoff function for a user u is a function $p_u : f(u) \rightarrow \mathbb{R}$ that assigns a real value for each action of the user. $\qquad\square$

A payoff function in this framework assigns to each action of the user an utility value in order to be able to compare the different actions. When the player u_1 performs the action a his turn finishes and is the turn of the player u_2, who decides what action should he apply in order to be closed to his goals. In this context the goals are represented with the payoff functions. Let us note that the goals of a user can be directly related to the goals of other user, therefore the user that performs the best strategy will win. Let us introduce this concept by using a classical game example where two users can go to prison or not depending on their answers and the answers of the other user.

Example 1. There are two users u_1 and u_2 that are involved in a crime. The policemen captured them and said to them the following rules in order to make their defense: If u1 and u2 are quite during the defense then both of them will spend one year in prison. If u_1 or u_2 but not both says that the other player (finks) is the guilty then who finks spends zero year in prison and the other one four. Finally, if u_1 and u_2 fink then each will spend three years in prison.

Following we formalize the strategic game (U, f, P). U is the set containing the two suspects $\{u1, u2\}$. We have that the set of actions for any user is

		u_2	
		quiet	fink
u_1	quiet	$(2,2)$	$(0,3)$
	fink	$(3,0)$	$(1,1)$

Fig. 1. Example of payoff functions for these users.

$\{quiet, fink\}$. Finally, the payoff functions for these users are presented in the Fig. 1:

In this table the two rows correspond to the two possible actions of the first player u1 and the two columns correspond to the two possible actions of the second player u_2. The numbers in each cell of this matrix are the payoffs of the players (u_1, u_2) respectively.

A high value in the box means that the player would prefer this option. □

In game theory, the next step is to consider what actions will be chosen by the players in a strategic game. In our framework we need to assume two hypothesis. The first one is that we have rational decision-maker, that is the players always choose the best available action. Therefore, when a player chooses her action she has to be in mind those actions that were previously selected by the other players. The second one is that every player belief that the others players actions were performed correctly. These two components are embodied in the following definition.

Definition 2. A strategy refers to one of the options that a user can choose during his turn. When all the users finish their turn, then the sequence of all the actions that they performed is called an action profile.

A strategy can be classified as

– Pure strategy:
  • Safe.
  • Risky.
– Mixed strategy.

The former provides a complete definition of how a player will play a game. The later provides a set of pure strategies for each user, with the probability to perform each strategy.

Finally, and additional classification of a pure strategy is if it is a safe strategy or not.

We say that a safe strategy for a player is the strategy for which the minimum payoff is as high as possible. A Nash equilibrium is an action profile with the property that no player can do better by unilaterally changing his or her strategy. □

Example 2. By examining the four possible pairs of actions in the Example 1, we see that $(fink, fink)$ is the unique Nash equilibrium. In particular, we say that $(fink, fink)$ is a Nash equilibrium because:

- Given that the u_2 chooses fink, then u_1 is better off choosing fink than quiet. Looking at the right column of the table we see that $fink$ yields u_1 a payoff of 1 whereas quiet yields her a payoff of 0.
- Given that u_1 chooses $fink$, then u_2 would choose better fink than quite for the same reason: Looking at the table we can observe that fink yields u_2 a payoff of 1 whereas quite yields a payoff of 0.   □

3 Monitoring

In this section we introduce in our framework how we can represent those entities that can be monitored in a system and how we can define some relationships with the collected data. To define the entities we need to introduce the notions of service, instance and attribute. An instance is anything connected to the network, in particular a module of a system. An instance is composed of attributes, and these attributes can be monitored. Finally, a service is a set of instances.

Example 3. Actually we can have several examples of servers, instances, etc. taking into account cloud computing.

In cloud computing we rent for a server. This server will contain different software programs, like database, web server, ssh, etc.

Each of this software programs would be an instance (we could have two similar instances in the same server by using different threads/jobs and daemons). I.e, a SQL server. With respect to attributes, they represent anything where a KPI can be applied. Number of open sessions, queries in IDLE, number of users, etc.   □

To define the relationships among the collected data we introduce the notion of *monitoring rule*. These formulas can be always evaluated into true or false. With true we represent that there is not any violation of the formula. The following two situations returns true:

1. There are not enough resources to compute the formula.
2. There are enough resources to compute the formula and the evaluation of the formula with these parameters is true[1].

Definition 3. We say that the sequence prop is a monitoring rule if it is defined according to the following EBNF:

$$prop ::= \quad service.(inst).op$$
$$op ::= \, \sim n | = n | \leq n | \leq n | \geq n | \geq n$$
$$inst ::= \quad i.a | i.a, inst$$

where we have that service represents any service of the system, $(i.a)$ is an instance and its attribute a, and $n \in \mathbb{R}$ is a value.   □

---

[1] While with false we represent when the previous two conditions do not hold.

Example 4. Let us consider a web service S. We could represent that the number of opened tables $NumOpTab$ of the software SQL instance must be at most 4.
This property is represented by:

$$S.(SQL.NumOpTab). \leq 4$$

The operators represent bigger than, less than or equal to, bigger than or equal to or equal respectively. The operator $\sim_{value}$ allows us to relate all the data that appear in the property. In particular, it returns **true** if all the values of this set belongs to $[av - value, av + value]$, where av is the average of all attributes.

In particular we have that $\sim_0$ represents that all the attributes contain the same value.

Let us consider that there are two Apache servers ($server_a$ and $server_b$) in S and we want to check that the number of total access ($NumTotAc$) to $server_a$ and $server_b$ only differs in 15 units. We can easily represent this property as:

$$S.(server_a.NumTotAc, server_b.NumTotAc). \sim_{15}$$

□

4   Combining Game Theory with Monitoring Task

Next we formulate the task of monitoring by using game theory. We take the same notation that some works presented in the area [1,2], where we simplify the framework in order to show only the relevant part that involves the monitoring task. Basically, there are two roles, the defender and the users.

According to our notation we have that the strategic game (U, f_a, P) that defines this situation is: Where we have that the set of users is $U = \{u1, ..., um\}$. This set can be divided into two classes of users $U = U_1 \cup U_2$, where U_1 and U_2 do not share any component.

Where U_1 represents the attackers, and U_2 represents the defenders. The sets of actions for each user are: for the attackers is $\{attack, noattack\}$, in short (a, na), and for the defenders $\{monitoring, nomonitoring\}$, in short (m, nm).

Next we identify and codify different variable that allows us to represent the payoff (see Fig. 2 for a graphical representation):

β_c Is the cost that the attacker suffers when she is discovered.
α_c Is the cost that the defender receives when an attack is discovered.
β_s Is the cost that the attacker receives when she can hack to the system.
α_s Is the cost that the defender should pay if a hacker can be in the system.
α_f Is the cost of the monitoring task.

Let us note that α_f depends on the number of the properties to be monitored. At this moment we consider that this number is fixed, but at the end of this Section we will extend this notion in order to introduce a dynamic behavior in the evaluation of this concept. Next we present the payoffs for the attackers and the defenders.

It does not exist a Nash equilibrium for the previous configuration [3]. Next we present two different strategies to find out a solution of this problem.

		Defender	
		m	nm
Attacker	a	$(-\beta_c, \alpha_c)$	$(\beta_s, -\alpha_s)$
	na	$(0, -\alpha_f)$	$(0, 0)$

Fig. 2. Payoff of attack, deffenders in a monitoring approach.

- In our monitoring environment, the a safe strategy would be:
  - Attacker: she decides not to attack, that is na. Her payoffs are 0.
  - Defender: she decides to monitor, that is m, if the cost of monitoring is less than the cost of loosing the information $\alpha_s > \alpha_f$, or to monitor if the cost of loosing the documents is bigger than to the cost of monitoring $\alpha_s \leq \alpha_f$.
- A mixed strategy for our framework is given as:

$$p_\alpha = \frac{\alpha_f}{\alpha_f + \alpha_c + \alpha_s}$$

$$p_m = \frac{\beta_s}{\beta_c + \beta_s}$$

Let us note that the mixed strategy provides the probability of monitoring/no monitoring, attack/not attack taking into account several factors.

As we previously mentioned, the cost that we assume for the monitoring task denoted by α_f was fixed. However, this assumption is not realistic. Consider that we monitor different entities and we describe those that we need to monitor by using the monitoring rules presented in Sect. 3. It is more realistic to assume that the cost of α_f instead of being a fix value, it can be represented by using an interval $[a, b]$, where a is the cost of monitoring those rules that the administrator considers more important and b is the cost of monitoring all the monitoring rules presented in the defender. So, the previous payoffs are changed into those that appear in Fig. 3.

		Defender	
		m	nm
Attacker	a	$(-\beta_c, \alpha_c)$	$(\beta_s, -\alpha_s)$
	na	$(0, -\alpha_f(t))$	$(0, 0)$

Fig. 3. Payoff using a mixed strategy

where $\alpha_f(t) \in [a, b]$ is a time value depending on the number of resources that are being monitored in time equal to t. Let us illustrate this concept with the following example.

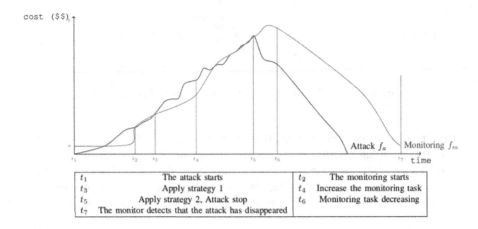

t_1	The attack starts	t_2	The monitoring starts
t_3	Apply strategy 1	t_4	Increase the monitoring task
t_5	Apply strategy 2, Attack stop	t_6	Monitoring task decreasing
t_7	The monitor detects that the attack has disappeared		

Fig. 4. Simulation scenario with a monitoring strategy.

Example 5. In Fig. 4 is represented an attack of a system. There are two players, the attacker and the defender. We identify seven different situations in this attack, denoted by $t_1, ..., t_7$. From t_1 to t_2 the attacker starts, increasing the possible cost that this action could cost in our system if it can be completely performed. The defender was monitoring with cost a, that is, checking only the most relevant monitoring properties. From t_2 to t_5 both players are attacking and defending. The defender is increasing the cost of monitoring activating new monitoring rules in order to be able to detect where is the attacker. Finally, at time t_5 the attacker was discovered and killed, and the cost of his attack decreases to zero. However, the defender waits until t6 in order to check that the cost of the attacking is decreasing very fast, and later, at t_7 it stop to monitor all monitoring rules except those that are the relevant one. □

In the previous example there are the following open issues: Why does the system decide to increase the monitoring task at t_2, and how do the system select different strategies to detect and kill the attack. To answer these questions we present our novel approach: MONGT. Each turn the defender will perform this loop. If there is not an equilibrium in the environment, then the defender will start monitoring in order to find the attack and eliminate it. On the contrary if there is an equilibrium, the defender will continue monitoring with cost a. Whenever the defender is not in equilibrium, the monitored traces will be analyzed using different diagnosis techniques in order to select the best strategy that presents those corrective actions that allow the defender to reduce the attack.

In MONGT we consider that the system under consideration is in the equilibrium state if all the monitoring properties considered crucial for the correct behavior of the system hold. Note that the equilibrium has to be defined on a system level. We mean by corrective actions, those behaviors that can either be performed manually or, preferably, automatically.

Hence, a self-healing system should recover from the abnormal (or unhealthy) state and return to the normative (healthy) state, and behave as it was supposed.

When the equilibrium is not met, corrective actions should be performed to bring the system back to the equilibrium state. In practice, there are many actions that will lead the system back to the equilibrium state. However, some actions are more appropriate than others.

Finally, it is worth mentioning that it is not always straightforward to know which strategy would be more adequate in order to tackle the current problem in the system. This is specially the case for, e.g., security, as there are several ways to attack a system. Therefore, there is the need not only to detect the problem but also to diagnose it before prescribing a corrective strategy. By inspecting the system's state, diagnosis is the process of attempting to determine a disorder in the system. In order to be able to inspect the state of the system by analyzing data of runtime behavior, the system has to be able to continuously monitor variables in the system that contribute to the overall system state. As monitoring causes a runtime overhead, it must be performed dynamically and only when needed. Our approach starts with minimal monitoring capabilities, and more variables are monitored only if needed to diagnose the current problem.

Therefore, with respect to Fig. 1, we can say that at t2 the equilibrium was broken, and the monitoring task is increased in order to prevent this attack, and that at time t6 the monitoring task starts decreasing due to the fact there are not necessary to monitor several traces because the attack was detected and eliminated. Moreover, the equation that represent the cost of monitoring with MONGT, and we try to minimize is:

$$\int_{t_2}^{t_7} f_m(x)dx.$$

where fm(x) is a function that depends on $[a, b]$ (the cost of monitoring).

5   Case Study: Load Balancing Scenario

In this section we describe an application example of MONGT to a component-based system provided by our industrial partner. For confidentiality reasons, we do not provide details about the system provided by our industrial partner. We only provide the necessary information for the reader to fully understand our proposed approach. The system under consideration represents a typical web server architecture where clients can interact with a pool of servers that have access to a common data store. Client HTTP requests are mediated by one or more dispatchers, selected randomly by a client, as is common in high-availability systems instances such as Oracle database systems, EMC Documentum, and DNS servers, which forward requests to a specific server in the pool.

Although relatively simple, this service is representative of a large class of applications, serving well to illustrate the need to handle security requirements. First, it could have hundreds of clients and hundreds of servers (for example, running on a Cloud computing platform), handling thousands of simultaneous

Instance	Attribute(Metric)	Description
Node	user	% CPU time in user space
Node	system	% CPU time in kernel space
Node	iowait	% CPU waiting time for I/O operation
Node	ctxt	context switches per second
Node	runq-sz	Number of processes waiting to run
Node	plist-sz	Total number of processes and threads
Node	ldavg-1	system load average for the last minute
Dispatcher	eth-rxbyt	Network bytes received per second
Dispatcher	eth-txbyt	Network bytes transmitted per second
Dispatcher	pgpgin	KBytes paged in from disk per second
Dispatcher	pgpgout	KBytes paged out to disk per second
Dispatched	fault	Page faults (major+minor) per second
Database	bread	Total bytes read from disk per second
Database	bwrtn	Total bytes written to disk per second

Fig. 5. Example of different instances, attributes and description.

requests. Hence scalability, concurrency, and distribution are important concerns. Second, when the system is being attacked by a mal-intentioned client, it is important to identify that the system is under attack and fix the problem as quick as possible (for example, attacking the dispatcher could drastically impact the overall ability of the system to deliver its services in a trustworthy manner). Third, there are many sources of uncertainty inherent in this system. For example, high latency in handling customer requests could be caused by faults in the system itself or due to malintentioned clients that attack the system (e.g., to cause a deny of service). Fourth, although certain kinds of problems may be easily detected and fixed (such as a server crash), softer failures like high latencies - because of a hacker - are just as important to detect and repair.

Linux is the running environment of our subject program (see Fig. 5). As mentioned before, we use operating system-level performance and/or traffic metrics to verify whether the system is executing normally or not (i.e., it is under attack or at fault). The performance metrics are gathered without requiring any instrumentation to the system under analysis. We use the program sadc provided by the Sysstat package 2 to collect the metrics (for your reference, as in [12], the 14 metrics are listed in the table of the Fig. 5), also defining the type of instance. The metrics are collected at a sampling interval of one second. For monitoring the origin of incoming network packages, tcpdump is used.

In this service S, the idea of equilibrium is that all instances in the scenario perform similar works. Formally, considering m different nodes $n_1, ..., n_m$, k different dispatcher $d_1, ..., d_k$, and i different databases $db_1, ..., db_i$, we have that is the conjunction of all the monitor rules:

$$S.(n_1.user, ..., n_m.user) \sim_{n_1} \wedge$$
$$S.(n_1.ctxt, ..., n_m.ctxt) \sim_{n_2} \wedge$$
$$...$$
$$S.(d_1.eth - rxbyt, ..., d_k.eth - rxbyt) \sim_{n_j} \wedge$$
$$...$$
$$S.db_1.bwrtn, ..., db_i.bwrtn \sim_{n_m}$$

where $n_k \in \mathbb{R}$.

Each row represents a monitoring rule. If the system is set to monitor the CPU load of each web server, then the system is in equilibrium if, and only if, the server's CPU loads are roughly the same. Otherwise, the system is potentially under an attack as the equilibrium criteria is not met. We have considered the following corrective actions in our experiments. First, when the equilibrium is not met, there is a subsequent analysis to detect which web-servers are overloaded. Based on the outcome of this analysis, there are four possible strategies:

1. Redistribute the jobs amongst the web-services, in case there are web-services that are not overloaded; or
2. Add more web-services to the system, from a pool of available web-services; or
3. Filter a node that is not working as expected; or
4. Disconnect a user.

Next we have identified different (problematic) scenarios are presented and discussed in this case study and how apply MONGT to deal with a correct solution.

5.1   DoS of 1 Web-Service

Suppose that there is an attempt to make one of the webservices unavailable to its intended users (also known as deniel-ofservice). Such attacks lead to a server overload as there is a client which consuming its resources so that it can no longer provide its intended service.

Hence, the CPU load of the web-service under attack is higher than all the others. As the equilibrium criteria is not met, the system is going to be diagnosed in order to decide which corrective strategy to take. The diagnosis phase will identify that there is one webservice with high CPU and recommends that the tasks that have to be performed by the web-service should be split with the other available web-services.

Such corrective answer will solve the problem of the system, and after a few seconds the system will be functioning as it was supposed to before the disruption.

5.2   DoS of Multiple Web-Services

An attacker discovers the corrective strategy taken by the system and decides to perform a denial-of-service to all web-services of the system. Obviously, the equilibrium criteria is not met, but now the diagnosis cannot pinpoint the web-service under attack. In order to be able to diagnose this problems, we need to refine the equilibrium criteria. This is done by specifying a threshold that is considered normal for each property that is being monitored. For simplicity, let us consider that we are only monitoring CPU load and that it should be lower than 20%. When the denial-of-service occurs, the load will be higher than the threshold. As the diagnosis will point out that all web-services are under attack, the strategy to recover from the attack is no add more web-services to the pool of available web-services and distribute evenly the work.

Meanwhile, the monitoring mechanism is changed to gather information about the incoming traffic. Once the attacker is diagnosed - by analyzing the incoming traffic - the system is instructed to block any traffic from the attacker

5.3   ICMP Flood

This attack involves at least three different players: the victim, the attacker, and a node that is not correctly implemented. The goal of this attack is to disconnect the victim from the service. To describe this attack we assume that there exists an erroneously con- figured node in our net that can receive broadcast messages and can send them inside the net. Moreover, it can also distribute the messages to the source again. Basically, a broadcast message is a message distributed to all nodes in a net, and when a node observes this message he replies.

The attack is following described. The attacker knows which node is incorrectly implemented and knows the IP address of the victim. Then, he starts sending several packages to the incorrectly node where the source IP is the victim IP and as destination IP he puts the broadcast IP. Therefore, if the node is not working as expected, then all these messages are sent inside the net, and all the nodes inside the net make a reply to the source IP, that is the victim. When the number of connexions of the victim increases then, it can be saturated and at the end to obtain a deniel of connexion of the client with the service.

When the equilibrium is broken we start monitoring our nodes and applying the following strategy:

1. First we select those nodes that are directly connected with the users. Save in NODES ← Connected nodes.
2. Try to send a broadcast message from the nodes that appear in NODES. If there exists a set of nodes that replies these messages then filter those nodes and check the equilibrium, else continue in 3.
3. Update the set of NODES with their neighbors, NODES ← neighbors (NODES). A node is a neighbor of another node if they are directly connected. Jump to 2.

We know that at least there exists a node that is sending broadcast messages due to the equilibrium that we represented. Thus, the previous strategy always allows us to detect at least one incorrect node.

6 Conclusions and Future Work

As our dependency on software becomes more notorious, applications also become more complex and less manageable. As a consequence, it is difficult to attain reasonable levels of availability, performance, and trustworthiness. This is particularly important for critical software applications (e.g., software that can lead to economic or life-threatening consequences). In an attempt to automatically manage such complex systems, in this paper, we propose a framework, dubbed MONGT, which uses a game theory approach to reduce the cost of monitoring complex systems. Our approach aims at automating the process of automating, diagnosis, and repair.

In order to demonstrate the practical utility of our approach, we use a case study with several scenarios. The case study is a typical and common web service scenario. We detail how the framework could be useful to improve the availability, performance, and trustworthiness of the systems under analysis.

Future works include experimenting the framework with more case studies in order to be able to generalize the results and applicability of our approach. We also plan to define a easy-to-use language to specify strategies and the equilibrium criteria.

References

1. Agah, A., Das, S.K., Basu, K., Asadi, M.: Intrusion detection in sensor networks: a non-cooperative game approach. In: Proceedings of the Third IEEE International Symposium on Network Computing and Applications (NCA 2004), pp. 343–346. IEEE (2004)
2. Alpcan, T., Basar, T.: A game theoretic approach to decision and analysis in network intrusion detection. In: Proceedings of 42nd IEEE Conference on Decision and Control, vol. 3, pp. 2595–2600. IEEE (2003)
3. Alpcan, T., Basar, T.: A game theoretic analysis of intrusion detection in access control systems. In: 43rd IEEE Conference on Decision and Control, CDC, vol. 2, pp. 1568–1573. IEEE (2004)
4. Aumann, R.J.: Game theory. In: Eatwell, J., Milgate, M., Newman, P. (eds.) Game Theory, The New Palgrave, pp. 1–53. Springer, Heidelberg (1989)
5. Bodden, E., Hendren, L., Lhoták, O.: A staged static program analysis to improve the performance of runtime monitoring. In: Ernst, E. (ed.) ECOOP 2007. LNCS, vol. 4609, pp. 525–549. Springer, Heidelberg (2007). doi:10.1007/978-3-540-73589-2_25
6. Boehm, B.W.: Software risk management: principles and practices. IEEE Softw. **8**(1), 32–41 (1991)
7. Kephart, J.O., Chess, D.M.: The vision of autonomic computing. Computer **36**(1), 41–50 (2003)
8. Leucker, M., Schallhart, C.: A brief account of runtime verification. J. Logic Algebraic Program. **78**(5), 293–303 (2009)
9. Manshaei, M.H., Zhu, Q., Alpcan, T., Bacşar, T., Hubaux, J.P.: Game theory meets network security and privacy. ACM Comput. Surv. **45**(3), 25:1–25:39 (2013)
10. Mok, A.K.: Fundamental design problems of distributed systems for the hard-real-time environment (1983)

11. Saad, W., Han, Z., Debbah, M., Hjorungnes, A., Basar, T.: Coalitional game theory for communication networks: a tutorial. CoRR, abs/0905.4057 (2009)
12. Tan, J., Pan, X., Marinelli, E., Kavulya, S., Gandhi, R., Narasimhan, P.: Kahuna: problem diagnosis for mapreduce-based cloud computing environments. In: 2010 IEEE Network Operations and Management Symposium-NOMS 2010, pp. 112–119. IEEE (2010)
13. Viega, J., McGraw, G.: Building Secure Software: How to Avoid Security Problems the Right Way, Portable Documents. Pearson Education, Upper Saddle River (2001)

Cryptography

High-Performance Elliptic Curve Cryptography by Using the CIOS Method for Modular Multiplication

Amine Mrabet[1,3,5(✉)], Nadia El-Mrabet[2], Ronan Lashermes[7],
Jean-Baptiste Rigaud[2], Belgacem Bouallegue[6], Sihem Mesnager[1,4],
and Mohsen Machhout[3]

[1] University of Paris XIII, CNRS, UMR 7539 LAGA, Paris, France
amine_mrabet_eniso@yahoo.fr
[2] Ecole des Mines de St-Etienne, SAS-CMP, Saint-Étienne, France
[3] EμE Lab, University of Monastir, Monastir, Tunisia
[4] Télécom ParisTech, Paris, France
[5] National Engineering School of Tunis, Tunis, Tunisia
[6] King Khalid University, Abha, Saudi Arabia
[7] LHS-PEC TAMIS INRIA-Rennes, Rennes, France

Abstract. Elliptic Curve Cryptography (ECC) is becoming unavoidable, and should be used for public key protocols. It has gained increasing acceptance in practice due to the significantly smaller bit size of the operands compared to RSA for the same security level. Most protocols based on ECC imply the computation of a scalar multiplication. ECC can be performed in affine, projective, Jacobian or others models of coordinates. The arithmetic in a finite field constitutes the core of ECC Public Key Cryptography. This paper discusses an efficient hardware implementation of scalar multiplication in Jacobian coordinates by using the Coarsely Integrated Operand Scanning method (CIOS) of Montgomery Modular Multiplication (MMM) combined with an effective systolic architecture designed with a two-dimensional array of Processing Elements (PE). As far as we know this is the first implementation of such a design for large prime fields. The proposed architectures are designed for Field Programmable Gate Array (FPGA) platforms. The objective is to reduce the number of clock cycles of the modular multiplication, which implies a good performance for ECC. The presented implementation results focuses on various security levels useful for cryptography. This architecture have been designed in order to use the flexible DSP48 on Xilinx FPGAs. Our architecture for MMM is scalable and depends only on the number and size of words.

Keywords: Hardware implementation · ECC · Modular multiplication · Montgomery algorithm · CIOS method · Systolic architecture · DSP48 · FPGA

© Springer International Publishing AG 2017
F. Cuppens et al. (Eds.): CRiSIS 2016, LNCS 10158, pp. 185–198, 2017.
DOI: 10.1007/978-3-319-54876-0_15

1   Introduction

The search for the most optimised architecture for arithmetic has always fascinated the embedded system world. In recent years this has been especially the case in finite fields for cyber security due to the invention of asymmetric encryption systems based on modular arithmetic operations. Throughout the history of cryptography for embedded systems, there has been a need for efficient architectures for these operations. The implementations must be cost-effective, both in terms of area and latency. Finite field arithmetic is the most important primitive of ECC, pairing and RSA. Since 1976, many Public Key Cryptosystems (PKC) have been proposed and all these cryptosystems base their security on the difficulty of some mathematical problem. The hardness of this underlying mathematical problem is essential for security. Elliptic Curve Cryptosystems which were proposed by Koblitz [10] and Miller [14], RSA [19] and the Pairing-Based Cryptography [8] are examples of PKCs. All these systems require an efficient finite field multiplication. As a consequence, the development of efficient architecture for modular multiplication has been a very popular subject of research. In 1985, Montgomery has presented a new method for modular multiplication [15]. It's one of the most suitable algorithm for performing modular multiplications in hardware and software implementations. The efficient implementation of the Montgomery Modular Multiplication (MMM) in hardware was considered by many authors [3,6,7,16,17,21]. There is a variety of ways to perform the MMM, considering if multiplication and reduction are separated or integrated. A systolic array architecture [11,22] is one possibility for the implementation of the Montgomery algorithm in hardware, with a design both parallel and pipelined [3,16–18,21]. A similar work [18] has been done for binary fields (field characteristic is a power of 2) without having to deal with carry propagation as a consequence. These architectures use a Processing Elements (PE) array where each Processing Element performs arithmetic additions and multiplications. In accordance with the number of words used, the architecture can employ a variable number of PEs. The systolic architecture uses very simple Processing Elements (as in a pipeline). As a consequence, the systolic architecture decreases the needs for logic elements in hardware implementations. Our contribution is to combine a systolic architecture, which is assumed to be the best choice for hardware implementations, with the CIOS method of Montgomery modular multiplication. We optimize the number of clock cycles required to compute a n-bit MMM and we reduce the utilization of FPGA resources. We have implemented the modular multiplication in a fixed number of clock cycles. To the best of our knowledge, this is the first time that a hardware or a software multiplier of modular Montgomery multiplication, suitable for various security level, is performed in just 33 clock cycles. Furthermore, as far as we know, our work is the first one dealing with systolic architecture and CIOS method over large prime characteristic finite fields. Using our efficient MMM hardware implementation, we propose an efficient design for ECC operations: point addition and doubling. This paper is organized as follows: Sect. 2 discusses related state-of-the-art works. Section 3 presents the CIOS method of Montgomery Modular Multiplication algorithm. The proposed architectures and results are presented in Sects. 4 and 5. Finally, the conclusion is drawn in Sect. 6.

2   State of the Art

2.1   Elliptic Curve Cryptography

The use of elliptic curves in cryptography has been independently introduced by Victor S. Miller [14] and N. Koblitz [10] during the 80 s. The main advantage of ECC is that the bit sizes of the key are reduced for the same security level when comparing with a classical RSA algorithm [20]. For instance, at the AES 128-bit security level the key for ECC is 256 bits, while RSA requires a 3072-bit key. The main operation in ECC is the scalar multiplication over the elliptic curve. This scalar multiplication consists in computing $\alpha \times P$, for α an integer and P a point of an elliptic curve. When such an operation is implemented on an embedded system such as a FPGA, it is subject to constraints of area and speed. Efficient scalar multiplication arithmetic is hence a central issue for cryptography. The interested reader is referred to [2] for a good overview of the question.

ECC Preliminaries. Let E be an elliptic curve defined over $\mathbb{F}_p$ with $p > 3$ according to the following short Weierstrass equation:

$$E : y^2 = x^3 + ax + b \tag{1}$$

where $a, b \in \mathbb{F}_p$ such that $4a^3 + 27b^2 \neq 0$. The elliptic curve $E(\mathbb{F}_p)$ is the set of points $(x, y) \in \mathbb{F}_p^2$ whose coordinates satisfy Eq. 1. The rational points of E, augmented with a neutral element O called point at infinity, have an abelian group structure. The associated addition law computes the sum of two points in affine coordinates $P = (x_1, y_1)$ and $Q = (x_2, y_2)$ as $P + Q = (x_3, y_3)$ where: $x_3 = \lambda^2 - x_1 - x_2$ and $y_3 = \lambda(x_1 - x_3) - y_1$ with

$$\lambda = \begin{cases} \dfrac{y_2 - y_1}{x_2 - x_1} & \text{if } P \neq Q, \\ \dfrac{3x_1^2 + a}{2y_1} & \text{if } P = Q. \end{cases} \tag{2}$$

The scalar multiplication of a point P by a natural integer α is denoted αP. The discrete logarithm problem is finding the value of α, given P and αP. The security of ECC is based on the hardness of the discrete logarithm problem. Point addition formulae such as in Eq. 2 are based on several operations over $\mathbb{F}_p$ (e.g. multiplication, inversion, addition, and subtraction) which have different computational costs.

ECC in Jacobian Coordinates. In Jacobian coordinates, we use $(x : y : z)$ to represent the affine point $(x/z^2; y/z^3)$. The elliptic curve equation becomes:

$$Y^2 = X^3 + aXZ^4 + bZ^6.$$

Doubling step: we represent the point $Q \in E(\mathbb{F}_p)$ in Jacobian coordinates as $Q = (X_Q, Y_Q, Z_Q)$. The formulae for doubling $T = 2Q = (X_T, Y_T, Z_T)$ can be computed as:

$$X_T = 9X_Q^4 - 8X_QY_Q^2. \quad Y_T = 3X_Q^2(4X_QY_Q - X_T) - 8Y_Q^4. \quad Z_T = 2Y_QZ_Q.$$

Algorithm 1. Scalar Multiplication

Input: $\alpha = (\alpha_n \alpha_{n-1} \ldots \alpha_1 \alpha_0)_2$ radix 2 decomposition $\in \mathbb{F}_p$, $P \in E(\mathbb{F}_p)$

Output: αP

1 $T \leftarrow P$

2 **for** $i = n - 1$ *to* 0 **do**

3 $\quad$ $T \leftarrow 2T$

4 $\quad$ **if** $\alpha_i = 1$ **then**

5 $\quad\quad$ $T \leftarrow T + P$

6 **return** T

Adding step: let $Q = (X_Q, Y_Q, Z_Q)$ and $T = (X_T, Y_T, Z_T) \in E(\mathbb{F}_p)$. Then the point $R = T + Q = (X_R, Y_R, Z_R)$, can be computed as:

$$X_R = (2Y_Q Z_T^3 - 2Y_T)^2 - 4(X_Q Z_T^2 - X_T)^3 - 8(X_Q Z_T^2 - X_T)^2 X_T.$$

$$Y_R = (2Y_Q Z_T^3 - 2Y_T)(4(X_Q Z_T^2 - X_T)^2 X_T - X_R) - 8Y_T(X_Q Z_T^2 - XT)^3.$$

$$Z_R = 2Z_T(X_Q Z_T^2 - X_T).$$

3   Our Architecture for MMM (CIOS Method)

The Coarsely Integrated Operand Scanning (CIOS) method presented in Algorithm 2, improves the Montgomery Algorithm by integrating the multiplication

---

Algorithm 2. CIOS algorithm for Montgomery multiplication [9]

Input: $p < 2^K$, $p' = -p^{-1} \bmod 2^w$, w, s , $K = s \cdot w$:bit length, $R = 2^K$, $a, b < p$

Output: $a \cdot b \cdot R^{-1} \bmod p$

1 $T \leftarrow 0$;

2 **for** $i \leftarrow 0$ *to* $s - 1$ **do**

3 $\quad$ $C \leftarrow 0$;

4 $\quad$ **for** $j \leftarrow 0$ *to* $s - 1$ **do**

5 $\quad\quad$ $(C, S) \leftarrow T[j] + a[i] \cdot b[j] + C$ $\qquad\qquad \left. \right\} \alpha$ cell

6 $\quad\quad$ $T[j] \leftarrow S$

7 $\quad$ $(C, S) \leftarrow T[s] + C$

8 $\quad$ $T[s] \leftarrow S$ $\qquad\qquad\qquad\qquad\qquad\quad \left. \right\} \alpha_f$ cell

9 $\quad$ $T[s + 1] \leftarrow C$

10 $\quad$ $m \leftarrow T[0] \cdot p' \bmod 2^w$ $\qquad\qquad\qquad \left. \right\} \beta$ cell

11 $\quad$ $(C, S) \leftarrow T[0] + m \cdot p[0]$

12 $\quad$ **for** $j \leftarrow 1$ *to* $s - 1$ **do**

13 $\quad\quad$ $(C, S) \leftarrow T[j] + m \cdot p[j] + C$ $\qquad\quad \left. \right\} \gamma$ cell

14 $\quad\quad$ $T[j - 1] \leftarrow S$

15 $\quad$ $(C, S) \leftarrow T[s] + C$

16 $\quad$ $T[s - 1] \leftarrow S$ $\qquad\qquad\qquad\qquad\quad \left. \right\} \gamma_f$ cell

17 $\quad$ $T[s] \leftarrow T[s + 1] + C$

18 **return** T;

and reduction. More specifically, instead of computing the product $a \cdot b$, then reducing the result, this method allows an alternation between iterations of the outer loops for multiplication and reduction. The integers (p, a and b) are seen as lists of s words of size w. This algorithm requires an array T of size only $s + 2$ to store the intermediate state. The final result of the CIOS algorithm is composed by the $s + 1$ least significant words of this array at the end.

The alternation between multiplications and reductions is possible since the value of m (in line 11 of the Algorithm 2) in the ith iteration of the outer loop for reduction depends only on the value $T[0]$, which is computed by the first iteration of the corresponding inner loop. In order to perform the multiplication, we have modified the CIOS algorithm of [9] and designed this method with a systolic architecture. Indeed, instead of using an array to store the intermediate result, we replace T by input and output signals for each Processing Element. As a consequence, our design uses fewer multiplexers decreasing as a consequence the number of slices taken by our design.

4   Hardware Implementation

4.1   Block DSP in Xilinx FPGAs

Modern FPGA devices like Xilinx Virtex-4, Virtex-5 and Artix-7 as well as Altera Stratix FPGAs have been equipped with arithmetic hardcore extensions to accelerate digital signal processing applications. These DSP blocks can be used to build a more efficient implementation in terms of performance and reduce at the same time the demand for area. DSP blocks can be programmed to perform basic arithmetic functions, multiplication, addition and subtraction of unsigned integers. Figure 1 shows the generic DSP structure in advanced FPGAs. DSP can operate on external input A,B and C as well as on feedback values from P or result PCIN.

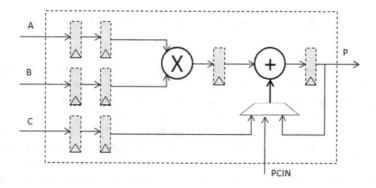

Fig. 1. Structure of DSP block in modern FPGA device.

4.2 Proposed Architecture

The idea of our design is to combine the CIOS method for the MMM presented in [9] with a two-dimensional systolic architecture in the model of [12, 18, 22]. As seen in Sect. 3, the CIOS method is an alternation between iterations of the loops for multiplication and reduction. The concept of the two-dimensional systolic architecture presented in Sect. 2 combines Processing Elements with local connections, which take external inputs and handle them with a predetermined manner in a pipelined fashion. This new architecture is directly based on the arithmetic operations of the CIOS method of Montgomery Algorithm. The arithmetic is performed in a radix-w base (2^w). The input operands are processed in s words of w bits. We present many versions of this method. We illustrate our design for $s = 16$ architecture, denoted NW-16 (for Number of Words). We describe it in detail as well as the various Processing Element behaviours. In order to have less states in our Final State Machine (FSM), we divided our Algorithm 2 of Montgomery in five kinds of PEs ($\alpha, \beta, \gamma, \alpha_f, \gamma_f$). Our efficient architecture comes from the fact that the data dependency in the CIOS algorithm allows to perform several operations in parallel. Figure 2 presents the dependency of the different cells. Below we describe precisely each cell. The letters MSW stand for the Most Significant Word and LSW for the Least Significant Word. In our notation the letter C denote the MSW of the result and the letter S the LSW.

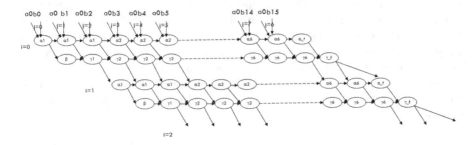

Fig. 2. Data dependency in general systolic architecture.

α *cell.* The α cell corresponds to lines 5 and 6 of Algorithm 2. Its operations are described in Algorithm 3. Notice how registers are embedded into the cell, avoiding in this manner the usage of an external memory. This cell corresponds to one iteration of the first inner loop. As such it must be used several times in a row (the number of iterations in the inner loop). This chain of α cells is terminated by an α_f cell (alpha final) corresponding to lines 7, 8 and 9 of Algorithm 2. Once the first α cell (for each outer loop) is computed, data is available for the β cell (it requires $T[0]$). It is preferable to consume this data as soon as it is available as to minimize memory usage.

Algorithm 3. α cell

Input: $a[i]$, $b[j]$, $C_{In}(=C)$, $S_{In}(=T[j])$
Output: C_{Out}, S_{Out}
1 $t1 \leftarrow S_{In} + C_{In}$
2 $t2 \leftarrow a[i] \cdot b[j]$
3 $t3 \leftarrow t2 + t1$
4 $C_{Out} \leftarrow \text{MSW}(t3)$
5 $S_{Out} \leftarrow \text{LSW}(t3)$
6 **return** C_{Out}, S_{Out}

Algorithm 4. α_f cell

Input: $C_{In}(=C)$, $S_{In}(=T[s])$
Output: $C_{Out}(=T[s+1])$, $S_{Out}(=T[s])$
1 $t1 \leftarrow S_{In} + C_{In}$
2 $C_{Out} \leftarrow \text{MSW}(t1)$
3 $S_{Out} \leftarrow \text{LSW}(t1)$
4 **return** C_{Out}, S_{Out}

Algorithm 5. β cell

Input: $S_{In}(=T[0])$, p', $p[0]$
Output: C_{Out}, S_{Out}
1 $t1 \leftarrow S_{In} \cdot p'$
2 $m \leftarrow \text{LSW}(t1)$
3 $t2 \leftarrow p[0] \cdot m$
4 $t3 \leftarrow S_{In} + t2$
5 $C_{Out} \leftarrow \text{MSW}(t3)$
6 **return** C_{Out}, m

α_f *cell.* The α_f cell corresponds to the end of the first inner loop. It is just an addition as shown in Algorithm 4.

β *cell.* The β cell is used to compute the m value for each outer loop as well as the first special iteration of the second inner loop. Its operations are described in Algorithm 5. Once the β cell computation has been done, it now becomes possible to compute the second inner loop with γ cells.

γ *cell.* The γ cell corresponds to one iteration of the second inner loop. As such these cells must be chained so as to complete the whole second inner loop. For each cell in this chain, the same m value is required. Value that is changed for each outer loop iteration (m is computed by the β cell). Since a new m value may be computed before the end of the γ chain, the value must be propagated along the cells in the same chain. Its operations are described in Algorithm 6.

Algorithm 6. γ cell

Input: $C_{In}(= C)$, $S_{In}(= T[j])$, m, $p[j]$
Output: C_{Out}, S_{Out}
1 $t1 \leftarrow S_{In} + C_{In}$
2 $t2 \leftarrow m \cdot p[j]$
3 $t3 \leftarrow t1 + t2$
4 $C_{Out} \leftarrow$ MSW$(t3)$
5 $S_{Out} \leftarrow$ LSW$(t3)$
6 **return** C_{Out}, S_{Out}, m

Algorithm 7. γ_f cell

Input: $C_{In}(= C)$, $S1_{In}(= T[s])$, $S2_{In}(= T[s+1])$
Output: $C_{Out}(= T[s])$, $S_{Out}(= T[s-1])$
1 $t1 \leftarrow S1_{In} + C_{In}$
2 $t2 \leftarrow$ MSW$(t1)$
3 $S_{Out} \leftarrow$ LSW$(t1)$
4 $C_{Out} \leftarrow$ LSW$(S2_{In} + t2)$
5 **return** $C_{Out}(= T[s])$, $S_{Out}(= T[s-1])$

γ_f *cell.* Finally, the γ_f cell terminate each γ cell chain. It consists in two additions as shown in Algorithm 7. The difference with the α_f cell is that in this case both output values S and C are used in the rest of the computation. C is used by the α_f cell and S by an α cell.

4.3 Our Architectures

Firstly, we will start with the NW-16 architecture which contains 6 PEs of type alpha and 6 of type gamma. An MMM can be performed with this architecture in 66 clock cycles. Similarly, in order to implement the NW-32 architecture and the NW-64 architecture it is required to double the number of cells each time. We provide a comparison of our architectures at the end of this section.

NW-16 Architecture. In this architecture, the operands and the modulo are divided in 16 words. The NW-16 architecture is designed in the same way as the NW-32 an NW-64. This example illustrates the scalability of our design. The NW-16 architecture is composed of 15 Processing Elements distributed in a two-dimensional array, where every Processing Elements are responsible for the calculus involving w-bit words of the input operands.

The 15 Processing Elements are divided like this: 6 α cells, 1 α_f cell, 1 β cell, 6 γ cells et 1 γ_f cell. As said previously, the number of other PE type (α_f, β, γ_f) remains unchanged whatever the number of words in the design. In order to evaluate the number of clock cycles of the NW-16 architecture, the first parameter is

$$6 = \max\{\text{number of } \alpha \text{ cells, number of } \gamma \text{ cells}\},$$

Table 1. Implementations of cells and MMM (NW-16).

Artix-7	DSP	Frequency	Clock cycles
MMM (s = 16/K = 256)	29	146	66
α	2	379	1
γ	2	379	1
β	2	453	1
α_f	1	460	1
γ_f	2	443	1

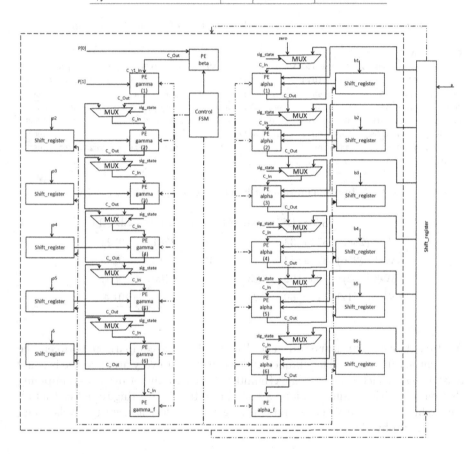

Fig. 3. Proposed Montgomery modular multiplication architecture of NW-16.

implying that our algorithm requires to loop $s + 6$ times. We can perform the multiplication with our design in 66 clock cycles since our design requires three states $(66 = 3 \times (s + 6))$. The different results of this architecture for bit-length 256 are given in Table 1.

Table 2. Comparison of our architectures

CIOS	$s = 8$	$s = 16$	$s = 32$	$s = 64$
$K = 256$	32	16	8	4
$K = 512$	64	32	16	8
$K = 1024$	128	64	32	16
$K = 2048$	256	128	64	32
Clock cycles $= 3 \times (s + nb)$	33	66	132	264
Number of cells	$6 + 3$	$12 + 3$	$24 + 3$	$48 + 3$

Table 3. Comparaison of our work with state-of-art implementations.

Xilinx FPGAs

	Our works A7		Our works V5		[17] V5		[16] VE		[5] VII	[4] VII	[13] V		[1] K7 and V5	
	512	1024	512	1024	512	1024	512	1024	1024	1024	512	1024	512 K7	512 V5
Freq	106	65	97	65	95	130	95.2	95.6	116.4	119	72.1	79.2	176	123
Cycles	66	66	66	66	96	384	1540	3076	1088	1167	–	–	66	66
Speed μs	0.622	1.013	0.680	1.015	1.010	2.953	16.031	32.021	9.34	9.80	–	–	0.374	0.536
Slice Reg	2164	4208	3046	6072	3876	6642	–	–	–	–	–	–	5076	4960
Slice LUTs	1789	5242	1781	5824	–	–	2972	5706	9319	9271	3125	6243	8757	10877
BRAM	0	0	0	0	128	256	–	–	–	–	–	–	0	0

Table 4. Implementations of ECC (Jacobian) in Xilinx FPGA.

	Slice	DSPs	BRAM	Freq	Slice FF	Slice LUT
NW-8 (256)	3745	33	12	98	8281	9722
NW-16 (256)	3770	34	12	130	8313	9255
NW-8 (512)	7066	92	23	59	16500	20394
NW-16 (512)	7116	60	23	74	16501	19199

Architectures Comparison. The Table 2 shows a comparison between the different architectures. The number of clock cycles for every architecture is equal to $3 \times (s + nb)$, such that $nb = \max\{$number of α cells number of γ cells$\}$, implying that our algorithm require to loop $s + nb$ times. It is interesting to notice that all our architectures are scalable and can target the different security levels useful in cryptography (Fig. 3).

4.4   ECC Implementation

ECC algorithms when implemented in a sequential way have the advantage that the number of finite field arithmetic modules can be reduced to a minimum. For example, only one adder, one multiplier and one subtraction unit (can be an adder) are needed for point addition and doubling. Parallelization between multiplication, addition and subtraction was achieved. We proposed in Figs. 4 and 5 the dataflow graphs for point addition and doubling. In this design we use our efficient systolic architecture of MMM to perform squaring or multiplication. The Table 4 summarizes the implementation results of the scalar multiplication. We present a results with both NW-8 and NW-16 architectures. To check the correctness of the hardware results, we compare the results given by the FPGA with sage software implementation.

5   Experimental Results

The Table 3 summarizes the FPGA post-implementation results for the proposed versions of MMM architectures. We present results for NW-16 architecture. The designs were described in a hardware description languages (VHDL) and synthesized for Artix-7 and Virtex-5 Xilinx FPGAs. We present the different results after implementation of bit-length k which are given in Table 3. As it is shown in Table 3, an interesting property of our design is the fact that the clock cycles are independent from the bit length. This property gives to our design the advantage of suitability to different security level. In order to implement the modular Montgomery multiplication for fixed security level, we must choose the most suitable architecture. The results presented in this work are compared with the previous work [4,5,16,17] in the Table 3. We can notice that our results are better than [17] considering every point of comparison i.e. the number of slice and the number of clock cycles. Considering the number of slices, we recall that [17] used an external memory to optimize the number of slices used by their algorithms. Considering the comparison with [16], our design requires less slices and can ran at a better frequency, without considering the huge progress in the number of clock cycles. Our design performed the MMM in 66 clock cycles for the 512 and 1024 bit length corresponding to AES-256 and AES-512 security level, while [16] performed the multiplication in 1540 clock cycles for the AES-256 security level and 3076 for the AES-512 security level.

6   Conclusion

In this paper we have presented an efficient hardware implementation of the CIOS method of MMM over large prime characteristic finite fields $\mathbb{F}_p$. We give the results of our design after routing and placement using a Artix-7 and Virtex-5 Xilinx FPGAs. Our systolic implementations is suitable for every implementation implying a modular multiplication, for example RSA, ECC and pairing-based cryptography. Our architectures and the designs were matched with features of the FPGAs. The NW-16 design presented a good performance considering *latency* × *area* efficiency. This architecture can run for all the bit length corresponding to classical security levels (128, 256, 512 or 1024 bits) in just 66 clock cycles. Our systolic design using this method CIOS is scalable for any other number of words. Then we showed that using this multiplier, it is possible to achieve an efficient scalar multiplication.

A   Elliptic Curve Operations Scheduling

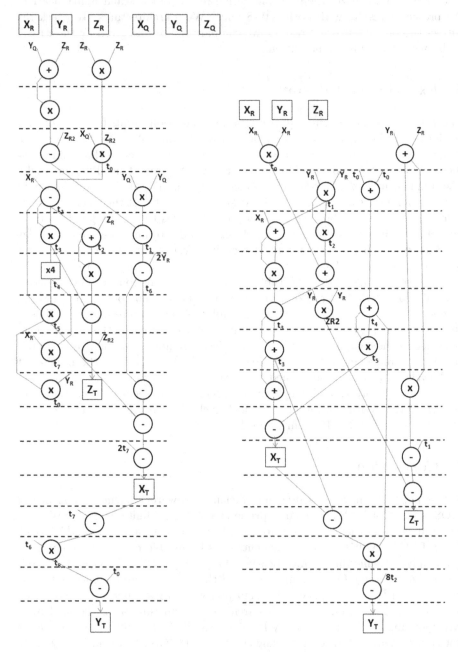

Fig. 4. DFG for the point addition algorithm.

Fig. 5. DFG for the point doubling algorithm.

References

1. Bigou, K., Tisserand, A.: Single base modular multiplication for efficient hardware RNS implementations of ECC. In: Güneysu, T., Handschuh, H. (eds.) CHES 2015. LNCS, vol. 9293, pp. 123–140. Springer, Heidelberg (2015). doi:10.1007/978-3-662-48324-4_7

2. Hankerson, D., Menezes, A.J., Vanstone, S.: Guide to Elliptic Curve Cryptography. Springer, New York (2006)

3. Hariri, A., Reyhani-Masoleh, A.: Bit-serial and bit-parallel montgomery multiplication and squaring over GF($2^\wedge$m). IEEE Trans. Comput. **58**(10), 1332–1345 (2009)

4. Harris, D., Krishnamurthy, R., Anders, M., Mathew, S., Hsu, S.: An improved unified scalable radix-2 montgomery multiplier. In: 17th IEEE Symposium on Computer Arithmetic, ARITH-17 2005, pp. 172–178, June 2005

5. Huang, M., Gaj, K., El-Ghazawi, T.: New hardware architectures for montgomery modular multiplication algorithm. IEEE Trans. Comput. **60**(7), 923–936 (2011)

6. Huang, M., Gaj, K., Kwon, S., El-Ghazawi, T.: An optimized hardware architecture for the montgomery multiplication algorithm. In: Cramer, R. (ed.) PKC 2008. LNCS, vol. 4939, pp. 214–228. Springer, Heidelberg (2008). doi:10.1007/978-3-540-78440-1_13

7. Iwamura, K., Matsumoto, T., Imai, H.: Systolic-arrays for modular exponentiation using montgomery method. In: Rueppel, R.A. (ed.) EUROCRYPT 1992. LNCS, vol. 658, pp. 477–481. Springer, Heidelberg (1993). doi:10.1007/3-540-47555-9_43

8. Joux, A.: A one round protocol for tripartite Diffie-Hellman. J. Crypt. **17**(4), 263–276 (2004). http://dx.doi.org/10.1007/s00145-004-0312-y

9. Koç, C., Acar, T., Kaliski, B.S.: Analyzing and comparing montgomery multiplication algorithms. IEEE Micro **16**(3), 26–33 (1996)

10. Koblitz, N.: Elliptic curve cryptosystems. Math. Comput. **48**(177), 203–209 (1987)

11. Kung, H.: Why systolic architectures? Computer **15**(1), 37–46 (1982)

12. i Lee, K.: Algorithm and VLSI architecture design for H.264/AVC inter frame coding. Ph.D. thesis, National Cheng Kung University, Tainan, Taiwan (2007)

13. Manochehri, K., Pourmozafari, S., Sadeghian, B.: Montgomery and rns for rsa hardware implementation. Comput. Inform. **29**(5), 849–880 (2012)

14. Miller, V.S.: Use of elliptic curves in cryptography. In: Williams, H.C. (ed.) CRYPTO 1985. LNCS, vol. 218, pp. 417–426. Springer, Heidelberg (1986). doi:10.1007/3-540-39799-X_31

15. Montgomery, P.L.: Modular multiplication without trial division. Math. Comput. **44**(170), 519–521 (1985)

16. Ors, S.B., Batina, L., Preneel, B., Vandewalle, J.: Hardware implementation of a montgomery modular multiplier in a systolic array. In: Proceedings of the International Parallel and Distributed Processing Symposium, p. 8. IEEE (2003)

17. Perin, G., Mesquita, D.G., Martins, J.B.: Montgomery modular multiplication on reconfigurable hardware: systolic versus multiplexed implementation. Int. J. Reconfig. Comput. **2011**, 61–610 (2011). http://dx.doi.org/10.1155/2011/127147

18. Reymond, G., Murillo, V.: A hardware pipelined architecture of a scalable montgomery modular multiplier over GF(2m). In: 2013 International Conference on Reconfigurable Computing and FPGAs (ReConFig), pp. 1–6, December 2013

19. Rivest, R., Shamir, A., Adleman, L.: A method for obtaining digital signatures and public-key cryptosystems. Commun. ACM **21**, 120–126 (1978)

20. Rivest, R.L., Shamir, A., Adleman, L.: A method for obtaining digital signatures and public-key cryptosystems. Commun. ACM **21**(2), 120–126 (1978)

21. Tenca, A.F., Koç, Ç.K.: A scalable architecture for montgomery nultiplication. In: Koç, Ç.K., Paar, C. (eds.) CHES 1999. LNCS, vol. 1717, pp. 94–108. Springer, Heidelberg (1999). doi:10.1007/3-540-48059-5_10

22. Vucha, M., Rajawat, A.: Design and FPGA implementation of systolic array architecture for matrix multiplication. Int. J. Comput. Appl. **26**(3), 18–22 (2011). ISSN 0975-8887

Improving Side-Channel Attacks Against Pairing-Based Cryptography

Damien Jauvart[1,2]([⊠]), Jacques J.A. Fournier[1], Nadia El-Mrabet[3],
and Louis Goubin[2]

[1] CEA-Tech PACA, Gardanne, France
{damien.jauvart2,jacques.fournier}@cea.fr
[2] UVSQ-PRiSM, Versailles, France
louis.goubin@uvsq.fr
[3] EMSE, Gardanne, France
nadia.el-mrabet@emse.fr

Abstract. Although the vulnerability of pairing-based algorithms to side-channel attacks has been demonstrated—pairing implementations were targeted on three different devices in a recent paper [41]—it nevertheless remains difficult to choose an adapted leakage model and detect points of interest. Our proposed approach evaluates the parameters of the attack and validates the data processing workflow. We describe weaknesses in the implementation of cryptographic pairings, and we show how information leakage can be fully exploited. Different leakage models, point-of-interest detection methods, and parameter dependencies are compared. In addition, practical results were obtained with a software implementation of twisted Ate pairing on Barreto–Naehrig curves with an ARM Cortex-M3 processor running at 50 MHz. We discuss countermeasures aimed at reducing side-channel leakage and review the available literature.

Keywords: Pairing-based cryptography · Twisted Ate pairing · Miller's algorithm · Side-channel attack · Points of interest · Countermeasures

1 Introduction

Side-channel attacks, which aim to recover secret data, are a serious threat to cryptographic devices. With embedded systems, the attacker can easily gain physical access to the device. Thus, side-channel attacks are a high-level concern [13,26,27]. Because identity-based encryption (IBE) [6] systems are not immune to these threats, the vulnerability of pairings used in IBE systems should be investigated. The basic modular multiplication algorithm used during a pairing calculation was recently attacked through correlation power analysis (CPA) [5,41].

Over the past few years, several works have highlighted the threat posed by attacks that target precise arithmetic operations during pairing computations. Side-channel attacks are based on exploiting the link between known (possibly

© Springer International Publishing AG 2017
F. Cuppens et al. (Eds.): CRiSIS 2016, LNCS 10158, pp. 199–213, 2017.
DOI: 10.1007/978-3-319-54876-0_16

malleable) data and secret data. A control device allows the attacker to execute a cryptographic algorithm with several known inputs. In IBE, such interactions appear during the decryption step. If the ciphertext to decrypt is $\{U, V\}$, then the first step consists in computing $e(s, U)$, where s is the secret key. The pairing algorithm then performs arithmetic operations between both sets of data. The attacks highlighted in [5,41] specifically target a modular multiplication algorithm. Once the target has been identified, a suitable leakage model must recreate the side-channel induced by calculating the targeted operation.

Studies on side-channel attacks share at least two important characteristics: the comparison of side-channel leakage models and the detection of points of interest associated with the models. The statistic tests that are used to detect points of interest can also be considered validators of the leakage model. In fact, if the statistical tool results in significant peaks, then the model can be validated. Our approach concerns a parameterized attack. Because of the large number of variables, we provide a detailed characterization of how side-channel attacks leak information concerning critical operations during pairings.

This study proposes a generic method for attacking pairing implementations and defines parameters to increase CPA efficiency (in terms of the number of measurement curves needed). To illustrate the application of our approach in the context of a cryptographic algorithm, we targeted one of the modular multiplications involved in the software implementation of an Ate pairing with the aim to retrieve (the secret) one of the two points in the pairing calculation. Compared with the best attacks on pairing calculations published so far [41], our results, based on taking real electromagnetic measurements on the chip of an embedded 32-bit ARM core processor, required significantly less computational time to retrieve the secret value.

The paper is organized as follows. Section 2 reviews existing research pertinent to the subject of the present paper, Sect. 3 gives some background information on pairing implementations, and Sect. 4 proposes an analysis of some general and specific techniques to defeat side-channel attacks. In addition, we describe our experimental results obtained with different techniques for the proposed attack scheme. Finally, possible countermeasures are discussed in Sect. 5, followed by our concluding statements in Sect. 6.

2   Related Work

Side-channel attacks on cryptographic algorithms have been studied extensively for more than two decades. Attacks targeting public key algorithms such as RSA or elliptic curve cryptography (ECC) have mainly been of the simple power analysis (SPA) type, whose objective is to reveal the secret exponent (in RSA) or the secret scalar (in ECC) used in a signature/decryption scheme. These algorithms use "public" variables, a long precision message (in RSA) or a base point (in ECC), that do not need to be attacked. One of the rare exceptions to this is a CPA-like attack on the final subtraction of a Montgomery Modular Multiplication (MMM), as described in [36]. CPA-type attacks on public key algorithms began to appear in attacks on implementations that were secured against SPA. For example, Joye [22] discusses this type of attack on protected versions of ECC. CPA attacks on algorithms such as RSA have been used to target protected implementations of the algorithm with a "horizontal" approach [10, 33]: the approach is horizontal in the sense that the statistical correlation analysis is done on portions of the same measured side-channel curve to defeat the random mask that is used as a countermeasure.

"Vertical" CPA (statistical correlation analysis of several measured side-channel curves for different input values) is relevant to and mainly studied in pairing-based cryptography (PBC), which is a field of public-key cryptography. When pairings are used (e.g., in IBE schemes), one of the two points of the pairing calculation is the secret decryption key; hence, it makes sense to use (vertical) CPA to attempt to retrieve this key.

Several papers have addressed side-channel attacks on pairings of fields in characteristic 2 or 3. These studies are merely mentioned for reference, considering that our implementation is based on large prime fields. Page and Vercauteren [31] published the first paper describing physical attacks (passive side-channel attacks and active fault attacks) on pairing algorithms. They targeted the Duursma–Lee algorithm [16], which is used to compute Tate pairings on elliptic curves over finite fields in characteristic 3. Data manipulation during the Duursma–Lee algorithm involves the product of a secret data item and a value derived from the known input point. The authors propose an SPA-like attack on field multiplication algorithms that are implemented using the shift-and-add method. They additionally describe a DPA attack that aims to recover the secret one bit at a time. Kim et $al.$ [24] proposed that timing, SPA, and DPA attacks used to target arithmetic operations also concern pairings over binary fields. In the context of Eta pairings over fields in characteristic 2, the targeted operation is $a(b + r)$, where a and b are derived from the secret, and r is derived from the known input. The authors conclude that, theoretically, the bitwise DPA proposed by Page and Vercauteren [31] would still be able to recover the secret point used in the pairing calculation. Pan and Marnane [32] proposed a practical CPA attack based on a Hamming distance model on an Eta pairing over a base field in characteristic 2 over supersingular curves.

One of the first papers describing side-channel attacks on pairings over large prime fields was proposed by Whelan and Scott [42], who used CPA to target the arithmetic operations to recover the secret: they calculated correlations between hypothetical outputs of the arithmetic operation $x \times k$ for all possible keys k and leakage traces. The resulting correlation curves were obtained for each key hypothesis; the correct one was the hypothesis with the highest peak. In the same paper, the authors discussed using word length (8, 16, 32, or 64) to represent long precision numbers; they further explain how partial correlation calculations can be used with CPA to target a portion of the word. El Mrabet et $al.$ [17] later proposed the first practical side-channel attack on Miller's algorithm for a pairing over prime fields equal to 251. The tangent line equation was targeted because it involves a modular multiplication of a coordinate derived from a public input point by a deterministic value derived from the secret point. Ghosh *et al.* [18] detailed a DPA attack on the modular subtraction in a Tate pairing over a Barreto–Naehrig elliptic curve [3]. Blömer *et al.* [5] then described side-channel attacks on modular additions and multiplications of finite field elements with large prime characteristics, showing that these attacks are possible even if the secret point is used as the first argument of the pairing calculation; their results were based on simulations. Unterluggauer and Wenger [41] have authored the most recent paper to investigate the use of SCA to target pairings. Using a CPA-like approach, as previously described in [42] for example, they targeted the modular operations during an Ate pairing to find the secret 16 bits at a time, taking advantage of the fact that the processor running the pairing calculation works with a 16-bit multiplier. Their configuration required more than 1500 measured curves to find the correct secret point.

3   Pairing-Based Cryptography

A pairing e is a bilinear and nondegenerate map such that $e : \mathbb{G}_1 \times \mathbb{G}_2 \to \mathbb{G}_3$, where $\mathbb{G}_1$, $\mathbb{G}_2$, and $\mathbb{G}_3$ are cyclic groups of the same prime order r. Let q be a prime number, let E be an elliptic curve over $\mathbb{F}_q$, and let r be a prime divisor of $\#E\,(\mathbb{F}_q)$. Efficient pairing algorithms are realized with $\mathbb{G}_1$, $\mathbb{G}_2$ subgroups of an elliptic curve $\#E\left(\mathbb{F}_{q^k}\right)$ with a point at infinity $\mathcal{O}$, and $\mathbb{G}_3$ is the subgroup of the rth roots of unity in $\mathbb{F}_{q^k}$, where k is the smallest integer such that r divides $(q^k - 1)$. A complete study of pairing-friendly elliptic curves can be found in [38]. The following properties complete the definition of a pairing:

- Nondegeneracy: $\forall P \in \mathbb{G}_1 \backslash \{\mathcal{O}\}$ $\exists Q \in \mathbb{G}_2$ such that $e(P,Q) \neq 1$, and $\forall Q \in \mathbb{G}_2 \backslash \{\mathcal{O}\}$ $\exists P \in \mathbb{G}_1$ such that $e(P,Q) \neq 1$,
- Bilinearity: $\forall a, b \in \mathbb{Z}, \forall P \in \mathbb{G}_1$ and $\forall Q \in \mathbb{G}_2$ then

$$e([a]P, [b]Q) = e(P,Q)^{ab}. \tag{1}$$

With the notation $[a]P = \underbrace{P + \ldots + P}_{a \text{ times}}$. More detailed definitions of pairings can be found in [39]; here, we are interested in physical attacks on cryptosystems that are based on Ate pairings.

For a 128-bit security level, Barreto–Naehrig (BN) curves [3] offer the highest security-level-to-computation-time ratio. Such curves take the form $E : y^2 = x^3 + b$ over a finite field $\mathbb{F}_q$, where $b \neq 0$ and q is a large prime integer.

For BN curves, the parameters q and r are defined as follows:

$$\begin{aligned} q(t) &= 36t^4 + 36t^3 + 24t^2 + 6t + 1, \\ r(t) &= 36t^4 + 36t^3 + 18t^2 + 6t + 1, \end{aligned} \tag{2}$$

for some $t \in \mathbb{Z}$ such that q is prime. Note that such curves have an embedded degree of $k = 12$.

The notation $E\,(\mathbb{F}_q)\,[r]$ is used to denote the $\mathbb{F}_q$-rational r-torsion group of E, (i.e., the set of points P in $E\,(\mathbb{F}_q)$ such that $[r]P = \mathcal{O}$).

Let $\mathbb{G}_1 = E(\mathbb{F}_q)[r] \cap \ker(\pi_q - [1])$, and let $\mathbb{G}_2 = E(\mathbb{F}_{q^{12}})[r] \cap \ker(\pi_q - [q])$, where π_q is the Frobenius endomorphism $\pi_q : E \to E : (x, y) \mapsto (x^q, y^q)$, and let $e = k/d$, where d is the degree of the twist, here $d = 6$. Let t be the trace of the Frobenius map over E.

Ate pairing [14,20] over BN curves gives the map

$$e : \mathbb{G}_1 \times \mathbb{G}_2 \to \mathbb{F}_{q^{12}}^{\star}$$
$$(P, Q) \to f_{(t-1)^e, P}(Q)^{\frac{q^k - 1}{r}}. \tag{3}$$

If the curves admit a sextic twist, then the elements of $E(\mathbb{F}_{q^{12}})$ can be on the twisted curve $E'(\mathbb{F}_{q^2})$. This improves processing efficiency considerably because the first input point P is now stored as two integers in $\mathbb{F}_q$ instead of as twelve integers.

Miller [28] provides an efficient method for calculating such pairings: Miller's algorithm is the main part of the pairing computation.

We recall the computation of twisted Ate pairings over BN curves using Miller's loop in Algorithm 1.

Algorithm 1. Computation of twisted Ate pairings using Miller's loop over BN curves

---

Input   : $P \in \mathbb{G}_1, Q \in \mathbb{G}_2$, t the Frobenius trace of E
Output : $e(P, Q)$

1 $T \leftarrow P$;
2 $f \leftarrow 1$;
3 $n \leftarrow t - 1$;   // $n = (n_{w-1} \ldots n_0)_2$ **radix 2 representation**
4 **for** $i = w - 2$ **downto** 0 **do**
5 $\quad f \leftarrow f^2 \cdot l_{T,T}(Q)$;
6 $\quad T \leftarrow [2]T$;
7 $\quad$ **if** $n_i == 1$ **then**
8 $\quad\quad f \leftarrow f \cdot l_{T,P}(Q)$;
9 $\quad\quad T \leftarrow T + P$;
10 $\quad$ **end**
11 **end**
12 **return** $f^{\frac{q^{12} - 1}{r}}$;

---

4   Analyzing Information Leakage in Side-Channel Attacks

From a theoretical standpoint, the security level of cryptographic algorithms corresponds to the level of computational difficulty of a well-known mathematical problem. In practice, the implementation of those cryptographic algorithms has to be tested for their resistance against physical attacks. Today, studies on physical attacks that aim to retrieve the secret keys used during cryptographic calculations represent a growing field of research, especially because cryptography is now being deployed in billions of connected objects.

Identity-based encryption (IBE) schemes solve several problems concerning the coupling of connected objects. In the context of pairing-based IBE implementations, the computational issues are solved by using pairing over elliptic curves. The principles of side-channel attacks are as follows: the decryption phase is calculated with a pairing between a point derived from the ciphertext (known) and a secret point, which constitutes the key. Hence, the aim of a side-channel attack is to target such pairing calculations in order to retrieve the secret key.

In pairing calculations, these critical operations are modular multiplications such as those identified in [5,31,41,42]. We describe how to identify these types of failures in Subsect. 4.1.

In Subsect. 4.2, we present a detailed study of the basic multiplication operation, which constitutes the basic building block of most public-key cryptographic algorithms, and provide a validated leakage model. So far, we have described a systematic method (based on predefined models) that finds the best parameters for using CPA to target a multiplication operation and, by extension, a modular multiplication, requiring only around 150 curves.

In the following, we use an efficient attack on a pairing computation to validate the usefulness of our approach.

4.1 Side-Channel Attack Strategy to Target Miller's Algorithm

Operations that occur during the pairing computation involve both known and secret data. This is the case in Algorithm 1 for the computation of the tangent line (see Line 5 in Algorithm 1). This interaction takes the form of a modular multiplication.

In our implementation, as is often the case in practice, the tangent line equation $l_{T,T}(Q)$ in Eq. 4 is in mixed affine–Jacobian coordinates. The equation of the tangent at T is evaluated at the point Q.

$$l_{T,T}(Q) = \frac{2y_Q Y_T Z_T^3 - 2Y_T^2 - (3X_T^2 + aZ_T^4)(x_Q Z_T^2 - X_T)}{2Y_T Z_T^3}. \tag{4}$$

For optimization, this equation can be written in mixed system coordinates as suggested in [1,25]:

– P and Q are in affine coordinates.
– T is in Jacobian coordinates.

The point T is initialized with P by $X_T \leftarrow x_P, Y_T \leftarrow y_P$ and $Z_T \leftarrow 1$ before Miller's loop. Thus, for the first iteration T is equal to P. Therefore, if we recover T, then we will directly obtain the secret P. Even if the input point is either P or Q, we can see that the multiplication $2y_Q Y_T Z_T^3$ involves known and secret data. We then attack the modular multiplication as described in Sect. 4.2.

Case 1. P is the Secret. In this case, we want to recover P (or T) with a side-channel attack. Our target is therefore the multiplication $(2y_Q) \cdot Y_T$. Knowledge of y_Q allows us to build a CPA to recover the coordinate $Y_T = Y_T^{(0)} + uY_T^{(1)} \in \mathbb{F}_{q^2}$. The multiplication $(2y_Q) \cdot Y_T$ applies to elements of $\mathbb{F}_q$, and $\mathbb{F}_{q^2}$ is similar to two multiplications in $\mathbb{F}_q$, that is, $(2y_Q) \cdot Y_T = (2y_Q) \cdot Y_T^{(0)} + u(2y_Q) \cdot Y_T^{(0)}$. Thus, a first CPA attack must target $(2y_Q) \cdot Y_T^{(0)}$ to recover $Y_T^{(0)}$, and a second attack then targets $Y_T^{(0)}$.

Case 2. Q is the Secret. In order to recover the input point Q, we target the modular multiplication $(2y_Q) \cdot Y_T$. After recovering $2y_Q \in \mathbb{F}_q$, we have y_Q, and we use the elliptic curve equation to recover x_Q.

4.2   Our Attack Principle and Practical Applications

We have seen that targeting the pairing amounts to an attack on a modular multiplication. We are not concerned with the method used to compute this multiplication (see Booth [7], Toom-Cook [11,40], Karatsuba [23], Brickell [8], Montgomery [29], or Quisquater [15,35]) because it is unimportant which method is chosen. The algorithm goes through a step of smaller integer multiplication. The size of these integers depends on the architecture of the device, for example, an integer of 256 bits needs to be stored in $n_{word} = 8$ registers of 32 bits in a 32-bit architecture.

In the following, we describe the processing chain of our attack. The aim is to understand the leakages induced by the multiplier during processing of the multiplication of two "small" integers (32 bits, for instance).

Using Correlation Power Analysis to Target Multiplication. We target the secret input $k = (k_{n-1} \ldots k_0)_2$ involved in $k \times x$. First, we record side-channel traces of this operation for several values of x. For all known inputs x and for all possible keys, we compute hypothetical outputs of the product $k \times x$. Then, we calculate correlations between the hypothetical outputs and the measured side-channel traces. To this end, we use the scheme detailed in Algorithm 2 to store two big matrices: the outputs and the traces.

Practical Set-Up. In order to support the method, we put in parallel our practical results. The targeted device is an ARM Cortex M3 processor working on 32-bit length registers. To target the multiplication operation, we place a trigger in the C code before this operation for synchronisation. This step is used for recording the traces just during the targeted time interval. The electromagnetic emanation (EM) measurements were done using a Langer EMV-Technik LF-U 5 probe equipped with a Langer Amplifier PA303 BNC (30 dB). The curves were collected using a Lecroy WaveRunner 640Zi oscilloscope. The acquisition frequency of the oscilloscope is 10^9 samples per second.

Algorithm 2. Using correlation power analysis to target multiplication

    Input   : $\mathcal{C}^{(l)}, \forall l = 1, \ldots, N$ the curves associated with $k \times x^{(l)}$ sampled on m points

    Output : $\widehat{k}$ candidate for k

 1 H is an empty matrix in $\mathcal{M}_{N \times 2^n}$;
 2 T is an empty matrix in $\mathcal{M}_{N \times m}$;
 3 **for** $l = 1$ **to** N **do**
 4     $T(l, \cdot) \leftarrow \mathcal{C}^{(l)}$;   `// Store the traces`
 5   **for** $j = 0$ **to** $2^n - 1$ **do**
 6         $H(l, j+1) \leftarrow \phi(j * x^{(l)})$;   `// `$\phi$`(Hypothetical output)`

 7 C is an empty matrix in $\mathcal{M}_{2^n \times m}$;
 8 **for** $i = 1$ **to** m **do**
 9   **for** $j = 1$ **to** 2^n **do**
10         $C(j, i) \leftarrow corr(T(\cdot, i), H(\cdot, j))$;   `// Correlation between traces`
             and predictions

11 $(\widehat{k}, t) \leftarrow argmax_{i,j} |C|$;
12 **return** $\widehat{k}$;

Statistical Tests to Evaluate Leakage Models. Ideally, CPA will recover the secret k if the leakage model ϕ is well chosen. In Algorithm 2, Line 6 can take numerous forms. Because we assume that the device leakage follows a Hamming weight (HW) model [13,27,30], the Hamming weight is a classic choice for ϕ. At the beginning, we considered two HW models for ϕ:

- $c = k \times x = (c_{2n-1} \ldots c_0)_2$ then $\phi_1(k, x) = \sum_{i=0}^{n-1} c_i$,
- $c = k \times x = (c_{2n-1} \ldots c_0)_2$ then $\phi_2(k, x) = \sum_{i=0}^{2n-1} c_i$.

Note that by taking the n least significant bits in the ϕ_1 model, we take in fact the bits of $a \times b \mod 2^n$.

We evaluate both models by computing the t-test (also known as the sum of squared pairwise t-differences [SOST] [19]). To this end, we use the fixed key and the variable plaintext obtained through our 1000 trace measurements. For each trace, we compute the supposed leakage $\phi(k, x)$, and we add the trace to the associated set. The size of each set is stored in $\eta_{\phi,i}, i = 1, \ldots, N_\phi$. In our case, $n = 8$; thus, for ϕ_1, there are $N_{\phi_1} = 9$ sets (9 possible HWs), and $N_{\phi_2} = 17$ for ϕ_2. We compute the mean $m_{\phi,i}$ for $i = 1, \ldots, N_\phi$ and the variance $\sigma_{\phi,i}^2$ of each set for ϕ_1 and ϕ_2. Thus, we are able to compute the SOST value for both models:

$$SOST_\phi = \sum_{i,j=1}^{N_\phi} \left(\frac{m_{\phi,i} - m_{\phi,j}}{\sqrt{\frac{\sigma_{\phi,i}^2}{\eta_{\phi,i}} + \frac{\sigma_{\phi,j}^2}{\eta_{\phi,j}}}} \right)^2 \quad \text{for } i \geq j \tag{5}$$

Figure 1 illustrates our experimental results. The leak is visibly confirmed for model ϕ_2: the peak is clearly always higher in this second case.

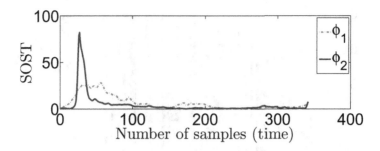

Fig. 1. The sum of squared pairwise t-differences (SOST)

Divide and Conquer. Using the previously described leakage model, we apply CPA in sequence to all four bytes of k in order to retrieve all 32 bits of k. First, we want to recover the 8 least significant bits of k, this is the attack of Algorithm 2, with either model ϕ_1 or ϕ_2. In this first instance of CPA, the 2^8-key hypotheses consider different values for plaintexts x. We thus obtain 2^8 values for the coefficient correlations. At this stage, we define an α-parameter, which means we will retain the key α-hypothesis corresponding to the best α-correlations. Then, for each of the α-hypotheses, we use CPA to target the following 8 bits of k. For each α, we also retain the best α-candidates. At the end of this step, the $\alpha \times \alpha$ key hypotheses correspond to the 16 least significant bits of k. We perform this process a third time to select candidates for the 24 least significant bits of k. The fourth step is identical to step three, and the candidate $\widehat{k}$ for k is the key corresponding to the best correlation found after this fourth instance of CPA.

Effects of the α-Parameters. Even though our comparison is based on differing α-values—$\alpha = 64$ with our method and $\alpha = 5$ for the attack proposed in [41]—Unterluggauer *et al.* specify that varying the α-parameter did not affect success for their attack. In fact, they observed no significant difference between $\alpha = 5$ and $\alpha = 10$.

Figure 2 shows the evolution of the success rate with respect to the number of traces used and the α-parameters of the CPA targeting the first 32-bit word. For each database size, the height of the bars of the corresponding column increases with α.

For example, for a database with 80 traces and with $\alpha \geq 40$ the success rate of the attack is greater than 80%. For 110 traces and $\alpha \geq 28$ the success rate of the attack is greater than 95%.

Resource Comparison with Unterluggauer et al. [41]. Our strategy consists in dividing $32 = 4 \times 8$ bits for a case with $\alpha = 64$ (a large α-value). By contrast, Unterluggauer *et al.* divided $32 = 2 \times 16$ bits with $\alpha = 5$. The resource comparison given in Table 1 quantifies the differences between both methods; "time" denotes the number of enumerated subkeys, and "memory" represents the resources used to store the subkeys.

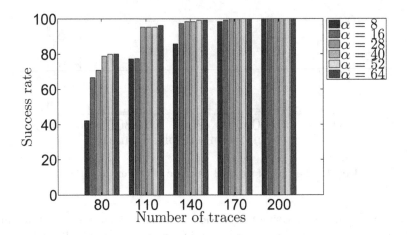

Fig. 2. Success rate for different database sizes and α-values

Table 1. Resource comparison

	Unterluggauer *et al.*	Our method (with $\alpha = 64$)
Time	$2^{18} < 2^{16} + 5 \times 2^{16} < 2^{19}$	$2^{15} < 2^8 + \alpha \times 2^8 + \alpha \times 2^8 + \alpha \times 2^8 < 2^{16}$
Memory	$2^{18} < 5 \times 2^{16} < 2^{19}$	$\alpha \times 2^8 = 2^{14}$

4.3 Practical Attack on the Pairing Algorithm

We implemented a twisted Ate pairing over BN curves in a real environment on an ARM Cortex M3 processor by manipulating 256-bit-long integers in $n_{\mathrm{word}} = 8$ words of 32 bits. We ran our algorithm and carried out experimental side-channel attacks using the same setup as described above. We chose to put the secret in the second input point Q. Therefore, thanks to our knowledge of P, we were able to use our attack to recover the secret, word for word, as previously described in Sect. 4.1.

Our method allowed us to recover the eight 32-bit words of the secret point of a pairing calculation using only around 150 curves. To enable a comparison with previously published practical results [41], we implemented the method described in [41] and ran the analysis on our curves. In terms of the required number of curves, our method only used 150 traces, compared with 1500 in [41]. Moreover, because we are working on 8-bit words ([41] are working on 16-bit words), our method is much faster. In addition, optimum leakage models can be identified based on our characterization of the multiplication calculation.

5 Countermeasures and Prospects

In this paper, we have shown how a thorough study of side-channel attacks—from leakage to multiplication—can be used to improve the attack. We were able to carry out an optimized side-channel attack on a pairing algorithm. Consequently, we are interested in how to protect implementations from such attacks. There are many methods to protect an implementation, for example the physical countermeasures. It based on create noise around the execution of sensitive operations. Here we are interrelated in the "mathematical" countermeasures.

Several countermeasures have already been proposed to protect pairing-based cryptographic algorithms against the kind of side-channel attacks described in the present paper. Most of these countermeasures aim to eliminate any predictable link between the manipulated data and the known input. In practice, pairing computations use various randomization levels. One category of countermeasures consists in randomizing the inputs before the pairing computation, another consists in adding a random mask directly to Miller's algorithm. In addition, a method based on arithmetic randomization can be adapted for pairing-based algorithms.

Input Randomization. Page and Vercauteren [31] proposed two countermeasures for their passive attack. The first one is based on the pairing bilinearity. Let a and b be two random values; thus, $e([a]P, [b]Q)^{1/ab} = e(P, Q)$. For each pairing computation, it is therefore possible to take different values for a and b and compute $e([a]P, [b]Q)^{1/ab}$. Evidently, this method is very costly in terms of computation time. Moreover, the randomization itself can be a target for side-channel attacks. In fact, some papers [4,9,10,33,34] have proposed horizontal attacks, which constitute a threat for protected exponentiation with a single trace.

The authors of [31] proposed another method (applicable, for example, to cases where P is secret) that consists in adding the mask to the point Q in the following way: select a random point $R \in \mathbb{G}_2$ and compute $e(P, Q + R)e(P, R)^{-1}$ instead of $e(P, Q)$, with different values of R at every call to e.

Based on this countermeasure, Blömer *et al.* [5] proposed to improve the Tate pairing. For a reduced Tate pairing, they note that the set of the second input argument is the equivalence class $E(\mathbb{F}_{q^k})/rE(\mathbb{F}_{q^k})$. They therefore choose a random point $R \in E(\mathbb{F}_{q^k})$ with order l and coprime to r. Thus, $Q + R \sim Q$. Hence, $e(P, Q + R) = e(P, Q)$. This method avoids the second pairing computation that is used to find the same result without a mask.

Randomization of Intermediate Variables. In 2005, Scott [37] proposed a countermeasure that involves randomizing the Miller variable. In this case, we would multiply instructions 5 and 8 in Algorithm 1 by a random $\lambda \in \mathbb{F}_q$, eliminated by the final exponentiation. This countermeasure is ineffective against our attack.

Kim *et al.* [24] use the third countermeasure proposed by Coron [12] (based on random projective coordinates) in order to protect the Eta pairing in characteristic 2. However, this countermeasure can be adapted to pairing algorithms that are based on large prime field characteristics. At the beginning of the algorithm, the authors implement this randomization based on the homogeneity of projective or Jacobian coordinates.

Arithmetic Randomization. All previous attacks on pairing algorithms have targeted arithmetic operations. The ability to secure multiplications was originally investigated in [21] to protect ECDSA against side-channel attacks with the aim to prevent all possible predictions during a modular multiplication. A "mask" is randomly chosen before processing a multiplication, rendering any hypothesis concerning the output of the internal modular multiplication impossible. Another masking technique proposed in [4] also aims to eliminate any predictable link between known and secret data directly in the arithmetic operations.

In addition, the well-known residue number system can be used to protect arithmetic operations [2].

Although arithmetic protection seems to be a robust method to protect against side-channel attacks, overhead costs must be evaluated. In fact, significant costs are associated with permutation changes in randomized multiplication and with base refreshing in RNS implementations.

Because none of these methods have been validated in the literature, we will apply the proposed countermeasures to our attack to measure their effectiveness. Different α-parameters were used in our attempts to defeat these countermeasures.

6   Conclusion

In this paper, we propose a revised version of the CPA attack provided in [41]. In fact, our investigation constitutes one of the first attempts to experimentally validate side-channel attacks on pairing-based algorithms. The paper makes two principal contributions: (1) We established the differences between two leakage models and described how to choose the appropriate model. The model is selected on the basis of using statistical tools applied to the multiplication of integers. Such tools also allowed us to find the points of interest used in future attacks. (2) We executed an attack on 32-bit multiplication, for which it was necessary to compute partial correlations (of just 8 bits, for example). Because the correlations are only partial, they are very sensitive to noise contained in the signals; to solve this problem, we introduced an α-parameter. The value of this parameter was varied in some experiments, which considerably improved the effectiveness of our attack. We demonstrated that our proposed attack method is less resource intensive (memory and processing time), even though the results obtained here focused exclusively on one chip. Consequently, through our detailed analysis, we achieved a substantial increase in the efficiency of side-channel attacks on pairing-based algorithms. We also discussed the countermeasures that can be used to thwart such an attack and considered their potential flaws.

Acknowledgments. This work was supported in part by the EUREKA Catrene programme under contract CAT208 MobiTrust and by a French DGA-MRIS scholarship.

References

1. Bajard, J., Mrabet, N.: Pairing in cryptography: an arithmetic point of view. In: Architectures, and Implementations, Advanced Signal Processing Algorithms (2007)

2. Bajard, J.-C., Imbert, L., Liardet, P.-Y., Teglia, Y.: Leak resistant arithmetic. In: Joye, M., Quisquater, J.-J. (eds.) CHES 2004. LNCS, vol. 3156, pp. 62–75. Springer, Heidelberg (2004). doi:10.1007/978-3-540-28632-5_5

3. Barreto, P.S.L.M., Naehrig, M.: Pairing-friendly elliptic curves of prime order. In: Preneel, B., Tavares, S. (eds.) SAC 2005. LNCS, vol. 3897, pp. 319–331. Springer, Heidelberg (2006). doi:10.1007/11693383_22

4. Bauer, A., Jaulmes, E., Prouff, E., Wild, J.: Horizontal and vertical side-channel attacks against secure RSA implementations. In: Dawson, E. (ed.) CT-RSA 2013. LNCS, vol. 7779, pp. 1–17. Springer, Heidelberg (2013). doi:10.1007/978-3-642-36095-4_1

5. Blömer, J., Günther, P., Liske, G.: Improved side channel attacks on pairing based cryptography. In: Prouff, E. (ed.) COSADE 2013. LNCS, vol. 7864, pp. 154–168. Springer, Heidelberg (2013). doi:10.1007/978-3-642-40026-1_10

6. Boneh, D., Franklin, M.: Identity-Based Encryption from the Weil Pairing, vol. 32. Springer, Heidelberg (2001)

7. Booth, A.D.: A signed binary multiplication technique. Q. J. Mech. Appl. Math. 4(2), 236–240 (1951)

8. Brickell, E.F.: A fast modular multiplication algorithm with application to two key cryptography. In: Chaum, D., Rivest, R.L., Sherman, A.T. (eds.) Advances in Cryptology, pp. 51–60. Springer, New York (1983)

9. Clavier, C., Feix, B., Gagnerot, G., Giraud, C., Roussellet, M., Verneuil, V.: ROSETTA for single trace analysis. In: Galbraith, S., Nandi, M. (eds.) INDOCRYPT 2012. LNCS, vol. 7668, pp. 140–155. Springer, Heidelberg (2012). doi:10.1007/978-3-642-34931-7_9

10. Clavier, C., Feix, B., Gagnerot, G., Roussellet, M., Verneuil, V.: Horizontal correlation analysis on exponentiation. In: Soriano, M., Qing, S., López, J. (eds.) ICICS 2010. LNCS, vol. 6476, pp. 46–61. Springer, Heidelberg (2010). doi:10.1007/978-3-642-17650-0_5

11. Cook, S.: On the minimum computation time of functions. Trans. Am. Math. Soc. 142(23), 291–291 (1969)

12. Coron, J.-S.: Resistance against differential power analysis for elliptic curve cryptosystems. In: Koç, Ç.K., Paar, C. (eds.) CHES 1999. LNCS, vol. 1717, pp. 292–302. Springer, Heidelberg (1999). doi:10.1007/3-540-48059-5_25

13. Coron, J.-S., Kocher, P., Naccache, D.: Statistics and secret leakage. In: Frankel, Y. (ed.) FC 2000. LNCS, vol. 1962, pp. 157–173. Springer, Heidelberg (2001). doi:10.1007/3-540-45472-1_12

14. Devegili, A.J., Scott, M., Dahab, R.: Implementing cryptographic pairings over Barreto-Naehrig curves. In: Takagi, T., Okamoto, T., Okamoto, E., Okamoto, T. (eds.) Pairing 2007. LNCS, vol. 4575, pp. 197–207. Springer, Heidelberg (2007). doi:10.1007/978-3-540-73489-5_10

15. Dhem, J.-F., Joye, M., Quisquater, J.-J.: Normalisation in diminished-radix modulus transformation. Electron. Lett. 33(23), 1931 (1997)

16. Duursma, I., Lee, H.-S.: Tate pairing implementation for hyperelliptic curves $y^2 = x^p - x + d$. In: Laih, C.-S. (ed.) ASIACRYPT 2003. LNCS, vol. 2894, pp. 111–123. Springer, Heidelberg (2003). doi:10.1007/978-3-540-40061-5_7

17. El Mrabet, N., Di Natale, G., Flottes, M.L.: A practical differential power analysis attack against the miller algorithm. In: PRIME, pp. 308–311 (2009)
18. Ghosh, S., Roychowdhury, D.: Security of prime field pairing cryptoprocessor against differential power attack. In: Joye, M., Mukhopadhyay, D., Tunstall, M. (eds.) InfoSecHiComNet 2011. LNCS, vol. 7011, pp. 16–29. Springer, Heidelberg (2011). doi:10.1007/978-3-642-24586-2_4
19. Gierlichs, B., Lemke-Rust, K., Paar, C.: Templates vs. stochastic methods. In: Goubin, L., Matsui, M. (eds.) CHES 2006. LNCS, vol. 4249, pp. 15–29. Springer, Heidelberg (2006). doi:10.1007/11894063_2
20. Hess, F., Smart, N.P., Vercauteren, F.: The Eta pairing revisited. IEEE Trans. Inf. Theor. **52**, 4595–4602 (2006)
21. Hutter, M., Medwed, M., Hein, D., Wolkerstorfer, J.: Attacking ECDSA-enabled RFID devices. In: Abdalla, M., Pointcheval, D., Fouque, P.-A., Vergnaud, D. (eds.) ACNS 2009. LNCS, vol. 5536, pp. 519–534. Springer, Heidelberg (2009). doi:10.1007/978-3-642-01957-9_32
22. Joye, M.: Elliptic curves and side-channel analysis. ST J. Syst. Res. **4**(1), 17–21 (2003)
23. Karatsuba, A., Ofman, Y.: Multiplication of multidigit numbers on automata. In: Soviet Physics Doklady, vol. 7, p. 595 (1963)
24. Kim, T.H., Takagi, T., Han, D.-G., Kim, H.W., Lim, J.: Side channel attacks and countermeasures on pairing based cryptosystems over binary fields. In: Pointcheval, D., Mu, Y., Chen, K. (eds.) CANS 2006. LNCS, vol. 4301, pp. 168–181. Springer, Heidelberg (2006). doi:10.1007/11935070_11
25. Koblitz, N., Menezes, A.: Pairing-based cryptography at high security levels. In: Smart, N.P. (ed.) Cryptography and Coding 2005. LNCS, vol. 3796, pp. 13–36. Springer, Heidelberg (2005). doi:10.1007/11586821_2
26. Kocher, P., Jaffe, J., Jun, B.: Differential power analysis. In: Advances in Cryptology - CRYPTO 1999, pp. 1–10 (1999)
27. Mayer-Sommer, R.: Smartly analyzing the simplicity and the power of simple power analysis on smartcards. In: Koç, Ç.K., Paar, C. (eds.) CHES 2000. LNCS, vol. 1965, pp. 78–92. Springer, Heidelberg (2000). doi:10.1007/3-540-44499-8_6
28. Miller, V.S.: Use of elliptic curves in cryptography. In: Williams, H.C. (ed.) CRYPTO 1985. LNCS, vol. 218, pp. 417–426. Springer, Heidelberg (1986). doi:10.1007/3-540-39799-X_31
29. Montgomery, P.L.: Modular multiplication without trial division (1985)
30. Oswald, E.: On side-channel attacks and the application of algorithmic countermeasures. na (2003)
31. Page, D., Vercauteren, F.: Fault and Side-Channel Attacks on Pairing Based Cryptography (2004)
32. Pan, W., Marnane, W.P.: A correlation power analysis attack against tate pairing on FPGA. In: Koch, A., Krishnamurthy, R., McAllister, J., Woods, R., El-Ghazawi, T. (eds.) ARC 2011. LNCS, vol. 6578, pp. 340–349. Springer, Heidelberg (2011). doi:10.1007/978-3-642-19475-7_36
33. Perin, G., Imbert, L., Maurine, P., Torres, L.: Vertical and horizontal correlation attacks on RNS-based exponentiations. J. Cryptographic Eng. **5**(3), 1–15 (2015)
34. Perin, G., Imbert, L., Torres, L., Maurine, P.: Attacking randomized exponentiations using unsupervised learning. In: Prouff, E. (ed.) COSADE 2014. LNCS, vol. 8622, pp. 144–160. Springer, Cham (2014). doi:10.1007/978-3-319-10175-0_11
35. Quisquater, J.-J.: Presentation at the rump session of Eurocrypt 90 (1990)

36. Sato, H., Schepers, D., Takagi, T.: Exact analysis of montgomery multiplication. In: Canteaut, A., Viswanathan, K. (eds.) INDOCRYPT 2004. LNCS, vol. 3348, pp. 290–304. Springer, Heidelberg (2004). doi:10.1007/978-3-540-30556-9_23

37. Scott, M.: Computing the tate pairing. In: Menezes, A. (ed.) CT-RSA 2005. LNCS, vol. 3376, pp. 293–304. Springer, Heidelberg (2005). doi:10.1007/978-3-540-30574-3_20

38. Scott, M.: On the efficient implementation of pairing-based protocols. In: Chen, L. (ed.) IMACC 2011. LNCS, vol. 7089, pp. 296–308. Springer, Heidelberg (2011). doi:10.1007/978-3-642-25516-8_18

39. Silverman, J.H.: The Arithmetic of Elliptic Curves. Graduate Texts in Mathematics, vol. 106, 2nd edn. Springer, New York (2009)

40. Toom, A.L.: The complexity of a scheme of functional elements realizing the multiplication of integers. Sov. Math. Dokl. **3**, 714–716 (1963)

41. Unterluggauer, T., Wenger, E.: practical attack on bilinear pairings to disclose the secrets of embedded devices. In: ARES, pp. 69–77 (2014)

42. Whelan, C., Scott, M.: Side channel analysis of practical pairing implementations: which path is more secure? In: Nguyen, P.Q. (ed.) VIETCRYPT 2006. LNCS, vol. 4341, pp. 99–114. Springer, Heidelberg (2006). doi:10.1007/11958239_7

A First DFA on PRIDE: From Theory to Practice

Benjamin Lac[1,5(✉)], Marc Beunardeau[2,6], Anne Canteaut[3],
Jacques J.A. Fournier[1], and Renaud Sirdey[4]

[1] CEATech/DPACA, Gardanne, France
{benjamin.lac,jacques.fournier}@cea.fr
[2] Ingenico Labs, Paris, France
marc.beunardeau@ingenico.com
[3] Inria, Paris, France
anne.canteaut@inria.fr
[4] CEATech/LIST, Saclay, France
renaud.sirdey@cea.fr
[5] ENSM-SE, Saint-Étienne, France
[6] ENS, Paris, France

Abstract. PRIDE is one of the most efficient lightweight block cipher proposed so far for connected objects with high performance and low-resource constraints. In this paper we describe the first ever complete Differential Fault Analysis against PRIDE. We describe how fault attacks can be used against implementations of PRIDE to recover the entire encryption key. Our attack has been validated first through simulations, and then in practice on a software implementation of PRIDE running on a device that could typically be used in IoT devices. Faults have been injected using electromagnetic pulses during the PRIDE execution and the faulty ciphertexts been used to recover the key bits. We also discuss some countermeasures that could be used to thwart such attacks.

Keywords: Lightweight cryptography · DFA · PRIDE · EM fault attacks

1   Introduction

With the emergence of the Internet of Things (IoT), new cryptographic primitives are needed to suit the high performance, low power and low resource constraints of IoT devices. Ciphers like AES, which are good enough for devices like smart cards, do not satisfy the constraints of devices like RFID tags or nodes in sensor networks. During the past years, several lightweight block ciphers have been proposed, like for example PRESENT [10], PRINCE [12], SIMON [6] or SPECK [6]. Among those, the NSA proposal SPECK is a highly efficient software-oriented cipher, but it does not have any 'linear diffusion layer' implying that it requires a huge number of rounds to guarantee an appropriate security level. In order to keep a small number of rounds, the PRIDE cipher [4]

© Springer International Publishing AG 2017
F. Cuppens et al. (Eds.): CRiSIS 2016, LNCS 10158, pp. 214–238, 2017.
DOI: 10.1007/978-3-319-54876-0_17

exploits an optimal linear layer which provides a high diffusion and has highly efficient implementations. Although hardware implementations are more efficient in terms of clock cycles than software implementations, design and study of software-oriented ciphers is nevertheless important since these implementations are used in practice because they are less expensive and more flexible than hardware implementations. To date, when looking at software implementations, PRIDE is one of the most efficient lightweight cryptographic ciphers as shown the performance comparisons given in [4,5]. This led us to study the security provided by PRIDE and its resistance to malicious attacks. In terms of security, two of the differential attacks proposed so far in the literature do not allow to recover the entire key [37,38], while a third one [14] does achieve this but under stringent conditions. Since PRIDE is to be used in IoT devices in pervasive environments, we ought to also look at implementation-related issues. In that respect, we propose in this paper the first Differential Fault Analysis (DFA) on PRIDE. DFA is a particular physical attack, in which we compare the results of a correct computation to one which has been disturbed at a precise time, in order to infer information about the key bits used in the algorithm. It is closely related to differential cryptanalysis, but much more efficient since it exploits differential characteristics on very few rounds only.

In this paper, we first present PRIDE before describing the theoretical DFA using different fault models. Then we validate our hypotheses and equations using data onto which fault models have been 'simulated'. In order to validate the practical feasibility of our attack, we used electromagnetic pulses to inject faults during the execution of the PRIDE cipher running on an off-the-shelf chip embedding an ARM Cortex-M3 micro-controller and applied our DFA on the corrupted results obtained. So as to taking advantage of the 32-bit architecture of the micro-controller, we have implemented PRIDE in ARM assembly language. Thereby, we show the practical feasibility of our attack from 32-bit random faults. Finally we discuss countermeasures that can be implemented to thwart such attacks before concluding the paper with some perspectives.

2 Fault Attacks Against Cryptographic Algorithms

2.1 Physical Attacks

Unlike mathematical attacks which target the actual definition of a cryptographic cipher, physical attacks target the way the cipher is implemented. Physical attacks can be divided into two categories: invasive and non-invasive ones. In this paper, we further focus on non-invasive techniques which mainly consist either in analysing side-channel information leakages or in injecting faults during a cryptographic computation.

Side-Channel Analyses [23,27] exploit the fact that some physical values or "side channels" such as the power consumption [22], the electromagnetic radiation [17,31] or the calculation time [16,21] of an integrated circuit depend on the operations and data manipulated during a given computation. Information about the internal processes of the chip and the data it is manipulating can be derived by observing such external physical characteristics. Such analyses can be quickly mounted with cheap equipment, without altering the physical integrity of the circuit. This dependency between the side channels and the internal computations can be analysed to infer information about the data manipulated using mathematical tools like correlation [13], mutual information [18], variance [25] or entropy [26] or using architecture-dependant behaviours such as cache accesses [7,29,30] or using branch predictions [1,2].

2.2 Fault Attacks

Fault Attacks, introduced in [11], consist in disturbing the behaviour of the circuit in order to alter the correct progress of the cipher. The faults are injected into the device by various means such as light pulses [34], laser [33], clock glitches [3], spikes on the voltage supply [9] or electromagnetic (EM) perturbations [15]. Some of those techniques, like the one using a laser, are invasive requiring the "decapsulation" of the chip using mechanical or chemical means. Laser allows to target one bit in a given register if well manipulated. However it is a very costly means of injection. Other techniques are not invasive such as glitches (power, clock, electromagnetic). Clock and voltage glitches disturb the whole component, and many injections have to be made before getting the faults required by theoretical attacks. EM glitches on the other hand allow to have relatively high spatial and temporal precisions using equipment at "affordable costs" [15].

One of the objectives of fault attacks, especially when considering cryptographic ciphers, is to perform Differential Fault Analysis (DFA). DFA, originally described in [8], consists in retrieving a cryptographic key by comparing the correct ciphertexts with the faulty ones. DFA techniques have been described and applied to most publicly known cryptographic ciphers going from symmetric-key algorithms like the DES [8] or the AES [32] to asymmetric algorithms like RSA [11] or even more complex schemes like pairing-based cryptography [24]. In the particular field of lightweight cryptography, differential fault attacks have been proposed against ciphers like PRESENT [39] (used in conjunction with a cube attack), SPECK [36] (although about a hundred faults are needed which is way more than usual), TRIVIUM [28] or PRINCE [35]. The latter PRINCE block cipher has an SPN structure similar to PRIDE and in that respect the DFA proposed in [35] is quite similar to the one proposed hereafter: in our case the attack is not only adapted to the PRIDE cipher but has also been validated in practice on an embedded device running PRIDE.

DFA techniques are very efficient in retrieving the keys used during a cryptographic computation, usually requiring a few executions only. It is also quite complex to devise countermeasures against such attacks because of the diversity of the possible injection methods and because the usually deployed countermeasures (like redundancy, error-correcting codes etc.) have serious impacts on the performance of the targeted cryptographic cipher. For all those reasons, in our approach of analysing the security of implementations of PRIDE, we decided to first focus on its resistance against fault attacks in order to identify possible attack paths and devise the most efficient countermeasures in order to keep the high performance characteristics of the original cipher.

3   The PRIDE Block Cipher

PRIDE is an iterative block cipher composed of 20 rounds and introduced by Albrecht et al. [4] in 2014. It takes as input a 64-bit block and uses a 128-bit key $k = k_0 || k_1$. The first 64 bits k_0 are used for pre- and post-whitening. The last 64 bits k_1 are used by a key schedule to produce the subkeys $f_r(k_1)$ for each round r. The key schedule simply adds round-constants to parts of the key.

We denote k_{1_i} the i-th byte of k_1 then

$$f_r(k_1) = k_{1_0} || g_r^{(0)}(k_{1_1}) || k_{1_2} || g_r^{(1)}(k_{1_3}) || k_{1_4} || g_r^{(2)}(k_{1_5}) || k_{1_6} || g_r^{(3)}(k_{1_7})$$

for round r with

$$g_r^{(0)}(x) = (x + 193r) \quad \mod 256$$
$$g_r^{(1)}(x) = (x + 165r) \quad \mod 256$$
$$g_r^{(2)}(x) = (x + 81r) \quad \mod 256$$
$$g_r^{(3)}(x) = (x + 197r) \quad \mod 256$$

In this paper, $X[n]$ denotes the n-th nibble (4 bits) of a binary word X while $X\{b\}$ denotes its b-th bit. Moreover, the bits and nibbles are numbered from left to right starting from 0. The following notation is used for the intermediate values of the state within the round function $\mathcal{R}$ of PRIDE (see Fig. 2):

I_r the input of the r-th round
X_r the state after the key addition layer of the r-th round
Y_r the state after the substitution layer of the r-th round input
Z_r the state after the permutation layer of the r-th round
W_r the state after the matrix layer of the r-th round
O_r the output of the r-th round

The r-th round, $1 \leq r \leq 19$, of PRIDE is then composed of the following steps (see Fig. 2).

i. Apply the inverse permutation layer $\mathcal{P}^{-1}$ given in [4] to $f_r(k_1)$ and XOR the permuted round subkey to the input state: $X_r = I_r \oplus \mathcal{P}^{-1}(f_r(k_1))$,
ii. Apply the S-box $\mathcal{S}$ given in Table 1 to each of the 16 nibbles of X_r (i.e. apply the substitution layer $\mathcal{S}$-layer to X_r): $Y_r = \mathcal{S}\text{-layer}(X_r)$,
iii. Apply the permutation layer $\mathcal{P}$ to Y_r: $Z_r = \mathcal{P}(Y_r)$,

iv. Multiply vector $\begin{pmatrix} Z_r\{16i\} \\ \vdots \\ Z_r\{16i+15\} \end{pmatrix}$ by $\mathcal{L}_i$ given in [4] for $i \in \{0, \cdots, 3\}$:

$$W_r = \mathcal{L}_0 \begin{pmatrix} Z_r\{0\} \\ \vdots \\ Z_r\{15\} \end{pmatrix} || \mathcal{L}_1 \begin{pmatrix} Z_r\{16\} \\ \vdots \\ Z_r\{31\} \end{pmatrix} || \mathcal{L}_2 \begin{pmatrix} Z_r\{32\} \\ \vdots \\ Z_r\{47\} \end{pmatrix} || \mathcal{L}_3 \begin{pmatrix} Z_r\{48\} \\ \vdots \\ Z_r\{63\} \end{pmatrix},$$

v. Apply the inverse permutation $\mathcal{P}^{-1}$ to W_r: $O_r = \mathcal{P}^{-1}(W_r)$.

Table 1. S-box of the block cipher PRIDE

x	0x0	0x1	0x2	0x3	0x4	0x5	0x6	0x7	0x8	0x9	0xa	0xb	0xc	0xd	0xe	0xf
$S(x)$	0x0	0x4	0x8	0xf	0x1	0x5	0xe	0x9	0x2	0x7	0xa	0xc	0xb	0xd	0x6	0x3

For the final round, denoted by $\mathcal{R}'$, only the first two steps are applied.

In order to encrypt a plaintext M, the cipher applies $\mathcal{P}^{-1}$ to M, then performs an XOR between the result and k_0. It then applies the 20 rounds as previously described and performs again an XOR with k_0. Finally, $\mathcal{P}$ is applied to the result to obtain the ciphertext C. Figure 1 shows the general structure of PRIDE.

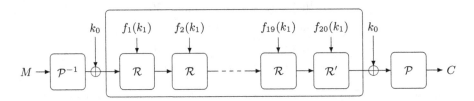

Fig. 1. The structure of PRIDE

The PRIDE round function $\mathcal{R}$ is depicted on Fig. 2.

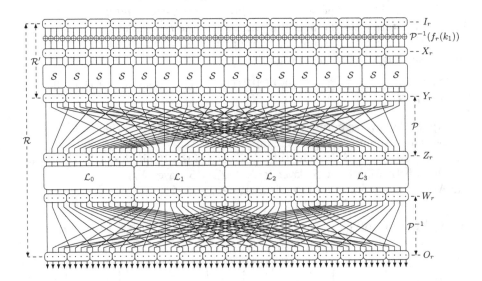

Fig. 2. The PRIDE round function

4   Differential Fault Analysis of PRIDE

In this section, we present a technique adapted from the proposed attack in [35] to retrieve the secret key using fault injections on PRIDE computations. The aim of our analysis is to minimize the number of fault injections needed. We use ideal fault models and we describe how to exploit them to retrieve the key.

4.1   General Principle

Despite their similarities, a DFA is different from a classical differential analysis. Indeed, for the latter, the differences must be injected on the input of the cipher while for a DFA they can be injected at the moments where the attacker wants. The DFA that we propose in this paper also differs from most classical DFA since it is not based on statistical methods: it is deterministic.

The attack is composed of two stages, one consists in corrupting data manipulated in the penultimate round to retrieve k_0 and the other in attacking the antepenultimate round to retrieve k_1. The general structure of the attack is to exploit the diffusion of a 16-bit word within the inverse permutation layer in order to get a known 4-bit difference at the input of each S-box on the following round. Together with the knowledge of the output difference of each S-box, which are derived from the correct and faulty ciphertexts, C and C^*, this allows us to retrieve information about the key. To this end, we exploit the difference distribution table of the PRIDE S-box given in Appendix A. Indeed, obtaining information on k_0 is possible from the following equation:

$$\Delta X_{20} = \mathcal{S}\text{-layer}^{-1}(\mathcal{P}^{-1}(C) \oplus k_0) \oplus \mathcal{S}\text{-layer}^{-1}(\mathcal{P}^{-1}(C^*) \oplus k_0),$$

where $\mathcal{S}\text{-layer} = \mathcal{S}\text{-layer}^{-1}$ denotes the substitution layer. We can use this equation for each nibble $0 \leq i \leq 15$:

$$x = \mathcal{P}^{-1}(C)[i] \oplus k_0[i] \text{ and } y = \mathcal{P}^{-1}(C^*)[i] \oplus k_0[i] \text{ satisfy}$$

$$x \oplus y = \Delta Y_{20}[i] = \mathcal{P}^{-1}(\Delta C)[i] \text{ and } \mathcal{S}^{-1}(x) \oplus \mathcal{S}^{-1}(y) = \Delta X_{20}[i].$$

From the knowledge of a nonzero input difference $\Delta Y_{20}[i]$ and of an output difference $\Delta X_{20}[i]$ for $\mathcal{S}^{-1}$, we deduce 2 or 4 candidates for the input value x, because the differential uniformity of $\mathcal{S}^{-1}$ equals 4 (see the difference distribution table in Appendix A). Moreover, Proposition 1 enables us to exhibit pairs of differentials for the S-box which are simultaneously satisfied for a single element. The proof to this proposition is given in Appendix A.

Proposition 1. *Let $\mathcal{S}$ be an n-bit S-box with differential uniformity 4. Let (a_1, b_1) and (a_2, b_2) be two differentials with $a_1 \neq a_2$ such that the system of two equations*

$$\mathcal{S}(x \oplus a_1) \oplus \mathcal{S}(x) = b_1 \tag{1}$$

$$\mathcal{S}(x \oplus a_2) \oplus \mathcal{S}(x) = b_2 \tag{2}$$

has at least two solutions. Then, each of the three Eqs. (1) *and* (2) *and*

$$S(x \oplus a_1 \oplus a_2) \oplus S(x) = b_1 \oplus b_2$$

has at least four solutions.

In other words, if we can find two differentials (a_1, b_1) and (a_2, b_2) such that one out of the three entries in the difference distribution table (a_1, b_1), (a_2, b_2) and $(a_1 \oplus a_2, b_1 \oplus b_2)$ equals to 2, then we can guarantee that the input satisfying these two differentials simultaneously is unique.

Note: if one of the three equations does not have any solution, then the system of two Eqs. (1) *and* (2) *does not have any solution neither.*

Once k_0 has been recovered (we will see in the next parts some strategies to achieve this end), X_{20} and X_{20}^* can be computed from the ciphertexts C and C^*. Let $\mathcal{L}$ denote the whole linear layer, i.e.,

$$\mathcal{L} = \mathcal{P}^{-1} \circ \begin{pmatrix} \mathcal{L}_0 & 0 & 0 & 0 \\ 0 & \mathcal{L}_1 & 0 & 0 \\ 0 & 0 & \mathcal{L}_2 & 0 \\ 0 & 0 & 0 & \mathcal{L}_3 \end{pmatrix} \circ \mathcal{P}.$$

Then ΔY_{19} can be computed and the following equation

$$\Delta X_{19} = S\text{-layer}^{-1}(\mathcal{L}^{-1}(S\text{-layer}^{-1}(\mathcal{P}^{-1}(C) \oplus k_0) \oplus \mathcal{P}^{-1}(f_{20}(k_1)))) \\ \oplus S\text{-layer}^{-1}(\mathcal{L}^{-1}(S\text{-layer}^{-1}(\mathcal{P}^{-1}(C^*) \oplus k_0) \oplus \mathcal{P}^{-1}(f_{20}(k_1)))),$$

allows the attacker to recover $\mathcal{P}^{-1}(f_{20}(k_1))$ and therefore k_1, with the same method but from fault injections in the 18-th round. Indeed, for $0 \le i \le 15$:

$$x = \mathcal{L}^{-1}(S\text{-layer}^{-1}(\mathcal{P}^{-1}(C) \oplus k_0) \oplus \mathcal{P}^{-1}(f_{20}(k_1)))[i] \text{ and} \\ y = \mathcal{L}^{-1}(S\text{-layer}^{-1}(\mathcal{P}^{-1}(C^*) \oplus k_0) \oplus \mathcal{P}^{-1}(f_{20}(k_1)))[i] \text{ satisfy} \\ x \oplus y = \Delta Y_{19}[i] = \mathcal{L}^{-1}(S\text{-layer}^{-1}(\mathcal{P}^{-1}(C \oplus k_0)) \oplus S\text{-layer}^{-1}(\mathcal{P}^{-1}(C^* \oplus k_0)))[i] \\ \text{and } S^{-1}(x) \oplus S^{-1}(y) = \Delta X_{19}[i].$$

4.2 Ideal Fault Model

The strategies we propose require at least 2 fault injections for each stage of the attack to retrieve a round key (i.e. 4 to retrieve the complete key). For the first stage, whose objective is to find k_0, one of the following approaches can be used:

$$\text{(i) Flip } Z_{19}^0 \text{ then } Z_{19}^3 \text{ or (ii) Flip } W_{19}^0 \text{ then } W_{19}^3,$$

where Z_r^i (resp. W_r^i) denotes the input (resp. output) of the matrix $\mathcal{L}_i$ at round r. Then, to retrieve the key k_1, and so the complete key, the possible fault injections are the same but are carried out on Z_{18} or W_{18}. A flip of Z_r^0 gives us a difference equal to 0xffff on the input of the matrix $\mathcal{L}_0$. The matrix being linear, we know that the output difference is also 0xffff. The latter being the same value than the one obtained with a flip of W_r^0. The other matrices have differences in input and output equal to zero. Then, the inverse permutation layer also being linear, we know the input difference of each S-box of the substitution layer at round $r + 1$. These values are equal to 0x8, so we obtain $\Delta X_{r+1}[i] = 0x8$ for all $i \in \{0, \cdots, 15\}$. Moreover, we recall that the output differences are known from the correct and faulty ciphertexts. Figure 3 shows the propagation of the difference (displayed in red) obtained by a flip of Z_{19}^0. In the same way, a flip of Z_r^3 or W_r^3 yields a difference of 0x1 on each S-box at round $r + 1$. Finally, with strategy (i) or (ii), we obtain pairs of differentials $(\Delta Y_{20}[i], \Delta X_{20}[i])_1 = (a_1, 0x1)$ and $(\Delta Y_{20}[i], \Delta X_{20}[i])_2 = (a_2, 0x8)$ for all $i \in \{0, \cdots, 15\}$ with a_1 and a_2 known. We get the same pairs for $(\Delta Y_{19}[i], \Delta X_{19}[i])$ from faults on the 18-th round. Since $0x1 \oplus 0x8 = 0x9$, from the Proposition 1 (and the difference distribution table in Appendix A), there is only one element in the intersection of the two sets of solutions obtained for each nibble. Therefore, we have shown that we get only one candidate for each nibble of $x = \mathcal{P}^{-1}(C) \oplus k_0$ from faults on the 19-th round and one candidate for each nibble of $x = \mathcal{L}^{-1}(\mathcal{S}-\text{layer}^{-1}(\mathcal{P}^{-1}(C) \oplus k_0) \oplus \mathcal{P}^{-1}(f_{20}(k_1)))[i]$. Finally, from the knowledge of C we retrieve k_0 and from the key schedule we retrieve k_1.

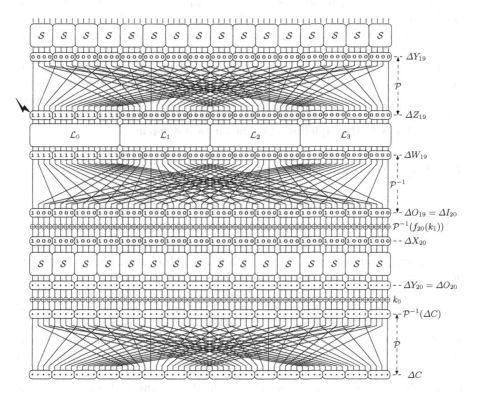

Fig. 3. Propagation on PRIDE of the difference obtained by a flip of Z_{19}^0 (Color figure online)

The strategies we have presented require 4 fault injections to retrieve the complete key. In case the attacker obtains fewer faults, Table 2 shows the time complexity, expressed as a number of encryptions, that an attacker can obtain to retrieve the secret key k with 1 to 3 faults following the ideal fault model. A proof of these values is given in Appendix B.

Table 2. Trade-offs between the time complexity, expressed as a number of encryptions, and the number of faults with the ideal fault model.

Number of faults	1	2	3
Time complexity	2^{64}	2^{32}	$2^{27.7}$

4.3   Random Fault Model

In order to achieve the attack, we must flip all the bits of four 16-bit words for the ideal fault model used in the preceding part. However, we can see that reversing one bit provides an active S-box, it is therefore enough to inverse all the bits of the desired 16-bit words. Indeed, if we flip the bit i of W_{19}^0 from one fault, we obtain 4 candidates for the nibble i of the subkey k_0. Moreover, if we flip the bit i of W_{19}^3 from an other fault, we retrieve (by intersection) the value of the nibble i of k_0.

It is easy to target a specific instruction from a simple power (or EM) analysis for example in practice. If the instruction is less than 16 bits, we can then reduce the key space from each active S-box, until it is enough small for an exhaustive search. Finally, we will see in the Sect. 5 that the attack is still effective from 32-bit faults, only the exploitation of the faults is different.

4.4   Properties Exploited by Our Attack

Our attack mainly exploits two properties of the building-blocks of PRIDE:

The design of the linear layer based on the so-called interleaved construction. Indeed, this construction aims at designing a diffusion layer with a high branch number (see Theorem 1 in [4]). For a SPN whose substitution layer is composed of n S-boxes over $\mathbb{F}_2^k$, the linear layer obtained by the interleaved construction is defined as $L = \mathcal{P}^{-1} \circ \mathcal{L} \circ \mathcal{P}$ where $\mathcal{P}$ is an isomorphism from $(\mathbb{F}_2^k)^n$ into $(\mathbb{F}_2^n)^k$. Then, we deduce from the definition of $\mathcal{P}$ that flipping the n bits of any word at the input of $\mathcal{P}^{-1}$ in $W = (W_1, \cdots, W_k)$ activates all S-boxes in the next round. Indeed, by construction, the n bits of any W_i go to different S-boxes. Hence flipping n consecutive bits in the linear layer of the penultimate round allows the attacker to recover information on all the n nibbles of the subkey used in the last round. The number of candidates for this last-round subkey is upper-bounded by $\delta(\mathcal{S})^n$, where $\delta(\mathcal{S})$ is the differential-uniformity of the S-box ($\delta(\mathcal{S}) = 4$ in the case of PRIDE and of most block ciphers using 4-bit S-boxes).

The differential properties of the S-box, which avoids the existence of differentials with high probability over a large number of rounds. The counterpart of this resistance against classical differential cryptanalysis is that the number of inputs which satisfy two valid differentials simultaneously is usually reduced to a single element. This property enables the attacker to drastically reduce the number of subkey candidates. In the case of PRIDE, two faults, each on n consecutive bits in the linear layer, are enough to obtain a single candidate for the subkey.

4.5   Simulation of the DFA on PRIDE

In order to validate our theoretical DFA against PRIDE and test the correctness of the proposed equations, we first performed a validation by simulation.

In this section we assume that a device executes PRIDE with a key $k = k_0 \| k_1$ where $k_0 = $ 0xefcdab8967452301 and $k_1 = $ 0x0123456789abcdef. We further assume that an attacker successfully flips all the bits of Z_{19}^0, Z_{19}^3, W_{18}^0 and W_{18}^3.

Then, she obtains the following ciphertexts from 5 executions of the same plaintext 0xfedcba9876543210:

i. 0xc40f2551f39c63a9 the correct ciphertext,
ii. 0xe7f325510dc3b7a8, 0xc40fdaaec89376f7 from a flip of Z_{19}^0, Z_{19}^3,
iii. 0x2857589433cbdead, 0x461720d9729c1956 from a flip of W_{18}^0, W_{18}^3.

The knowledge of the plaintext is not necessary, it is sufficient to ensure that the same plaintext is used for each execution.[1] The attacker obtains the following differentials for the last substitution layer from the first two faulty ciphertexts:

i. $(\Delta X_{20}, \Delta Y_{20})_1 = ($0x8888888888888888, 0x33a323a88a8aaa23$)$,
ii. $(\Delta X_{20}, \Delta Y_{20})_2 = ($0x1111111111111111, 0x4467656745457776$)$.

From the first differential, she obtains a set of candidates for each nibble of $\mathcal{P}^{-1}(C) \oplus k_0$ where C is the correct ciphertext. She can then find a set of candidates for each nibble of k_0 from $\mathcal{P}^{-1}(C) = $ 0xab720c373416ba8d. Table 3 shows the obtained sets of candidates.

Table 3. Sets of candidates obtained from $(\Delta X_{20}, \Delta Y_{20})_1$

$k_0[0]$	$k_0[1]$	$k_0[2]$	$k_0[3]$	$k_0[4]$	$k_0[5]$	$k_0[6]$	$k_0[7]$	$k_0[8]$	$k_0[9]$	$k_0[10]$	$k_0[11]$	$k_0[12]$	$k_0[13]$	$k_0[14]$	$k_0[15]$
0x5	0x4	0x4	0x5	0x0	0x0	0x0	0x1	0x5	0x5	0x4	0x5	0x0	0x1	0x0	0x1
0x6	0x7	0x6	0x6	0x2	0x3	0x2	0x2	0x6	0x7	0x7	0x7	0x2	0x3	0x2	0x2
0xd	0xc	0xc	0xd	0x8	0x8	0x8	0x9	0xd	0xd	0xc	0xd	0x8	0x9	0x8	0x9
0xe	0xf	0xe	0xe	0xa	0xb	0xa	0xa	0xe	0xf	0xf	0xf	0xa	0xb	0xa	0xa

From the last differential, the attacker obtains another set of candidates for each nibble of k_0. Table 4 shows the resulting candidates.

---

[1] If it is not the case, the attacker can mount an attack if she knows, for each faulty ciphertext, the corresponding correct ciphertext - to obtain differentials for the S-boxes. But the key may not be recovered in this case since the information obtained by the attacker depends on the value of the correct ciphertext.

Table 4. Sets of candidates obtained from $(\Delta X_{20},\, \Delta Y_{20})_2$

$k_0[0]$	$k_0[1]$	$k_0[2]$	$k_0[3]$	$k_0[4]$	$k_0[5]$	$k_0[6]$	$k_0[7]$	$k_0[8]$	$k_0[9]$	$k_0[10]$	$k_0[11]$	$k_0[12]$	$k_0[13]$	$k_0[14]$	$k_0[15]$
0xa	0xa	0xa	0xa	0xa	0xa	0x8	0x8	0x2	0x2	0x0	0x0	0x2	0x2	0x0	0x0
0xb	0xb	0xb	0xb	0xb	0xb	0x9	0x9	0x3	0x3	0x1	0x1	0x3	0x3	0x1	0x1
0xe	0xe	0xc	0xc	0xc	0xe	0xe	0xe	0x6	0x6	0x4	0x4	0x4	0x4	0x6	0x6
0xf	0xf	0xd	0xd	0xd	0xf	0xf	0xf	0x7	0x7	0x5	0x5	0x5	0x5	0x7	0x7

By doing the intersection of the obtained two sets for each nibble, the attacker gets k_0. Then, with this value of k_0, she obtains the following differences for the antepenultimate substitution layer from the flip of W_{18}^0 and W_{18}^3:

i. $(\Delta X_{19},\, \Delta Y_{19})_1 = (0\mathrm{x}8888888888888888,\, 0\mathrm{x}23a2288338832828)$,

ii. $(\Delta X_{19},\, \Delta Y_{19})_2 = (0\mathrm{x}1111111111111111,\, 0\mathrm{x}7777456474776476)$.

From the first differential, she obtains sets of candidates for each nibble Nib_i of $\mathcal{L}^{-1}(\mathcal{S}(\mathcal{P}^{-1}(C) \oplus k_0) \oplus \mathcal{P}^{-1}(f_{20}(k_1)))$ with $i \in \{0, \cdots, 15\}$. Table 5 shows the sets of candidates she gets.

Table 5. Sets of candidates obtained from $(\Delta X_{19},\, \Delta Y_{19})_1$

Nib_0	Nib_1	Nib_2	Nib_3	Nib_4	Nib_5	Nib_6	Nib_7	Nib_8	Nib_9	Nib_{10}	Nib_{11}	Nib_{12}	Nib_{13}	Nib_{14}	Nib_{15}
0x0	0x4	0x1	0x0	0x0	0x5	0x5	0x4	0x4	0x5	0x5	0x4	0x0	0x5	0x0	0x5
0x2	0x7	0x3	0x2	0x2	0x6	0x6	0x7	0x7	0x6	0x6	0x7	0x2	0x6	0x2	0x6
0x8	0xc	0x9	0x8	0x8	0xd	0xd	0xc	0xc	0xd	0xd	0xc	0x8	0xd	0x8	0xd
0xa	0xf	0xb	0xa	0xa	0xe	0xe	0xf	0xf	0xe	0xe	0xf	0xa	0xe	0xa	0xe

From the last differential, the attacker obtains other sets of candidates for each nibble Nib_i of $\mathcal{L}^{-1}(\mathcal{S}(\mathcal{P}^{-1}(C) \oplus k_0) \oplus \mathcal{P}^{-1}(f_{20}(k_1)))$ with $i \in \{0, \cdots, 15\}$. Table 6 shows the sets of candidates obtained.

Table 6. Sets of candidates obtained from $(\Delta X_{19},\, \Delta Y_{19})_2$

Nib_0	Nib_1	Nib_2	Nib_3	Nib_4	Nib_5	Nib_6	Nib_7	Nib_8	Nib_9	Nib_{10}	Nib_{11}	Nib_{12}	Nib_{13}	Nib_{14}	Nib_{15}
0x8	0x8	0x8	0x8	0x0	0x2	0xa	0x0	0x8	0x0	0x8	0x8	0xa	0x0	0x8	0xa
0x9	0x9	0x9	0x9	0x1	0x3	0xb	0x1	0x9	0x1	0x9	0x9	0xb	0x1	0x9	0xb
0xe	0xe	0xe	0xe	0x4	0x6	0xc	0x4	0xe	0x4	0xe	0xc	0x4	0xe	0xc
0xf	0xf	0xf	0xf	0x5	0x7	0xd	0x5	0xf	0x5	0xf	0xf	0xd	0x5	0xf	0xd

By intersecting the obtained two sets for each nibble, the attacker gets

$$\mathcal{L}^{-1}(\mathcal{S}(\mathcal{P}^{-1}(C) \oplus k_0) \oplus \mathcal{P}^{-1}(f_{20}(k_1))) = 0\mathrm{x}8f9806d4f5efa58d.$$

Then, she computes

$$\mathcal{S}(\mathcal{P}^{-1}(C) \oplus k_0) \oplus \mathcal{P}^{-1}(f_{20}(k_1)) = \text{0x24c39cc978f41dd4}$$

and from $\mathcal{S}(\mathcal{P}^{-1}(C) \oplus k_0) = \text{0x11c3a9c65f5f772b}$, she retrieves

$$\mathcal{P}^{-1}(f_{20}(k_1)) = \text{0x3500350f27ab6aff}.$$

Finally she deduces $f_{20}(k_1) = \text{0x0137454b89ffcd53}$, she gets k_1 from the key scheduling and so she retrieves the complete key.

5   Practical Implementation of the DFA on PRIDE

In order to test the feasibility of our attack against the PRIDE block cipher, we have implemented and run the cipher on an STM32 chip embedding an ARM Cortex-M3 micro-controller. That particular chip was chosen because it is quite representative of the off-the-shelf devices used for IoT applications. Note that the chip does not embed any countermeasures against the kind of the fault attacks implemented in this paper. We validated the attack on an implementation in ARM assembly language taking advantage of the 32-bit architecture of the micro-controller. We present in this section the full analysis conducted on this implementation. The source code is given in Appendix C and Table 7 compares the performances of this implementation with that of the implementation in AVR assembly language whose source code and performances are given in [4].

Table 7. Comparison between AVR and ARM assembly implementation

	Time (cycle)	Size (bytes)
AVR assembly implementation (given in [4])	1514	266
ARM assembly implementation (Appendix C)	2375	490

So as to inject exploitable faults into such a chip, we used EM pulses because with this approach we did not need to decapsulate the chip and we were able to inject faults at precise enough instants to target specific instructions of the cipher during its execution. The set-up we used is quite similar to the one described in [15], with the difference that we did not need any motorized X-Y stage: injecting faults 'in the center' of the chip was good enough for having a fault model close to a random fault model (one chance over two to flip a bit). Indeed, it is possible to target a precise 32-bit word (more precisely a specific instruction) but the injected faults follow a random pattern. In order to obtain pairs of differentials $(\Delta X_{20}[i], \Delta Y_{20}[i])$ (resp. $(\Delta X_{19}[i], \Delta Y_{19}[i])$) for $i \in \{0, \cdots, 15\}$, we injected the faults on the first and on the second 32-bit word of the state before the inverse permutation in the 19-th (resp. 18-th) round. by as many faults as necessary. Each fault on the first word provided us differences on each nibble of ΔX_{20} equal to 0x0, 0x4, 0x8 or 0xc and equal to 0x0, 0x1, 0x2 or 0x3 from each fault on the second word. We validated the attack from these 32-bit faults, we will see that the faults exploitation is different (some pairs of differentials do not allow us a single candidate) but the attack is nevertheless still effective.

In our experiment, we used a key $k = k_0 \| k_1$ where $k_0 = 0xf3f721cb1c882658$ and $k_1 = 0xe417d148e239ca5d$. The plaintext used for all executions was 0x0132546 798badcfe and the correct ciphertext was 0x9aecb37ea45a6c89. We used a simple EM analysis to identify in time the 18-th and 19-th rounds. Figure 4 shows the curve obtained on the oscilloscope, the 20 rounds are displayed in red.

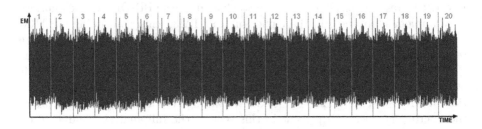

Fig. 4. EM curve measured of PRIDE cipher (Color figure online)

Then we used an electromagnetic pulse generator to disrupt the PRIDE's execution. Table 8 (resp. Table 9) shows the faults we have obtained from the electromagnetic injection on W_{19} (resp. W_{18}) numbered from 1 to 25. For each fault, Table 8 (resp. Table 9) provides the value of ΔX_{20} and ΔY_{20} (resp. ΔX_{19} and ΔY_{19}), only obtained from the correct and the faulty ciphertexts. We denote respectively by θ, β, γ, δ the possible pair of values (0x2,0x3), (0x4,0x8), (0x4,0xc), (0x8,0xc). Indeed, some differences in output of the S-boxes can be obtained from two distinct differences in input. Finally, we give in each table the fault value computed after retrieving the key.

Note: Out of 2,000 shots, we don't get any cipher for 1,219 cases and we get 247 faulty ciphers including 13 exploitable (i.e. which satisfied the conditions for our DFA). Non exploitable faulty ciphers came from a dysfunction of the UART due to the faults.

We now give, among the obtained faults, those that give as much information as all faults and all sets of candidates that we can extract from each fault. Table 10 shows all sets of candidates obtained for each nibble of k_0 from the differentials (ΔY_{20}, ΔX_{20}) and from $\mathcal{P}^{-1}(C) = 0xe17c93c49ec6fc61$ with C the correct ciphertext. Symbol $\emptyset$ means that the fault does not provide any information about the nibble (i.e. the 16 values are possible).

Table 8. Faults obtained on the 19-th round

No.	Faulty ciphertext	Value of the fault on W_{19}	Value of ΔY_{20}	Value of ΔX_{20}
1	0x1aad3b972c92ec09	0x00000000804108e8	0xf00060007e40600c	0xθ000100010101000θ
2	0x7b4c93dea55a6d89	0x00000000e1a0a0a0	0x88c0000bc0c00000	0x$\theta\theta$00000$\theta\theta$00θ00000
3	0x1b6c733e255aadc9	0x0000000081804040	0xf500000b85000000	0xθ100000$\theta\theta$1000000
4	0x71ecd27ee55a6d89	0x00000000eb00e900	0x8ec0808f00000000	0x$\theta\theta$0θ0θ0θ00000000
5	0x9aecb324a4426cdb	0x000000000000005a	0x0000000005076050	0x0000000001011010
6	0x9a57b33fa4626cf1	0x0000000000bb005a	0x0000000085bbb08c	0x00000000θ1θ0θ000
7	0x9a57b365a4606cb9	0x0000000000bb0000	0x0000000080bfe0ec	0x0000000000θ0$\theta\theta$00
8	0x77aa24313111ed8c	0x00000000ed461f4d	0xf8868e4f0e006de7	0xθ00100100θ0001θ01
9	0x9ae8b37ac15a6989	0x6500040400000000	0x0220030300000c00	0x0$\delta\delta$0δ0δ00000γ00
10	0x8aecb27e415abc89	0xe400d10000000000	0x3329020600000000	0x$\delta\delta\delta\gamma$0δ0400000000
11	0xa3e692ed909ee688	0x355fab9300000000	0x10ea921c620482c5	0x40c$\beta\gamma\delta$4γ4δ0c8$\delta\gamma$c
12	0x05ecb27e565a7289	0xf3001f0000000000	0xa22b99bc00000000	0x$\beta\delta\delta$c$\gamma\gamma$cγ00000000

Table 9. Faults obtained on the 18-th round

No.	Faulty ciphertext	Value of the fault on W_{18}	Value of ΔY_{19}	Value of ΔX_{19}
13	0xf24690de8df8cc89	0x0000000082000000	0xc00000b000000000	0xθ000000θ000000000
14	0x2df93aebf5935009	0x0000000041c0d0d0	0x7807000bd8050000	0x1θ01000$\theta\theta\theta$010000
15	0xa9a4a34f84604dde	0x0000000003010707	0x000004cd0000065c	0x000001θ000000110θ
16	0x52c367c49a9b8786	0x0000000000b55858	0x05077000b6d84808	0x01011000θ1θ01θ0θ
17	0x00632c247f18e99e	0x0000000058580000	0x0e0bb0000d0ef000	0x0θ0θ0000000θ0θ000
18	0xecbc98d50864ad3a	0x00000000a7a70000	0xc0f008bbb0d00888	0xθ0θ00θ0θ000θ000$\theta\theta$
19	0x43b733ec34c1ec11	0x0093000000000000	0x00000000300a0022	0x00000000δ00β000$\delta\delta$
20	0xcabdf870ee423736	0x75e5575700000000	0x0c8c0b123baf049e	0x0γ8γ0c4$\delta\delta$cβ40cγc
21	0x46eb59132610ef55	0x01e0c60100000000	0x6f0001133aa00006	0x4400044$\delta\delta\beta\beta$00004
22	0x9d13b57cf2211618	0x13974cd400000000	0x0f036133290c0422	0x040δ44$\delta\delta\delta\gamma$0γ0c$\delta\delta$
23	0x1247352b2400c0ed	0x0000006700000000	0x0000000009900c96	0x000000000$\gamma\gamma$00$\gamma\gamma$4
24	0x770a084c5528c599	0x6363000000000000	0x0a8000330aa00022	0x0$\beta\beta$8000$\delta\delta$0$\beta\beta$000$\delta\delta$
25	0xc80ca16eb67b9711	0x3600a90000000000	0x6043623a00000000	0x40cδ4$\delta\delta\beta$00000000

We eventually get 4 possible values for k_0 with $k_0[8] \in \{0x0, 0x1\}$ and $k_0[10] \in \{0x8, 0x9\}$. In order to reduce the number of possible keys, we then used faulty ciphers obtained from fault injection on the 18-th round. For this, we compute the difference output ΔY_{19} from the remaining 4 candidates for the key. Then we can observe that some differentials $(\Delta X_{19}, \Delta Y_{19})$ are not possible and therefore remove the corresponding candidate.

Indeed, from the faulty ciphertext 0xf24690de8df8cc89 obtained from a fault on W_{18}, we obtain the 4 following values for ΔY_{19} for each possible value of k_0:

k_0	ΔY_{19}
f3f721cb0c882658	0xc000009022000000
f3f721cb0c982658	0xe000009022220000
f3f721cb1c882658	0xc00000b000000000
f3f721cb1c982658	0xe00000b000220000

Table 10. Sets of candidates obtained from $(\Delta Y_{20}, \Delta X_{20})$

No.	$k_0[0]$	$k_0[1]$	$k_0[2]$	$k_0[3]$	$k_0[4]$	$k_0[5]$	$k_0[6]$	$k_0[7]$	$k_0[8]$	$k_0[9]$	$k_0[10]$	$k_0[11]$	$k_0[12]$	$k_0[13]$	$k_0[14]$	$k_0[15]$
1	0x0 0x1 0xe 0xf	∅	∅	∅	0x2 0x3 0x4 0x5	∅	∅	∅	0x0 0x1 0x6 0x7	0x2 0x3 0xc 0xd	0x8 0x9 0xc 0xd	∅	0x2 0x3 0x4 0x5	∅	∅	0x4 0x5 0x8 0x9
3	0x0 0x1 0xe 0xf	0x2 0x3 0x6 0x7	∅	∅	∅	∅	∅	0x0 0x1 / 0x2 0x3 / 0x8 0x9 / 0xa 0xb	0x0 0x1 / 0x2 0x3 / 0x8 0x9 / 0xa 0xb	0x8 0x9 0xc 0xd	∅	∅	∅	∅	∅	∅
6	∅	∅	∅	∅	∅	∅	∅	∅	0x0 0x1 / 0x2 0x3 / 0x8 0x9 / 0xa 0xb	0x8 0x9 0xc 0xd	0x0 0x1 / 0x2 0x3 / 0x8 0x9 / 0xa 0xb	0x0 0x1 / 0x2 0x3 / 0x8 0x9 / 0xa 0xb	0x0 0x1 / 0x2 0x3 / 0x8 0x9 / 0xa 0xb	∅	0x4 0x5 / 0x6 0x7 / 0xc 0xd / 0xe 0xf	0x4 0x5 0x8 0x9
8	0x0 0x1 0xe 0xf	0x0 0x1 / 0x2 0x3 / 0x8 0x9 / 0xa 0xb	0x4 0x5 / 0x6 0x7 / 0xc 0xd / 0xe 0xf	0x0 0x1 0x6 0x7	0x0 0x1 / 0x2 0x3 / 0x8 0x9 / 0xa 0xb	0x0 0x1 0xe 0xf	0x8 0x9 0xc 0xd	0x4 0x5 0xa 0xb	∅	0x2 0x3 0xc 0xd	∅	∅	0x2 0x3 0x4 0x5	0x6 0x7 0xa 0xb	0x4 0x5 0xa 0xb	0x8 0x9 0xe 0xf
11	0xa 0xb 0xe 0xf	∅	0x1 0xf	0x1 0x5 0x7 0xb 0xd 0xf	0x2 0x4 0xb 0xd	0x1 0x3 0x4 0x6 0x9 0xb	0x8 0x9 0xc 0xd	0x1 0x2 0x7 0xb 0xe	0x0 0x1 0x6 0x7	0x4 0x6 0x9 0xb 0xc 0xe	∅	0x8 0xc	0x1 0x2 0x9 0xa	0x6 0x9 0xb 0xc 0xe	0x0 0x5 0x9 0xc	0x8 0xd
12	0x3 0x5 0x7 0x9 0xd 0xf	0x1 0x3 0x4 0x6 0x9 0xb	0x0 0x2 0x5 0x7 0xd 0xf	0x7 0xc	0x2 0x4 0xb 0xd	0x1 0x7 0x8 0xe	0x7 0xc	0x2 0x7 0xb 0xe	∅	∅	∅	∅	∅	∅	∅	∅

and since we know that we injected faults on the last 32 bits of W_{18}, we know that each nibble of ΔX_{19} is either 0x0, 0x1, 0x2 or 0x3. From the difference distribution table of the S-box, we see that an input difference equal to 0x1, 0x2 or 0x3 can lead to an output difference in {0x4, 0x5, 0x6, 0x7, 0x8, 0xb, 0xc, 0xd, 0xe, 0xf} only. Consequently, we retrieve k_0 (displayed in red).

Then, Table 11 shows all sets of candidates obtained for each nibble Nib_i of $\mathcal{L}^{-1}(\mathcal{S}(\mathcal{P}^{-1}(C) \oplus k_0) \oplus \mathcal{P}^{-1}(f_{20}(k_1)))$ with $i \in \{0, \cdots, 15\}$, from differentials $(\Delta Y_{19}, \Delta X_{19})$. We again denote by ∅ when the fault does not provide any information about the nibble (i.e. the 16 values are possible).

Finally, by intersecting sets for each nibble, we deduce 8 candidates for k_1 from k_0 and C and we retrieve the correct value of k by testing all. With this we provide, to the best of our knowledge, the first practical validation of a DFA against PRIDE, even against any light weight SPN-block cipher.

Note: We observed that injecting 32-bit random faults allows us to have lower complexity than with 16-bit random faults. Indeed, although the differential pairs obtained do not always provide a single candidate in the case of 32-bit faults, the probability to obtain a differential is greater than with 16-bit faults. Finally we showed that flipping one bit give us a known difference on a nibble, we can so lead the attack with faults from 1 to 32 bits.

Table 11. Sets of candidates obtained from (ΔY_{19}, ΔX_{19})

No.	Nib$_0$	Nib$_1$	Nib$_2$	Nib$_3$	Nib$_4$	Nib$_5$	Nib$_6$	Nib$_7$	Nib$_8$	Nib$_9$	Nib$_{10}$	Nib$_{11}$	Nib$_{12}$	Nib$_{13}$	Nib$_{14}$	Nib$_{15}$
16	∅	0x2 0x3 0x6 0x7	∅	0x8 0x9 0xe 0xf	0x8 0x9 0xe 0xf	∅	∅	∅	0x4 0x5 0x6 0x7 0xc 0xd 0xe 0xf	0xa 0xb 0xc 0xd	0x6 0x7 0xa 0xb	0x0 0x1 0x2 0x3 0x8 0x9 0xa 0xb	0x0 0x1 0x4 0x5	0x0 0x1 0x2 0x3 0x8 0x9 0xa 0xb	∅	0x0 0x1 0x2 0x3 0x8 0x9 0xa 0xb
17	∅	0x2 0x3 0xa 0xb	∅	0x4 0x5 0x6 0x7 0xc 0xd 0xe 0xf	0x4 0x5 0x6 0x7 0xc 0xd 0xe 0xf	∅	∅	∅	∅	0x6 0x7 0xa 0xb	∅	0x2 0x3 0xa 0xb	0x0 0x1 0xe 0xf	∅	∅	∅
18	0x4 0x5 0x8 0x9	∅	0x0 0x1 0xe 0xf	∅	∅	0x0 0x1 0x2 0x3 0x8 0x9 0xa 0xb	0x4 0x5 0x6 0x7 0xc 0xd 0xe 0xf	0x4 0x5 0x6 0x7 0xc 0xd 0xe 0xf	0x4 0x5 0x6 0x7 0xc 0xd 0xe 0xf	∅	0x6 0x7 0xa 0xb	∅	∅	0x0 0x1 0x2 0x3 0x8 0x9 0xa 0xb	0x0 0x1 0x2 0x3 0x8 0x9 0xa 0xb	0x0 0x1 0x2 0x3 0x8 0x9 0xa 0xb
20	∅	0x3 0x6 0xa 0xf	0x5 0x6 0xd 0xe	0x3 0x6 0xa 0xf	∅	0x0 0xb	0x0 0x1 0x4 0x5	0x0 0x2 0x5 0x7 0x8 0xa	0x1 0x2 0x4 0x7 0xc 0xf	0x0 0xb	0x1 0x3 0x7 0x9 0xb 0xd	0x3 0xc	∅	0xa 0xe	0x2 0x4 0xb 0xd	0x6 0x8
22	∅	0x3 0xc	∅	0x1 0x2 0x4 0x7 0xc 0xf	0x8 0x9 0xe 0xf	0x0 0x1 0x4 0x5	0x1 0x2 0x4 0x7 0xc 0xf	0x1 0x2 0x4 0x7 0xc 0xf	0x0 0x2 0x5 0x7 0x8 0xa	0x2 0x4 0xb 0xd	∅	0x3 0x6 0xa 0xf	∅	0xa 0xe	0x0 0x2 0x5 0x7 0x8 0xa	0x0 0x2 0x5 0x7 0x8 0xa
23	∅	∅	∅	∅	∅	∅	∅	∅	∅	∅	0x2 0x4 0xb 0xd	0x2 0x4 0xb 0xd	∅	0x3 0x6 0xa 0xf	0x2 0x4 0xb 0xd	0x8 0x9 0xe 0xf
25	0x8 0x9 0xe 0xf	∅	0xa 0xe	0x1 0x2 0x4 0x7 0xc 0xf	0x8 0x9 0xe 0xf	0x0 0x2 0x5 0x7 0x8 0xa	0x1 0x2 0x7 0x7 0xc 0xf	0x1 0x3 0x7 0x9 0xb 0xd	∅	∅	∅	∅	∅	∅	∅	∅

6 Countermeasures

We present and briefly analyze three possible countermeasures. This list of countermeasures is not exhaustive and any combination of those three can be used in practice to thwart the DFA proposed in this paper.

6.1 Duplication of Computations

Description: A simple countermeasure is to make two computations for the last two rounds. We save the state of the cipher W_{17} in memory, possibly k times for more security - since we are in lightweight cryptography is seems reasonable to take $k = 1$ or $k = 2$. Then we make the computations up to O_{20} and save the state again. We repeat the computation with the saved state (W_{17}) and compare with the first result - possibly k times again. If two different computations give different results we trap the cipher and no output is produced by the system. Else the execution performs normally.

Cost: This countermeasure uses, for encryption and decryption, two additional matrix layer and three additional substitution layers, subkey updates and subkey additions. The cost can be bounded from above by 15% of the total PRIDE cost.

6.2 Desynchronization

Description: This countermeasure consists in adding time randomization during the cipher so that the temporal position of the 18-th and the 19-th round will not be the same for each execution. For the time randomization generation we can use a simple Linear Feedback Shift Register (LFSR) whose value indicates the 'random' delay time. Those random delay functions can be added before the 18-th round.

Cost: The cost depends on the time randomization generation - a simple LFSR implemented in hardware has a low cost with respect to IoT constraints, it also depends on the duration of the 'random delay' and on the time needed to access the random output of the LFSR.

6.3 Masking

Description: Another countermeasure proposed by Guilley *et al.* [20] is to add a random mask to the message to prevent two consecutive executions of the same plaintext. More precisely, in its original description, it consists in generating a 64-bit random mask different at each execution, XOR it with the asked plaintext and the ciphertext obtained is sent with the mask.

In our case, we use a simple LFSR defined by a minimal primitive polynomial of degree 64 ($X^{64} + X^{63} + X^{61} + X^{60} + 1$ for example) and by an initialization made public. The LFSR thus generates $2^{64} - 1$ different masks. It must not be again accessible by the user to prevent its reset. For this, it must be correctly implemented in hardware. We apply the mask by an XOR on the input of the 10-th round. This allows to prevent the adversary to get two encryption of the same plaintext, and therefore to make a DFA. For decryption, we apply an XOR between the mask and the output of the 10-th round and get the correct plaintext. We then have two options. The first is to send the mask with the ciphertext. Unfortunately in this case, this method does not protect against an attack on decryption. Indeed, the attacker can choose the same mask on each decryption. However, in the context of IoT it is common that the card is only used for encryption and decryption is carried out on a protected server. The second is to synchronize the encryption and the decryption. They both use the same LFSR with the same initialization and the decryption must be applied in the same order as ciphertexts received. Therefore, the countermeasure protects both the encryption and the decryption but with an additional synchronisation constraint.

Cost: The cost depends on the choice of the random mask generation. A simple LFSR - like the one we cited - implemented in hardware has a low cost with respect to IoT constraints. Moreover, applying the mask requests an additional cost of an XOR for encryption and the same for decryption in the second case.

7   Conclusion

In this paper we propose the first differential fault analysis on the block cipher
PRIDE. We explain how this attack can be optimized and we demonstrate it,
with 4 faults only to retrieve the full secret key. We show that our attack is indeed
feasible from 32-bit random faults obtained with electromagnetic injection, which
is a low-cost means of injection. We believe that the resistance against DFA is
important for a cipher like PRIDE, which is expected to be largely deployed in
low-end devices thanks to its lightness. At last we propose some countermeasures
which leave the cipher still very efficient for IoT devices. They can be combined
to provide more security and are not exhaustive. An optimization of these countermeasures is possible for make them less costly and keep the light side of the
cipher. It is also necessary to be careful that the protections to prevent the DFA
do not open doors to further attacks. Finally, it appears that our attack applies
to any SPN-based block ciphers with a linear layer similar to the one used in
PRIDE, like the LS-Designs family introduced by Grosso et al. [19] in 2014. The
details of this generalization will be studied in a future work.

Acknowledgement. Benjamin Lac's research work is partly supported by the French
DGA-MRIS scholarship.

A   Differential Properties of the PRIDE S-Box

A.1   Difference Distribution Table of the PRIDE S-Box

Table 12 shows the difference distribution table T of the PRIDE S-box which is
defined by $T(i,j) = \#\{(x,y) \in \{0,1\}^4 \times \{0,1\}^4 \mid x \oplus y = i, \mathcal{S}(x) \oplus \mathcal{S}(y) = j\}$.

A.2   Proof of Proposition 1

We can see that, from the knowledge of a nonzero input $(x \oplus y)$ and of an output
difference $(\mathcal{S}(x) \oplus \mathcal{S}(y))$ for $\mathcal{S}$ we deduce 0, 2 or 4 candidates for the input value
x. Moreover, we can easily find pairs of differentials (a_1, b_1) and (a_2, b_2) which
are satisfied by a single input x. For this, we use Proposition 1 that we prove
here.

Proof (of Proposition 1). Let $\mathcal{D}(a, b)$ denote the set of solutions of the equation

$$\mathcal{S}(x \oplus a) \oplus \mathcal{S}(x) = b.$$

Let us consider (a_1, b_1) and (a_2, b_2) be two differentials with $a_1 \neq a_2$ such that

$$\#\mathcal{D}(a_1, b_1) \cap \mathcal{D}(a_2, b_2) \geq 2.$$

Let us first prove that both $\mathcal{D}(a_1, b_1)$ and $\mathcal{D}(a_2, b_2)$ have at least 4 elements. If
these two sets have two elements only, $\mathcal{D}(a_1, b_1) = \{x, x \oplus a_1\}$ and $\mathcal{D}(a_2, b_2) =
\{x, x \oplus a_2\}$, implying that they cannot be the same since $a_1 \neq a_2$. Then, at least

Table 12. difference distribution table of the PRIDE S-box

T	0x0	0x1	0x2	0x3	0x4	0x5	0x6	0x7	0x8	0x9	0xa	0xb	0xc	0xd	0xe	0xf
0x0	16	0	0	0	0	0	0	0	0	0	0	0	0	0	0	0
0x1	0	0	0	0	4	4	4	4	0	0	0	0	0	0	0	0
0x2	0	0	0	0	0	0	0	0	4	0	0	4	2	2	2	2
0x3	0	0	0	0	0	0	0	0	4	0	0	4	2	2	2	2
0x4	0	4	0	0	0	0	4	0	0	2	2	0	2	0	0	2
0x5	0	4	0	0	0	4	0	0	0	2	2	0	2	0	0	2
0x6	0	4	0	0	4	0	0	0	0	2	2	0	0	2	2	0
0x7	0	4	0	0	0	0	0	4	0	2	2	0	0	2	2	0
0x8	0	0	4	4	0	0	0	0	4	0	4	0	0	0	0	0
0x9	0	0	0	0	2	2	2	2	0	0	0	0	2	2	2	2
0xa	0	0	0	0	2	2	2	2	4	0	4	0	0	0	0	0
0xb	0	0	4	4	0	0	0	0	0	0	0	0	2	2	2	2
0xc	0	0	2	2	2	2	0	0	0	2	0	2	2	0	2	0
0xd	0	0	2	2	0	0	2	2	0	2	0	2	0	2	0	2
0xe	0	0	2	2	0	0	2	2	0	2	0	2	2	0	2	0
0xf	0	0	2	2	2	2	0	0	0	2	0	2	0	2	0	2

one of the two sets contains at least four elements. Suppose that $\#\mathcal{D}(a_1, b_1) = 4$ and $\#\mathcal{D}(a_2, b_2) = 2$. Then, $x \oplus a_2 \in \mathcal{D}(a_1, b_1)$, with $\mathcal{D}(a_2, b_2) = \{x, x \oplus a_2\}$. Consequently,

$$\mathcal{S}(x \oplus a_1 \oplus a_2) \oplus \mathcal{S}(x \oplus a_2) = b_1 = \mathcal{S}(x \oplus a_1) \oplus \mathcal{S}(x)$$

implying that

$$\mathcal{S}(x \oplus a_2) \oplus \mathcal{S}(x) = \mathcal{S}(x \oplus a_1 \oplus a_2) \oplus \mathcal{S}(x \oplus a_1).$$

Thus $x \oplus a_1 \in \mathcal{D}(a_2, b_2)$, a contradiction. We have proved that $\#\mathcal{D}(a_2, b_2) = 4$. Now, it is clear that any element x in $\mathcal{D}(a_1, b_1) \cap \mathcal{D}(a_2, b_2)$ is a solution of

$$\mathcal{S}(x \oplus a_2) \oplus \mathcal{S}(x \oplus a_1) = b_1 \oplus b_2,$$

i.e., $x \oplus a_1 \in \mathcal{D}(a_1 \oplus a_2, b_1 \oplus b_2)$ and $x \oplus a_2 \in \mathcal{D}(a_1 \oplus a_2, b_1 \oplus b_2)$.
  Suppose now that $\{x, x \oplus a_4\} \subseteq \mathcal{D}(a_1, b_1) \cap \mathcal{D}(a_2, b_2)$ for some $a_4 \neq 0$, we deduce that the four elements $x \oplus a_1$, $x \oplus a_2$, $x \oplus a_1 \oplus a_4$ and $x \oplus a_2 \oplus a_4$ belong to $\mathcal{D}(a_1 \oplus a_2, b_1 \oplus b_2)$. These four elements are either distinct or satisfy $a_4 = a_1 \oplus a_2$ which implies that $x \oplus a_4 \oplus a_2 = x \oplus a_1$ belongs to $\mathcal{D}(a_2, b_2)$, i.e., $x \oplus a_1 \in \mathcal{D}(a_1, b_1) \cap \mathcal{D}(a_2, b_2)$. Therefore, $x \oplus a_1$, $x \oplus a_2$, x and $x \oplus a_1 \oplus a_2$ all belong to $\mathcal{D}(a_1 \oplus a_2, b_1 \oplus b_2)$ and $\#\mathcal{D}(a_1 \oplus a_2, b_1 \oplus b_2) = 4$. □

B Other Trade-Offs Between the Number of Faults and the Time Complexity

We have shown that 4 faults with an appropriate strategy enable the attacker to recover the whole key. In this section, we evaluate the number of key candidates that an attacker can obtain with fewer faults. This number then corresponds to the time complexity of the complete key recovery. Indeed, if the attacker knows a pair of plaintext-ciphertext, encrypting the known plaintext under each key candidate until the correct ciphertext is recovered leading to a complete key recovery[2]. Firstly, the number of remaining candidates for the subkey k_0 (resp. k_1) that an attacker can obtain with one fault on the 19-th round (resp. 18-th round) is 2^{32}. We now use this result to estimate the cost of the full key recovery from a few faults only.

With a single fault. We want to determine the cost of the key recovery if the attacker can inject a single fault. If this fault is injected in the 19-th round, then the possible values of k_0 is reduces to a list of 2^{32} candidates. This corresponds to a total of 2^{96} candidates for the whole 128-bit key. If the attacker knows two plaintext-ciphertext pairs, he can then encrypt the first known plaintext under each of these 2^{96} key candidates, until the corresponding ciphertext is recovered. Only $2^{96-64} = 2^{32}$ key candidates then remain, and the second plaintext-ciphertext pair can then be exploited for recovering the key. The main part of the time complexity in this attack is the cost of the exhaustive search over the 2^{96} candidates, which corresponds to 2^{96} encryptions.

If the fault is now injected in the 18-th round, then the attack consists in successively examining all 2^{64} possible values for k_0. For each of these 2^{64} candidates, the attacker inverts the last encryption round for both the correct and the faulty ciphertexts C and C^*. He deduces the value of ΔX_{20}, and then of ΔY_{19}. When choosing a random k_0, ΔX_{20} varies in the set of all input differences which can appear when the output difference equals ΔY_{20}. From the difference distribution table of the S-box, the average number of valid input differences corresponding to a fixed output difference is

$$\frac{1}{16}(1 + 4 \times 2 + 6 \times 8 + 8 \times 5) = 6.0625.$$

Therefore, ΔX_{20} (and then ΔY_{19}) takes in average $6.0625^{16} = 2^{41.6}$ different values, and each of these differences appears for $2^{22.4}$ values of k_0 in average.

But, the difference ΔX_{20} is not valid if the corresponding value of ΔY_{19} does not have the form expected from the value of the fault. As the fault has been injected on Z_{18}^0 or Z_{18}^3, each nibble of ΔX_{19} is equal either to 0x1, or to 0x8.

---

[2] provided that the number of key candidates is smaller than 2^{64}. Otherwise, two plaintext-ciphertext pairs are needed.

Then, the corresponding nibble ΔY_{19} can take 4 values only. Therefore, the proportion of valid values for ΔY_{19} is $4^{16} \times 2^{-64} = 2^{-32}$. It follows that, among the $2^{41.6}$ values of ΔY_{19} which are obtained from the partial decryption, only $2^{9.6}$ are valid, implying that only 2^{32} values of k_0 need to be considered. For each of these 2^{32} values of k_0, the value of the fault, and then of ΔX_{19} provides 2^{32} candidates for k_1 as proved in the previous section. This step then leads to a list of 2^{64} candidates for the whole 128-bit key, with a time complexity which mainly corresponds to the cost for decrypting one round of PRIDE 2^{64} times. The bottleneck of the attack is then the final key recovery procedure, which consists in testing the 2^{64} remaining keys on two plaintext-ciphertext pairs. The overall cost of the attack is then roughly the cost of 2^{64} encryption.

With two faults. If the two faults are injected in the 18-th round, then the previously described technique which enables the attacker to eliminate some candidates for k_0 is repeated twice. Only a proportion of 2^{-64} values of ΔY_{19} will be valid, implying that only the correct value of ΔY_{19} will remain after this step. As previously explained, each value of ΔY_{19} is obtained for $2^{22.4}$ values of k_0 in average. Therefore, this sieving procedure leads to a list of $2^{22.4}$ candidates for k_0. Now, exploiting the two faults injected in the 18-th round provides one candidate for k_1. Therefore, we get $2^{22.4}$ candidates for the whole key. The total time complexity of the attack then corresponds to 2^{64} decryption of a single round, and to an exhaustive search among the $2^{22.4}$ remaining keys. The first step is then the bottleneck and its cost is less than the cost of $2^{64}/20 = 2^{59.7}$ complete encryptions.

If the first fault is now injected in the 19-th round, then the list of possible values for k_0 is first reduced to a list of size 2^{32} as explained in the previous section. The second fault, injected on the 18-th round, then enables to reduce this list to $2^{32-32} = 1$ possible value for k_0. For this value of k_0, a list of 2^{32} candidates for k_1 is obtained from the second fault. The number of candidates for the whole key, which need to tested, is then 2^{32}. The bottleneck of the attack is then the exhaustive search over the 2^{32} remaining key candidates, which corresponds to a time complexity equal to the cost of 2^{32} encryptions.

With three faults. The best strategy with three faults consists in injecting one fault in the 19-th round, and two in the 18-th round. From the fault in the 19-th round, the attacker gets a list of 2^{32} candidates for k_0. By decrypting the last round under these 2^{32} values of k_0, we roughly get 2^{32} pairs of values for ΔY_{19} among which one is expected to be consistent with the two faults injected in the 18-th round. Moreover, these two faults lead to one candidate for k_1, i.e., one candidate for the whole key. The time complexity of the attack then corresponds to the cost of 2^{32} encryptions of a single round, i.e., $2^{27.7}$ full encryptions.

C   ARM Source Code

C.1   L-Layer

; $\mathcal{L}_0$ and $\mathcal{L}_1$
; State s_0
; Temporary registers $t_0, \cdots, t_6$
(1) MOV t_0, #0x00F0
(2) MOVT t_0, #0xF0F0
(3) AND t_1, t_0, s_0, LSL#4
(4) LSR t_0, #4
(5) AND t_2, t_0, s_0, LSR#4
(6) AND t_0, s_0, #0xFF000000
(7) AND t_3, s_0, #0XFF0000
(8) EOR t_1, t_1, t_2
(9) AND s_0, s_0, #0xFF00
(10) EOR s_0, s_0, t_1
(11) AND t_1, s_0, #0x8000
(12) AND t_2, s_0, #0x01
(13) AND t_4, s_0, #0xFF00
(14) AND t_5, s_0, #0x00FF
(15) MOV t_6, #0xFF000000
(16) AND t_6, t_6, s_0, LSL#8
(17) EOR s_0, s_0, r10
(18) AND t_6, s_0, #0xFF000000
(19) EOR t_0, t_0, t_6
(20) BIC s_0, s_0, #0xFF0000
(21) EOR s_0, s_0, t_0, LSR#8
(22) EOR s_0, s_0, t_3, LSL#8
(23) MOV t_0, #0xFF00
(24) AND t_0, t_0, t_4, LSL#1
(25) EOR t_0, t_0, t_1, LSR#7
(26) LSR t_3, t_5, #1
(27) EOR t_3, t_3, t_2, LSL#7
(28) EOR s_0, s_0, t_3, LSL#8
(29) AND t_3, s_0, #0xFF00
(30) EOR s_0, s_0, t_0
(31) EOR s_0, s_0, t_3, LSR#8

; $\mathcal{L}_2$ and $\mathcal{L}_3$
; State s_1
; Temporary registers $t_0, \cdots, t_5$
(1) MOV t_0, #0xF0F0
(2) MOVT t_0, #0xF000
(3) AND t_1, t_0, s_1, LSL#4
(4) LSR t_0, #4
(5) AND t_2, t_0, s_1, LSR#4
(6) AND t_0, s_1, #0xFF00
(7) AND t_3, s_1, #0X00FF
(8) AND s_1, s_1, #0xFF0000
(9) EOR t_1, t_1, t_2
(10) EOR s_1, s_1, t_1
(11) AND t_1, s_1, #0x80000000
(12) AND t_2, s_1, #0x00010000
(13) MOV t_4, #0xFF000000
(14) AND t_5, s_1, t_4
(15) AND t_4, t_4, t_5, LSL#1
(16) EOR t_1, t_4, t_1, LSR#7
(17) MOV t_4, #0x00FF0000
(18) AND t_5, s_1, t_4
(19) AND t_4, t_4, t_5, LSR#1
(20) EOR t_2, t_4, t_2, LSL#7
(21) EOR s_1, s_1, t_2, LSL#8
(22) AND t_2, s_1, #0xFF000000
(23) EOR s_1, s_1, t_1
(24) EOR s_1, s_1, t_2, LSR#8
(25) AND t_4, s_1, #0x00FF
(26) EOR s_1, s_1, t_4, LSL#8
(27) AND t_4, s_1, #0xFF00
(28) EOR t_3, t_3, t_4, LSR#8
(29) EOR t_0, t_0, t_3
(30) BIC s_1, s_1, #0x00FF
(31) EOR s_1, s_1, t_0

C.2   S-Layer

; State s_0, s_1
; Temporary registers t_0, t_1
(1) MOV t_1, s_0
(2) AND t_0, s_0, s_0, LSL#16
(3) EOR t_0, t_0, s_1

(4) AND s_0, s_0, s_1, LSR#16

(5) EOR s_0, s_0, t_0

(6) AND t_0, s_0, s_0, LSL#16

(7) EOR t_0, t_0, t_1

(8) AND s_1, s_0, t_0, LSR#16

(9) EOR s_1, s_1, t_0

References

1. Acıiçmez, O., Koç, Ç.K., Seifert, J.-P.: Predicting secret keys via branch prediction. In: Abe, M. (ed.) CT-RSA 2007. LNCS, vol. 4377, pp. 225–242. Springer, Heidelberg (2006). doi:10.1007/11967668_15

2. Acıiçmez, O., Koç, Ç.K., Seifert, J.P.: On the power of simple branch prediction analysis. In: 2007 ACM Symposium on Information, Computer and Communications Security (ASIACCS 2007), pp. 312–320. ACM Press (2007)

3. Agoyan, M., Dutertre, J.-M., Naccache, D., Robisson, B., Tria, A.: When clocks fail: on critical paths and clock faults. In: Gollmann, D., Lanet, J.-L., Iguchi-Cartigny, J. (eds.) CARDIS 2010. LNCS, vol. 6035, pp. 182–193. Springer, Heidelberg (2010). doi:10.1007/978-3-642-12510-2_13

4. Albrecht, M.R., Driessen, B., Kavun, E.B., Leander, G., Paar, C., Yalçın, T.: Block ciphers – focus on the linear layer (feat. PRIDE). In: Garay, J.A., Gennaro, R. (eds.) CRYPTO 2014. LNCS, vol. 8616, pp. 57–76. Springer, Heidelberg (2014). doi:10.1007/978-3-662-44371-2_4

5. Baysal, A., Şahin, S.: RoadRunneR: a small and fast bitslice block cipher for low cost 8-bit processors. In: Güneysu, T., Leander, G., Moradi, A. (eds.) Light-Sec 2015. LNCS, vol. 9542, pp. 58–76. Springer, Heidelberg (2016). doi:10.1007/978-3-319-29078-2_4

6. Beaulieu, R., Shors, D., Smith, J., Treatman-Clark, S., Weeks, B., Wingers, L.: SIMON and SPECK: block ciphers for the internet of things. Cryptology ePrint Archive, report 2015/585 (2015). http://eprint.iacr.org/2015/585

7. Bertoni, G., Zaccaria, V., Breveglieri, L., Monchiero, M., Palermo, G.: AES power attack based on induced cache miss and countermeasure. In: ITCC, Las Vegas, Nevada, USA, vol. 1, pp. 586–591. IEEE Computer Society, 4–5 April 2005

8. Biham, E., Shamir, A.: Differential fault analysis of secret key cryptosystems. In: Kaliski, B.S. (ed.) CRYPTO 1997. LNCS, vol. 1294, pp. 513–525. Springer, Heidelberg (1997). doi:10.1007/BFb0052259

9. Blömer, J., Seifert, J.-P.: Fault based cryptanalysis of the advanced encryption standard (AES). In: Wright, R.N. (ed.) FC 2003. LNCS, vol. 2742, pp. 162–181. Springer, Heidelberg (2003). doi:10.1007/978-3-540-45126-6_12

10. Bogdanov, A., Knudsen, L.R., Leander, G., Paar, C., Poschmann, A., Robshaw, M.J.B., Seurin, Y., Vikkelsoe, C.: PRESENT: an ultra-lightweight block cipher. In: Paillier, P., Verbauwhede, I. (eds.) CHES 2007. LNCS, vol. 4727, pp. 450–466. Springer, Heidelberg (2007). doi:10.1007/978-3-540-74735-2_31

11. Boneh, D., DeMillo, R.A., Lipton, R.J.: On the importance of checking cryptographic protocols for faults. In: Fumy, W. (ed.) EUROCRYPT 1997. LNCS, vol. 1233, pp. 37–51. Springer, Heidelberg (1997). doi:10.1007/3-540-69053-0_4

12. Borghoff, J., et al.: PRINCE – a low-latency block cipher for pervasive computing applications. In: Wang, X., Sako, K. (eds.) ASIACRYPT 2012. LNCS, vol. 7658, pp. 208–225. Springer, Heidelberg (2012). doi:10.1007/978-3-642-34961-4_14

13. Brier, E., Clavier, C., Olivier, F.: Correlation power analysis with a leakage model. In: Joye, M., Quisquater, J.-J. (eds.) CHES 2004. LNCS, vol. 3156, pp. 16–29. Springer, Heidelberg (2004). doi:10.1007/978-3-540-28632-5_2

14. Dai, Y., Chen, S.: Cryptanalysis of full PRIDE block cipher. Cryptology ePrint Archive, Report 2014/987 (2014). http://eprint.iacr.org/2014/987

15. Dehbaoui, A., Dutertre, J., Robisson, B., Tria, A.: Electromagnetic transient faults injection on a hardware and a software implementations of AES. In: Bertoni, G., Gierlichs, B. (eds.) FDTC, Leuven, Belgium, pp. 7–15. IEEE Computer Society, 9 September 2012

16. Dhem, J.-F., Koeune, F., Leroux, P.-A., Mestré, P., Quisquater, J.-J., Willems, J.-L.: A practical implementation of the timing attack. In: Quisquater, J.-J., Schneier, B. (eds.) CARDIS 1998. LNCS, vol. 1820, pp. 167–182. Springer, Heidelberg (2000). doi:10.1007/10721064_15

17. Gandolfi, K., Mourtel, C., Olivier, F.: Electromagnetic analysis: concrete results. In: Koç, Ç.K., Naccache, D., Paar, C. (eds.) CHES 2001. LNCS, vol. 2162, pp. 251–261. Springer, Heidelberg (2001). doi:10.1007/3-540-44709-1_21

18. Gierlichs, B., Batina, L., Tuyls, P., Preneel, B.: Mutual information analysis. In: Oswald, E., Rohatgi, P. (eds.) CHES 2008. LNCS, vol. 5154, pp. 426–442. Springer, Heidelberg (2008). doi:10.1007/978-3-540-85053-3_27

19. Grosso, V., Leurent, G., Standaert, F.-X., Varıcı, K.: LS-designs: bitslice encryption for efficient masked software implementations. In: Cid, C., Rechberger, C. (eds.) FSE 2014. LNCS, vol. 8540, pp. 18–37. Springer, Heidelberg (2015). doi:10.1007/978-3-662-46706-0_2

20. Guilley, S., Sauvage, L., Danger, J., Selmane, N.: Fault injection resilience. In: Breveglieri, L., Joye, M., Koren, I., Naccache, D., Verbauwhede, I. (eds.) FDTC 2010, Santa Barbara, California, USA, pp. 51–65. IEEE Computer Society, 21 August 2010. http://dx.doi.org/10.1109/FDTC.2010.15

21. Kocher, P.C.: Timing attacks on implementations of Diffie-Hellman, RSA, DSS, and Other Systems. In: Koblitz, N. (ed.) CRYPTO 1996. LNCS, vol. 1109, pp. 104–113. Springer, Heidelberg (1996). doi:10.1007/3-540-68697-5_9

22. Kocher, P., Jaffe, J., Jun, B.: Differential power analysis. In: Wiener, M. (ed.) CRYPTO 1999. LNCS, vol. 1666, pp. 388–397. Springer, Heidelberg (1999). doi:10.1007/3-540-48405-1_25

23. Koeune, F., Standaert, F.-X.: A tutorial on physical security and side-channel attacks. In: Aldini, A., Gorrieri, R., Martinelli, F. (eds.) FOSAD 2004-2005. LNCS, vol. 3655, pp. 78–108. Springer, Heidelberg (2005). doi:10.1007/11554578_3

24. Lashermes, R., Fournier, J., Goubin, L.: Inverting the final exponentiation of tate pairings on ordinary elliptic curves using faults. In: Bertoni, G., Coron, J.-S. (eds.) CHES 2013. LNCS, vol. 8086, pp. 365–382. Springer, Heidelberg (2013). doi:10.1007/978-3-642-40349-1_21

25. Maghrebi, H., Danger, J.L., Flament, F., Guilley, S., Sauvage, L.: Evaluation of countermeasure implementations based on Boolean masking to thwart side-channel attacks. In: International Signals, Circuits and Systems Conference - SCS 2009, pp. 1–6 (2009)

26. Maghrebi, H., Guilley, S., Danger, J., Flament, F.: Entropy-based power attack. In: Plusquellic, J., Mai, K. (eds.) HOST, Anaheim Convention Center, California, USA, pp. 1–6. IEEE Computer Society, 13–14 June 2010

27. Mangard, S., Oswald, E., Popp, T.: Power Analysis Attacks - Revealing the Secrets of Smart Cards. Springer, New York (2007)

28. Mohamed, M.S.E., Bulygin, S., Buchmann, J.: Using SAT solving to improve differential fault analysis of trivium. In: Kim, T., Adeli, H., Robles, R.J., Balitanas, M. (eds.) ISA 2011. CCIS, vol. 200, pp. 62–71. Springer, Heidelberg (2011). doi:10.1007/978-3-642-23141-4_7

29. Page, D.: Theoretical use of cache memory as a cryptanalytic side-channel. Cryptology ePrint Archive, Report 2002/169 (2002). http://eprint.iacr.org/2002/169

30. Page, D.: Defending against cache based side-channel attacks. Inf. Secur. Tech. Rep. 8(1), 30–44 (2004)

31. Quisquater, J.-J., Samyde, D.: ElectroMagnetic Analysis (EMA): measures and counter-measures for smart cards. In: Attali, I., Jensen, T. (eds.) E-smart 2001. LNCS, vol. 2140, pp. 200–210. Springer, Heidelberg (2001). doi:10.1007/3-540-45418-7_17

32. Sakiyama, K., Li, Y., Iwamoto, M., Ohta, K.: Information-theoretic approach to optimal differential fault analysis. IEEE Trans. Inf. Forensics Secur. 7(1), 109–120 (2012)

33. Skorobogatov, S.: Semi-invasive attacks - a new approach to hardware security analysis. Technical report 630, University of Cambridge, April 2005

34. Skorobogatov, S.P., Anderson, R.J.: Optical fault induction attacks. In: Kaliski, B.S., Koç, Ç.K., Paar, C. (eds.) CHES 2002. LNCS, vol. 2523, pp. 2–12. Springer, Heidelberg (2003). doi:10.1007/3-540-36400-5_2

35. Song, L., Hu, L.: Differential fault attack on the PRINCE block cipher. Cryptology ePrint Archive, Report 2013/043 (2013). http://eprint.iacr.org/2013/043

36. Tupsamudre, H., Bisht, S., Mukhopadhyay, D.: Differential fault analysis on the families of SIMON and SPECK ciphers. Cryptology ePrint Archive, Report 2014/267 (2014). http://eprint.iacr.org/2014/267

37. Yang, Q., Hu, L., Sun, S., Qiao, K., Song, L., Shan, J., Ma, X.: Improved differential analysis of block cipher PRIDE. In: Lopez, J., Wu, Y. (eds.) ISPEC 2015. LNCS, vol. 9065, pp. 209–219. Springer, Heidelberg (2015). doi:10.1007/978-3-319-17533-1_15

38. Zhao, J., Wang, X., Wang, M., Dong, X.: Differential analysis on block cipher PRIDE. Cryptology ePrint Archive, Report 2014/525 (2014). http://eprint.iacr.org/2014/525

39. Zhao, X., Wang, T., Guo, S.: Improved side channel cube attacks on PRESENT. Cryptology ePrint Archive, Report 2011/165 (2011). http://eprint.iacr.org/2011/165

Author Index

Printed in the United States
By Bookmasters